Design and Craft

SECOND EDITION

A. Yarwood
S. Dunn

HODDER AND STOUGHTON
LONDON SYDNEY AUCKLAND TORONTO

Preface to the first edition

The methods advocated in this book have been developed and tested at the High Ridge Comprehensive School, Scunthorpe. The book is intended as a text and reference book covering a two-year course for fourth and fifth year pupils in secondary schools. Its contents are aimed at examinations such as 'Design and Technology'; 'Craftwork, Design Communication and Application'; 'Design, Craft and Technology' for candidates at the age of 16+ (CSE, GCE Ordinary level, etc.).

The contents of the book have been influenced by the published results of the Schools Council 'Design and Craft Education' project which was set up at Keele University. A. Yarwood was, until 1977, a member of the Crafts, Applied Science and Technology subjects committee of the Schools Council.

The aim of the book is to describe in detail a systematic approach which can be applied to design and craft taught in schools. Craft techniques as such are not described in its pages. The value of teaching traditional craft skills is fully recognised. When these craft skills are coupled to the intellectual challenge of solving design situations, the educational value of craft teaching is greatly enhanced. Many examples of craft designs illustrate the book. The materials for these fall mainly in the three groups commonly found in secondary school workshops —metals, woods and plastics. It must however be emphasised that the design process recommended here can be applied to designing in any material.

This design process strengthens the links which already exist between design, crafts and technical drawing. The technical drawing methods employed could be more properly referred to as technical graphics.

Preface to the second edition

This book has been very well received in schools and colleges and, mainly because of its success, this new edition incorporating the revised content and new approach required by the GCSE examination has been prepared. The new edition is eminently suitable as a textbook for candidates preparing for CDT: Design and Realisation examinations set in accordance with the GCSE CDT National Criteria. The amendments included in this second edition are as follows:

First—some pages now include examples of simple colour work, suitable for applications to the graphics associated with design and craft.

Second—the examples of projects shown in pages 12 to 33 have been revised to include more graphics and some colour work, together with a greater variety of methods of presentation of sheets of drawings from design folios.

Third—a greater emphasis has been placed on graphics and communication by placing all the various aspects of graphics within Section 3 of the book.

Fourth—the pages concerned with models have been revised to include examples of methods of development such as can be employed for the making of models suitable for project work in Design and Craft.

Books by A. Yarwood
Design and Technology by A. Yarwood and A. H. Orme
Design and Woodwork
Tools and Processes
Teach Yourself Woodwork
Teach Yourself Graphical Communication

Contents

THE DESIGN PROCESS

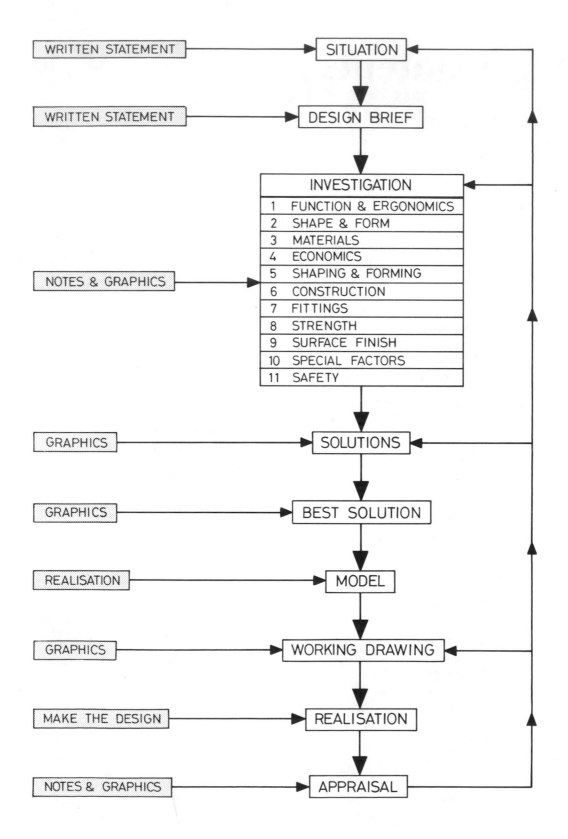

SECTION 1

Introduction

The design process

The flow chart on page 4 shows the design process followed throughout this book. Each part of the process will be explained in detail in later pages. In this book the process has been applied mainly to craft work involving woods, metals and plastics.

Situation
All designs are the results of attempts to find solutions to situations which have arisen from human needs. If a design does not meet the requirements of the situation for which it has been made, it is unsuccessful. The first step must be to define the situation and to write it down. An example: 'A bed-ridden old lady finds difficulty in placing a tray on her knees when eating a meal.' Such a statement helps ensure that a design is to be made to overcome a problem in a given situation. In this example, if the completed design does not overcome the old lady's difficulty, the design has failed.

Design brief
Again, the design brief should be written down. From the given design situation above, a design brief might be: 'Design a bed-table which will assist the old lady to eat in greater comfort.' The design brief should state quite clearly what is required within a given design situation. When a design has been realised, the designer should refer back to the design brief to make sure the design meets its requirements. If the design does not meet these requirements, the design is unsuccessful.

Investigation
All details related to solving the problem stated in the design brief should be investigated. The eleven details shown in the flow chart should be analysed and possibly tested. Notes should be made of the results of this research and, where necessary, drawings made to enlarge on the notes. When working to some design briefs, you may not need to look at all eleven details. Some details may be more important than others.

Solutions
At the same time as the various aspects of the investigation are being considered, freehand or instrument-assisted drawings of possible solutions which might satisfy the design brief should be made. It may well be that some details of an investigation can only be considered when a number of solutions have been drawn. For example, after notes considering function and ergonomics have been written, the shape and form of possible solutions may need to be drawn. Suggestions for materials may only be possible when some ideas of constructions suitable for possible solutions have been considered. Thus the drawing of solutions should proceed at the same time as the notes (and drawings) for the investigation are being compiled. Aim at a minimum of at least three ideas for solutions, but the more solutions you can consider, the greater will be the choice of ideas from which you will be able to attain a good answer to the design brief.

Best solution
From the solutions drawn, select and develop the one which is considered as being the best. Make a clear and neat drawing of the chosen best solution. Add notes to this drawing as necessary.

Model
Always consider whether it is advisable to make a model of the best solution. Imperfections not seen when drawing solutions may show up in a model.

Working drawing
Always make a clear, neat, fully-dimensioned working drawing of the best solution. This will usually be in the form of an instrument-assisted drawing, but could also be a well-drawn freehand drawing. The working drawing must be complete in that anybody working from it would be able to make the design.

Realisation
The design can now be made.

Appraisal
When the design has been realised, look at it, test it and make notes as to whether you consider it has satisfied the design brief and, as a result, meets the requirements of the situation for which it was designed. Be honest about this appraisal. State clearly why it is considered that the design has succeeded and—just as important—where or why it has failed.

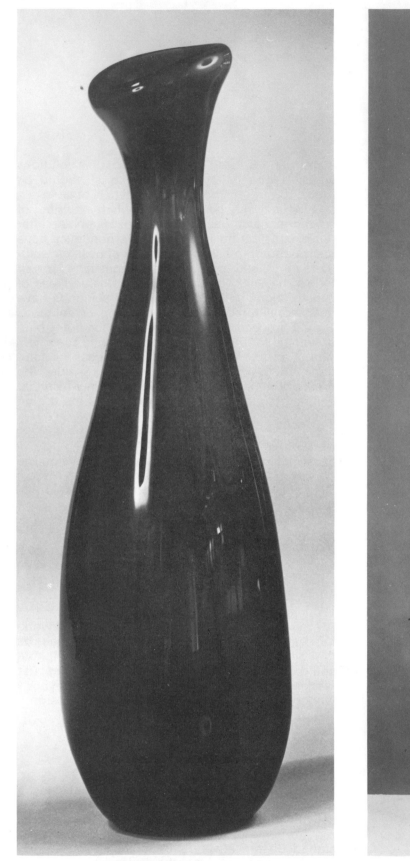

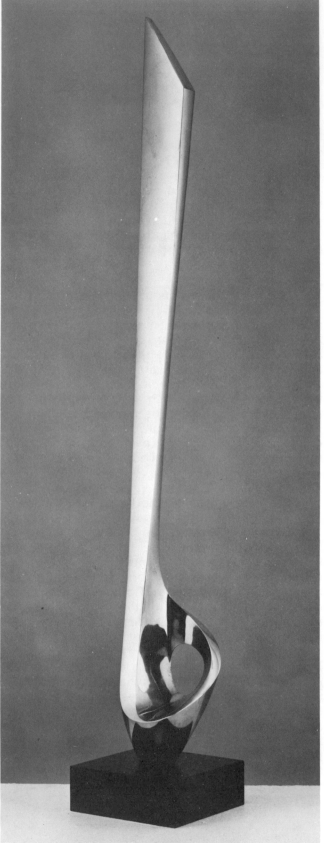

Glass vessel by Dominick Labino

Praze by Denis Mitchell

6

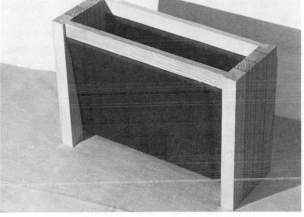

The photographs on this page are of items of craftwork designed and made by Danielle and Selwyn Holmes at their Design Workshop and Craftwork Gallery at Abbotsbury, Dorset.

Comparisons with industrial design

An interesting exercise is to compare the designing of a single piece of craft work made by a pupil at school with the designing processes employed in an industrial concern. The illustration on page 9 opposite makes this comparison. The designing of a small fruit dish by a pupil in a school is compared with the design process followed in a large industrial organisation when designing mass-produced articles for sale to the public.

Design in industry
Large organisations can employ specialists to undertake certain parts of the design process. These employees must consult and co-operate with each other throughout if successful designing is to be achieved.

Situation
The situation will be defined by the directors of the company after reading and listening to reports from market research and sales departments. Market research firms may be commissioned to decide on the sales possibilities of some products designed to meet specified situations.

Brief
The board of directors or a management committee will decide on the brief to be followed. This brief may be amended later as the design process continues.

Investigation
A group of employees will be brought together from such departments as market research, design, drawing office and accounts to discuss and investigate the brief passed to them by management. This group will report back to management at regular intervals. Any models or 'hardware' required to assist the investigation will be made at this stage in the workshops of the research department—for testing ergonomics, strength, special fittings required and other such details. Details such as working conditions, wages and special machinery which may be needed will be discussed and reported on at this stage. Design consultancy firms may be employed to assist with specialised information or the whole investigation may be passed to such a firm. Some production firms rely completely upon design consultancies.

Solutions
The same team or group of people will now prepare possible solutions to the design brief. Research, design and drawing-office departments will prepare drawings at this stage. Some of the solutions will be made up as models, some even actually made as 'prototypes'. These drawings, models and prototypes will be carefully examined and tested by all the personnel concerned and will also be passed back to managers and directors for examination.

Best solution
From the variety of possible solutions so far obtained the assistance of the production department may be required to assist in deciding the best solution to the design brief. Sales and service departments may also be called in for specialised advice.

Model
Models will be made of the proposed best design. Some may be tested to destruction to decide on length of life, others may not need such testing. If now the design looks as if it could be a successful commercial proposition with good sales prospects, the whole information gained so far will be placed before the board of directors. They will decide whether to continue with the design. At this stage the proposed selling price may be decided.

Working drawings
Some working drawings will have been made during the stage when a best solution was being decided. From these a series of final drawings will be required. These final drawings will be made in the drawing office, although again consultation with other departments will be necessary. Assembly drawings will be needed on the production lines, detailed drawings of parts will be required in machine shops and by supply departments where individual components are made. Parts lists and perhaps cutting lists may be used by stock controllers, stores, accounts personnel and materials suppliers.

Realisation
The company may make everything connected with the product within its own factories or may sub-contract some of the work involved. At this stage production and assembly lines need to be carefully and thoroughly planned and the delivery and movement of parts for the design organised.

Appraisal
Completed products may be sent to specialised testing organisations for appraisal. Good Design Centre and magazine test results will help to promote sales. The company itself will test the completed product—it doesn't want faulty products carrying its name. Such faulty products can harm sales of future products. Finally the market research department will wish to know whether its original forecasting was good and whether sales meet their expectations.

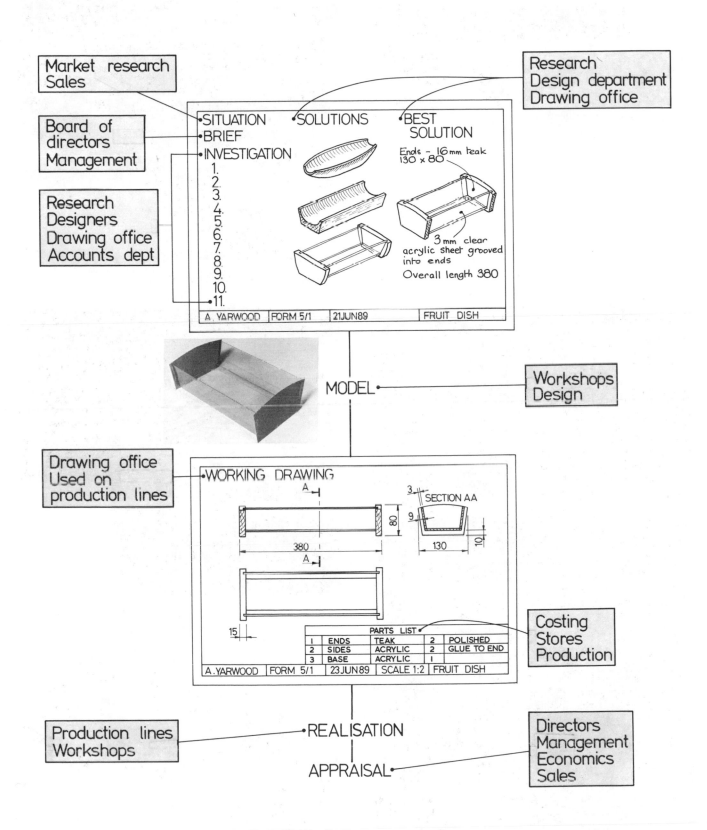

Market research
Sales

Research
Design department
Drawing office

Board of
directors
Management

Research
Designers
Drawing office
Accounts dept

SITUATION   SOLUTIONS   BEST
BRIEF   SOLUTION
INVESTIGATION
1.
2.
3.
4.
5.
6.
7.
8.
9.
10.
11.

Ends – 16mm teak
130 x 80

3 mm clear
acrylic sheet grooved
into ends
Overall length 380

A. YARWOOD | FORM 5/1 | 21 JUN 89 | FRUIT DISH

MODEL

Workshops
Design

Drawing office
Used on
production lines

WORKING DRAWING

A

SECTION AA

80

3

9

380

130

10

A

15

PARTS LIST				
I	ENDS	TEAK	2	POLISHED
2	SIDES	ACRYLIC	2	GLUE TO END
3	BASE	ACRYLIC	I	

A. YARWOOD | FORM 5/1 | 23 JUN 89 | SCALE 1:2 | FRUIT DISH

Costing
Stores
Production

Production lines
Workshops

REALISATION

APPRAISAL

Directors
Management
Economics
Sales

Design drawing for Sierra motor car

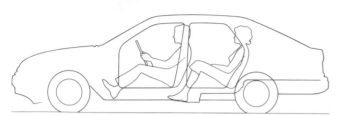

Ergonomics drawing of seating for Sierra

Sierra production line Dagenham

Sierra robot production at Dagenham

Testing a Sierra in a wind tunnel

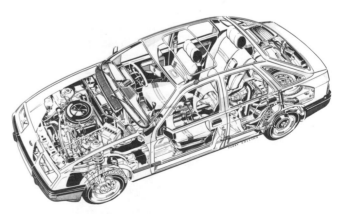

Drawing of Sierra for maintenance manual

Alternative descriptions

The words and phrases describing the design process throughout this book are in common use. However, alternative descriptions will be found in other books, in examination syllabuses and in examination papers.

On this page the design process chart from page 4 has been re-drawn using some of the symbols designed for computer flow charts (from British Standard BS:4058). Alternative descriptions of each step in the design process are shown linked to the descriptions found in this book.

Note that no matter which words or phrases describe stages in the design process, there is always a basic system which should be followed. This can be summarised as follows:
1. Write down the situation and design brief.
2. Investigate and analyse the problems involved in finding ideas for solutions to the design brief.
3. Select what is considered to be your best solution and make a working drawing.
4. Make the design, preferably after making and testing a model.
5. The design is then appraised.

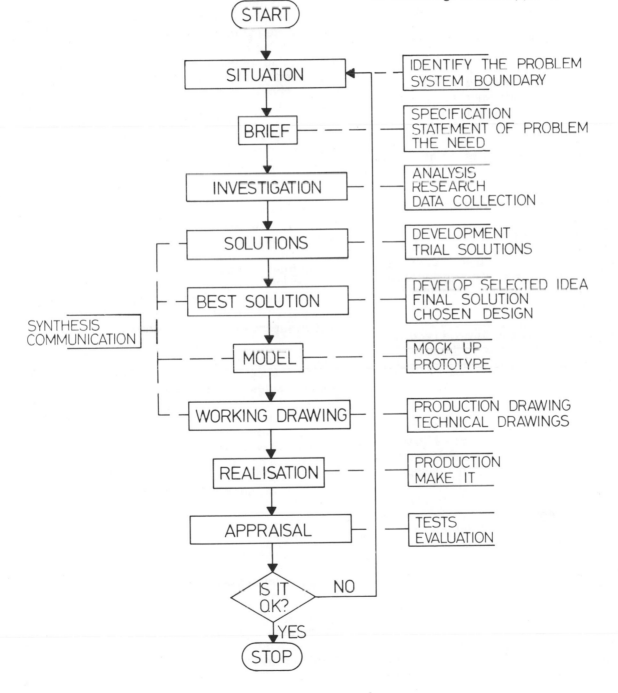

Examples of school designs

Eleven examples of school design and craft are given on pages 13 to 33. Each of these follows the design process described on pages 4 and 5. Each stage of the design process is more fully described later in this book. The eleven examples show that every piece of craft work is planned in notes and drawings. The common practice is to work on A4 or A3 sheets of drawing paper, but any other size or type of paper may be suitable.

A variety of methods of drawing, as well as a variety of styles of presenting notes and drawings are shown in the eleven examples. The following methods of drawing and styles of presentation are included:

Pencil and pen drawings, using pencils of grades B, HB or 2H; ball-point pens; technical pens; other 'mechanical' pens.

Freehand and instrument-assisted drawings.

Technical drawing methods such as: isometric drawing; cabinet oblique drawing; orthographic projections in First Angle; single-view drawing; sheet development; estimated perspective drawing; electrical circuit drawing. These methods have been applied using both freehand and instrument-assisted techniques.

Shading of drawings with pencils, crayons or water colour.

Colour wash of parts of drawings.

The use of dry transfer lettering such as Letraset.

Notes have been written in pencil or with pens, employing methods such as long hand, script writing, capital letters. Some notes have been typed. In some examples notes have been included in the printed text.

The number of drawing sheets included with each example varies from a single sheet in the case of the neck pendant, to as many as six sheets in the case of the marbles game project.

Investigation and solutions

1. The notes of the investigation may either be written in columns on the drawing sheets on which the solutions are to be drawn (the neck pendant, page 13, is an example) or written on separate sheets of paper.
2. Start the investigation notes with written statements of the design situation and the design brief arising from the situation. These statements should be as short, but as clear as is possible.
3. After writing the situation and design brief statements, the investigation notes can commence with notes on the function of the design.
4. Ergonomics will always be an important consideration. A simple drawing explaining the ergonomics problem will often assist.
5. The drawing of ideas for solutions can now commence. Draw anything that comes to mind.

Even if an idea seems silly or absurd, a drawing should be made. Some seemingly silly ideas may be developed into good designs. Aim for at least three different solutions but, as can be seen in the examples which follow, many more ideas for solutions are often possible.

6. As solutions are drawn, investigation notes can be written. For example, as solutions are drawn, the shape and form of a design will become more apparent; suitable materials will be noted; the time taken and the costs involved can be estimated; and so on. Thus, solutions and investigation notes build up side by side as the design work develops.
7. After a number of ideas for solutions have been drawn and investigation notes become more complete, a best solution will be evolving from the suggestions in the solutions drawings. A careful and neat drawing of a chosen best solution should be made at this stage. Notes and explanatory drawings may be added to the best solution drawing.
8. The sheets of drawings and notes should be collected together in the form of a folio. An attractive cover for such a folio should be considered as part of a design and craft project. This could be particularly important if the design sheets are part of a folio for presentation at an examination or at an interview.

Model
It is always advisable to consider making a model at this stage. A model enables the designer to ensure that a design will look right and fulfil its function before a final decision about the design is made. The model may suggest changes or modifications that are needed, and these should be put into effect before you make a working drawing from which the final design is made. Photographs of some of the models for the examples are shown.

Working drawing
If, after inspecting and testing the model, the designer decides that the work so far is satisfactory, a working drawing should now be made. This would normally be drawn with technical drawing instruments, although a well-drawn clear and neat freehand drawing may suffice. It should be possible to make the final design from this working drawing. In some design work a working drawing may not be essential—as shown in the neck pendant design on page 13.

Realisation
The design can now be made, from the information given in the working drawing. Photographs of all the eleven examples are given.

Appraisal
An appraisal of the design should always be attempted. Space does not allow for an appraisal in all the examples given.

Neck pendant

In this example the drawings and notes are complete on a single sheet of paper. The sheet is divided into three parts, with spaces each side of a central larger space.

All drawings have been drawn freehand in pencil outlines. Shading has been by colour wash or colour crayons. All notes are in lower-case script written in pencil.

Many more solutions than truly necessary are shown, but the variety of possibilities is limitless.

The model of the chosen solution was made from white drawing-paper glued to a piece of teak wood veneer. Both paper and veneer were cut to shape with sharp scissors. The actual model was twice full size, measuring 120 mm high.

The finished pendant was made from thin sheet stainless steel, glued with epoxy resin glue on 5 mm thick rosewood. All edges were sanded smooth and rounded, and the pendant was finished with clear fingernail lacquer spray.

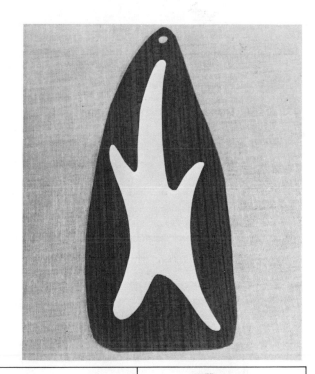

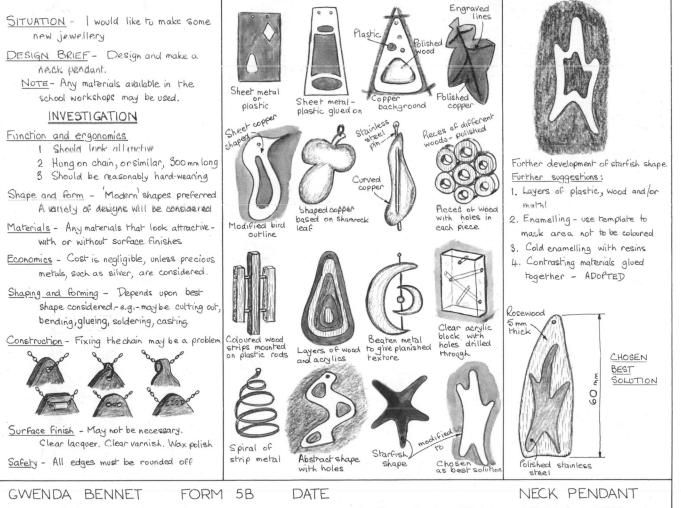

SITUATION - I would like to make some new jewellery

DESIGN BRIEF - Design and make a neck pendant.

NOTE - Any materials available in the school workshops may be used.

INVESTIGATION

Function and ergonomics
1 Should look attractive
2 Hung on chain, or similar, 300 mm long
3 Should be reasonably hard-wearing

Shape and form - 'Modern' shapes preferred
A variety of designs will be considered

Materials - Any materials that look attractive - with or without surface finishes

Economics - Cost is negligible, unless precious metals, such as silver, are considered.

Shaping and forming - Depends upon best shape considered - e.g. - maybe cutting out, bending, glueing, soldering, casting.

Construction - Fixing the chain may be a problem

Surface Finish - May not be necessary.
Clear lacquer. Clear varnish. Wax polish

Safety - All edges must be rounded off

Sheet metal or plastic

Sheet metal - plastic glued on

Plastic
Polished wood
Copper background
Polished copper

Engraved lines

Sheet copper shaped
Modified bird outline

Shaped copper based on shamrock leaf

Stainless steel pin
Curved copper

Pieces of different woods - polished
Pieces of wood with holes in each piece

Further development of starfish shape.
Further suggestions:
1. Layers of plastic, wood and/or metal
2. Enamelling - use template to mask area not to be coloured
3. Cold enamelling with resins
4. Contrasting materials glued together - ADOPTED

Coloured wood strips mounted on plastic rods

Layers of wood and acrylics

Beaten metal to give planished texture

Clear acrylic block with holes drilled through

Spiral of strip metal

Abstract shape with holes

Starfish shape

modified to
Chosen as best solution

Rosewood 5 mm thick

CHOSEN BEST SOLUTION

60 mm

Polished stainless steel

GWENDA BENNET   FORM 5B   DATE   NECK PENDANT

13

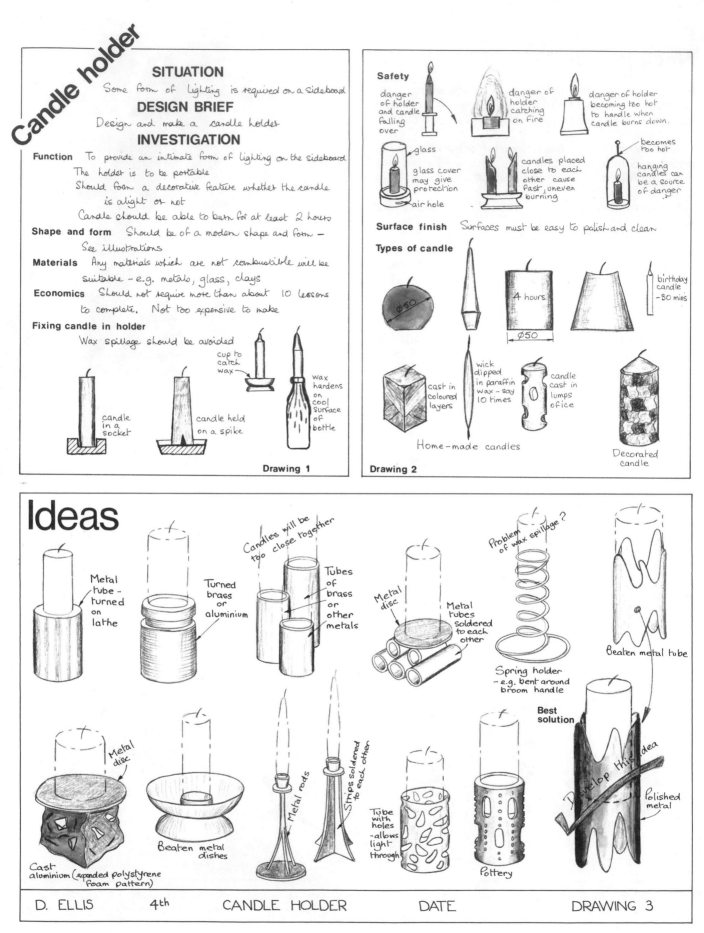

Candle holder

SITUATION
Some form of lighting is required on a sideboard

DESIGN BRIEF
Design and make a candle holder

INVESTIGATION

Function To provide an intimate form of lighting on the sideboard
The holder is to be portable
Should form a decorative feature whether the candle is alight or not
Candle should be able to burn for at least 2 hours

Shape and form Should be of a modern shape and form — See illustrations

Materials Any materials which are not combustible will be suitable — e.g. metals, glass, clays

Economics Should not require more than about 10 lessons to complete. Not too expensive to make

Fixing candle in holder
Wax spillage should be avoided

candle in a socket

cup to catch wax

candle held on a spike

wax hardens on cool surface of bottle

Drawing 1

Safety

danger of holder and candle falling over

danger of holder catching on fire

danger of holder becoming too hot to handle when candle burns down.

glass
glass cover may give protection
air hole

candles placed close to each other cause fast, uneven burning

becomes too hot
hanging candles can be a source of danger.

Surface finish Surfaces must be easy to polish and clean

Types of candle

Ø50

4 hours
Ø50

birthday candle — 30 mins

cast in coloured layers

wick dipped in paraffin wax — say 10 times

candle cast in lumps of ice

Home-made candles

Decorated candle

Drawing 2

Ideas

Metal tube — turned on lathe

Turned brass or aluminium

Candles will be too close together
Tubes of brass or other metals

Metal disc
Metal tubes soldered to each other

Problem of wax spillage?
Spring holder — e.g. bent around broom handle

Beaten metal tube

Metal disc
Cast aluminium (expanded polystyrene foam pattern)

Beaten metal dishes

Metal rods
Strips soldered to each other

Tube with holes — allows light through

Pottery

Best solution
Develop this idea
Polished metal

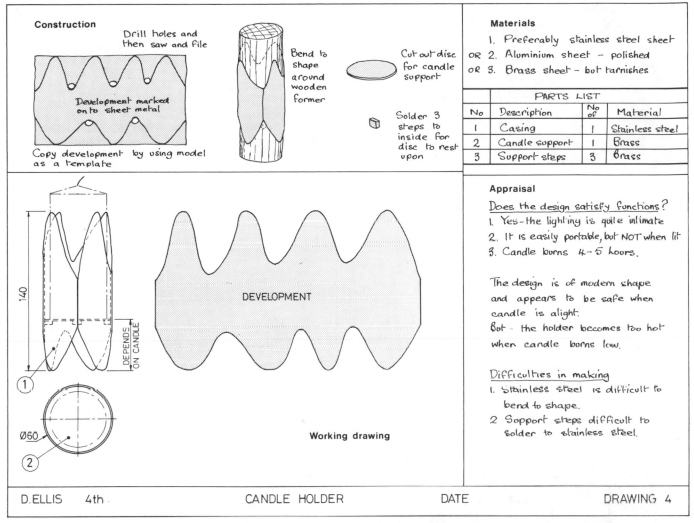

Construction

Drill holes and then saw and file

Development marked onto sheet metal

Copy development by using model as a template

Bend to shape around wooden former

Cut out disc for candle support

Solder 3 steps to inside for disc to rest upon

Materials

1. Preferably stainless steel sheet
OR 2. Aluminium sheet – polished
OR 3. Brass sheet – but tarnishes

	PARTS LIST		
No	Description	No of	Material
1	Casing	1	Stainless steel
2	Candle support	1	Brass
3	Support steps	3	Brass

140

DEPENDS ON CANDLE

DEVELOPMENT

①

Ø60

②

Working drawing

Appraisal

Does the design satisfy functions?
1. Yes – the lighting is quite intimate
2. It is easily portable, but NOT when lit
3. Candle burns 4 – 5 hours.

The design is of modern shape and appears to be safe when candle is alight.
But the holder becomes too hot when candle burns low.

Difficulties in making
1. Stainless steel is difficult to bend to shape.
2. Support steps difficult to solder to stainless steel.

D.ELLIS 4th.	CANDLE HOLDER	DATE	DRAWING 4

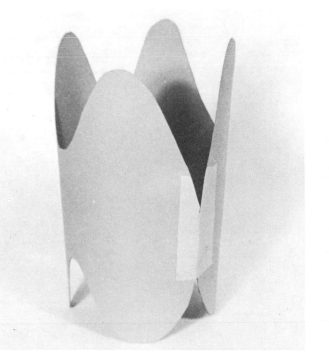

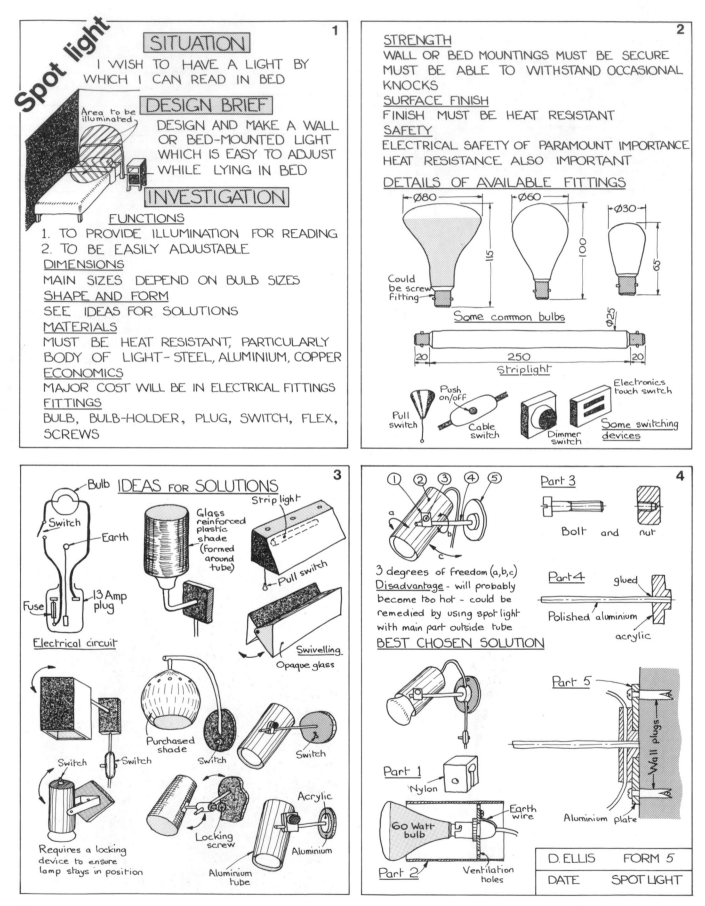

Spot light

Panel 1

SITUATION

I WISH TO HAVE A LIGHT BY WHICH I CAN READ IN BED

Area to be illuminated

DESIGN BRIEF

DESIGN AND MAKE A WALL OR BED-MOUNTED LIGHT WHICH IS EASY TO ADJUST WHILE LYING IN BED

INVESTIGATION

FUNCTIONS
1. TO PROVIDE ILLUMINATION FOR READING
2. TO BE EASILY ADJUSTABLE

DIMENSIONS
MAIN SIZES DEPEND ON BULB SIZES

SHAPE AND FORM
SEE IDEAS FOR SOLUTIONS

MATERIALS
MUST BE HEAT RESISTANT, PARTICULARLY BODY OF LIGHT- STEEL, ALUMINIUM, COPPER

ECONOMICS
MAJOR COST WILL BE IN ELECTRICAL FITTINGS

FITTINGS
BULB, BULB-HOLDER, PLUG, SWITCH, FLEX, SCREWS

Panel 2

STRENGTH
WALL OR BED MOUNTINGS MUST BE SECURE MUST BE ABLE TO WITHSTAND OCCASIONAL KNOCKS

SURFACE FINISH
FINISH MUST BE HEAT RESISTANT

SAFETY
ELECTRICAL SAFETY OF PARAMOUNT IMPORTANCE HEAT RESISTANCE ALSO IMPORTANT

DETAILS OF AVAILABLE FITTINGS

Ø80   Ø60   Ø30
115   100   65

Could be screw fitting

Some common bulbs

Ø25
20   250   20
Striplight

Pull switch
Push on/off
Cable switch
Dimmer switch
Electronics touch switch
Some switching devices

Panel 3

IDEAS FOR SOLUTIONS

Bulb
Switch
Earth
Fuse
13 Amp plug

Electrical circuit

Glass reinforced plastic shade (formed around tube)

Strip light
Pull switch
Swivelling
Opaque glass

Purchased shade
Switch   Switch   Switch   Switch

Requires a locking device to ensure lamp stays in position

Locking screw
Acrylic
Aluminium
Aluminium tube

Panel 4

① ② ③ ④ ⑤
a   b   c

3 degrees of freedom (a,b,c)
Disadvantage - will probably become too hot - could be remedied by using spot light with main part outside tube

BEST CHOSEN SOLUTION

Part 3
Bolt   and   nut

Part 4
glued
Polished aluminium
acrylic

Part 5
Wall plugs
Aluminium plate

Part 1
Nylon

Part 2
60 Watt bulb
Earth wire
Ventilation holes

D. ELLIS	FORM 5
DATE	SPOT LIGHT

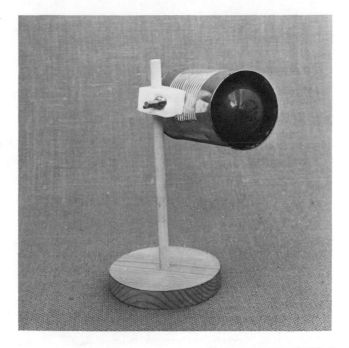

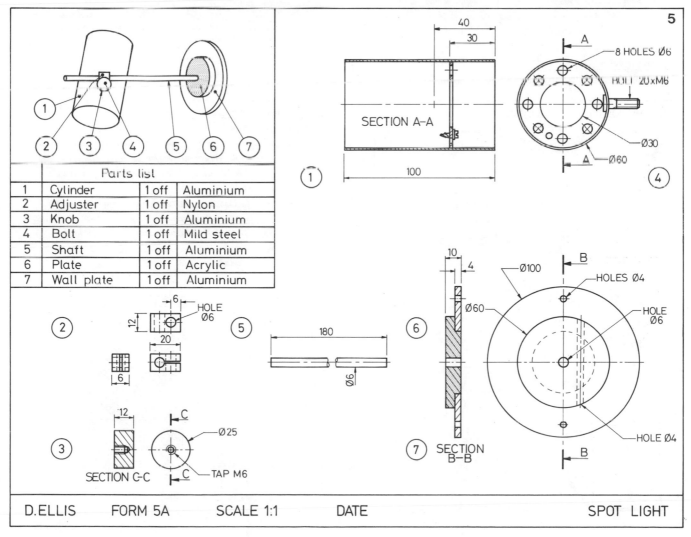

Parts list

1	Cylinder	1 off	Aluminium
2	Adjuster	1 off	Nylon
3	Knob	1 off	Aluminium
4	Bolt	1 off	Mild steel
5	Shaft	1 off	Aluminium
6	Plate	1 off	Acrylic
7	Wall plate	1 off	Aluminium

SECTION A–A

40
30
100

8 HOLES Ø6
BOLT 20 x M6
Ø30
Ø60
A
A

HOLE Ø6

6
12
20
6

180
Ø6

Ø25
TAP M6
SECTION C-C
12
C
C

10
4
Ø100
Ø60
HOLES Ø4
HOLE Ø6
HOLE Ø4
B
B
SECTION B–B

D.ELLIS   FORM 5A   SCALE 1:1   DATE   SPOT LIGHT

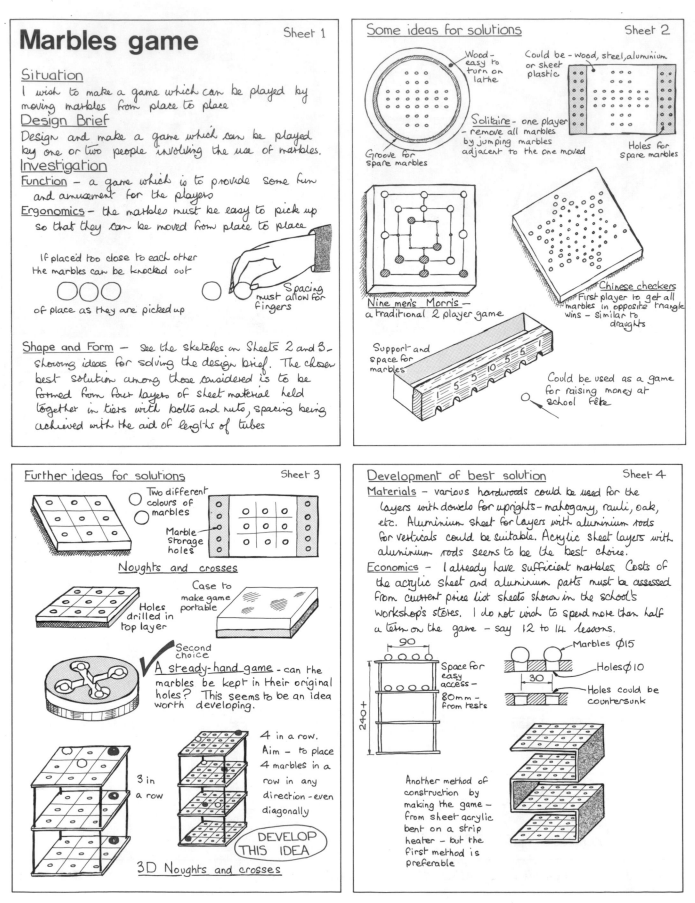

Marbles game

Situation
I wish to make a game which can be played by moving marbles from place to place

Design Brief
Design and make a game which can be played by one or two people involving the use of marbles.

Investigation
Function – a game which is to provide some fun and amusement for the players

Ergonomics – the marbles must be easy to pick up so that they can be moved from place to place

If placed too close to each other the marbles can be knocked out

of place as they are picked up

Spacing must allow for fingers

Shape and Form – See the sketches on Sheets 2 and 3 showing ideas for solving the design brief. The chosen best solution among those considered is to be formed from four layers of sheet material held together in tiers with bolts and nuts, spacing being achieved with the aid of lengths of tubes

---

Some ideas for solutions

Wood – easy to turn on lathe

Groove for spare marbles

Could be – wood, steel, aluminium or sheet plastic

Solitaire – one player – remove all marbles by jumping marbles adjacent to the one moved

Holes for spare marbles

Nine men's Morris – a traditional 2 player game

Chinese checkers – First player to get all marbles in opposite triangle wins – similar to draughts

Support and space for marbles

1 5 5 10 5 5 1

Could be used as a game for raising money at school fête

Further ideas for solutions

Two different colours of marbles

Marble storage holes

Noughts and crosses

Case to make game portable

Holes drilled in top layer

Second choice

✓ A **steady-hand game** – can the marbles be kept in their original holes? This seems to be an idea worth developing.

3 in a row

4 in a row. Aim – to place 4 marbles in a row in any direction – even diagonally

DEVELOP THIS IDEA

3D Noughts and crosses

Development of best solution

Materials – various hardwoods could be used for the layers with dowels for uprights – mahogany, rauli, oak, etc. Aluminium sheet for layers with aluminium rods for verticals could be suitable. Acrylic sheet layers with aluminium rods seems to be the best choice.

Economics – I already have sufficient marbles. Costs of the acrylic sheet and aluminium parts must be assessed from current price list sheets shown in the school's workshop's stores. I do not wish to spend more than half a term on the game – say 12 to 14 lessons.

90

240+

Space for easy access – 80mm – from tests

Marbles Ø15

Holes Ø10

30

Holes could be countersunk

Another method of construction by making the game – from sheet acrylic bent on a strip heater – but the first method is preferable

---

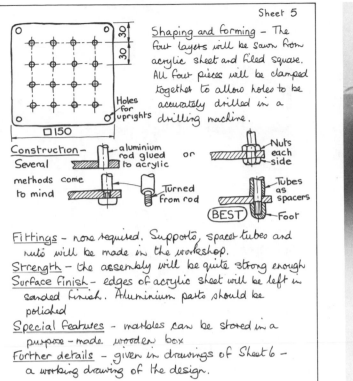

□150

30 30 30

Holes for uprights

<u>Shaping and forming</u> - The four layers will be sawn from acrylic sheet and filed square. All four pieces will be clamped together to allow holes to be accurately drilled in a drilling machine.

<u>Construction</u> - Several methods come to mind

aluminium rod glued to acrylic   or   Nuts each side

Turned from rod

Tubes as spacers

(BEST)   Foot

<u>Fittings</u> - none required. Supports, spacer tubes and nuts will be made in the workshop.

<u>Strength</u> - the assembly will be quite strong enough

<u>Surface finish</u> - edges of acrylic sheet will be left in sanded finish. Aluminium parts should be polished

<u>Special features</u> - marbles can be stored in a purpose-made wooden box

<u>Further details</u> - given in drawings of Sheet 6 - a working drawing of the design.

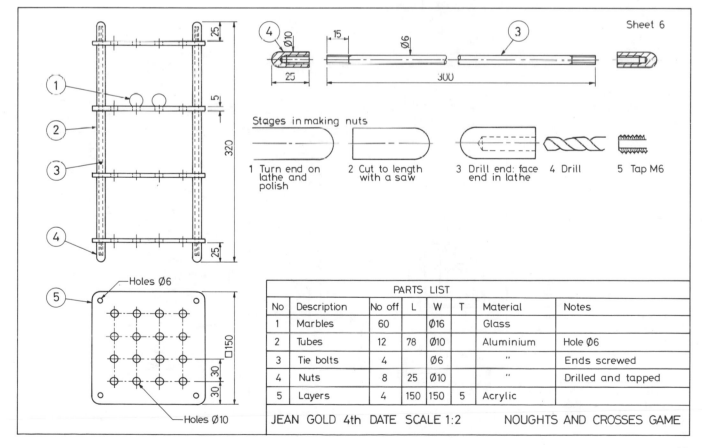

Sheet 6

④ Ø10   15   Ø6   ③   300   25

25   5   320   25

⑤ Holes Ø6   □150   30 30   30 30   Holes Ø10

Stages in making nuts

1 Turn end on lathe and polish   2 Cut to length with a saw   3 Drill end: face end in lathe   4 Drill   5 Tap M6

PARTS LIST							
No	Description	No off	L	W	T	Material	Notes
1	Marbles	60		Ø16		Glass	
2	Tubes	12	78	Ø10		Aluminium	Hole Ø6
3	Tie bolts	4		Ø6		"	Ends screwed
4	Nuts	8	25	Ø10		"	Drilled and tapped
5	Layers	4	150	150	5	Acrylic	

JEAN GOLD 4th   DATE   SCALE 1:2   NOUGHTS AND CROSSES GAME

Cacti stand

This is an example of outline drawings made with a black ball-point pen. Water colour wash has been applied by brush to all drawings.

All printing is in capitals and lower case using black ball-point pen.

Note the ergonomic problem stated with two drawings of cacti.

The selected best solution is really a development of one of the suggested solutions.

The model was made from cardboard and drinking straws. The model is about one-fifth full size. Holes for the straws were made with a leather punch with a variable hole-cutter head.

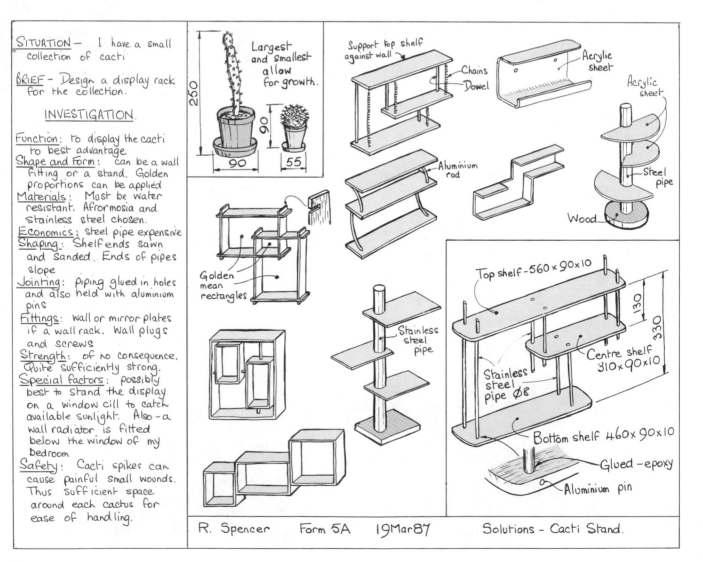

SITUATION – I have a small collection of cacti

BRIEF – Design a display rack for the collection.

INVESTIGATION.

Function: to display the cacti to best advantage
Shape and Form: can be a wall fitting or a stand. Golden proportions can be applied
Materials: Must be water resistant. Afrormosia and stainless steel chosen.
Economics: steel pipe expensive
Shaping: Shelf ends sawn and sanded. Ends of pipes slope
Jointing: piping glued in holes and also held with aluminium pins
Fittings: Wall or mirror plates if a wall rack. Wall plugs and screws
Strength: of no consequence. Quite sufficiently strong.
Special factors: possibly best to stand the display on a window cill to catch available sunlight. Also - a wall radiator is fitted below the window of my bedroom
Safety: Cacti spikes can cause painful small wounds. Thus sufficient space around each cactus for ease of handling.

Largest and smallest allow for growth.

Support top shelf against wall

Chains
Dowel

Acrylic sheet

Acrylic sheet

Aluminium rod

Steel pipe

Wood

Golden mean rectangles

Stainless steel pipe

Top shelf – 560 × 90 × 10

Centre shelf 310 × 90 × 10

Stainless steel pipe Ø8

Bottom shelf 460 × 90 × 10

Glued – epoxy

Aluminium pin

R. Spencer   Form 5A   19 Mar 87   Solutions – Cacti Stand.

20

Working drawing

Three-view orthographic drawing made with 0.6 and 0.2 Rotring automatic pens and Indian ink.

All printing drawn with a 0.5 Rotring pen using a 6 mm Rotring lettering stencil.

All dimensions drawn with the aid of the same Rotring stencil.

Note the use of a scale. All parts of the drawing are made to half full size. However, full size dimensions are shown.

The completed cacti stand was made from 10 mm thick mahogany. In place of the suggested stainless steel pipes for the uprights, 8 mm diameter aluminium rod was used. This was because stainless steel piping could not be purchased in the locality.

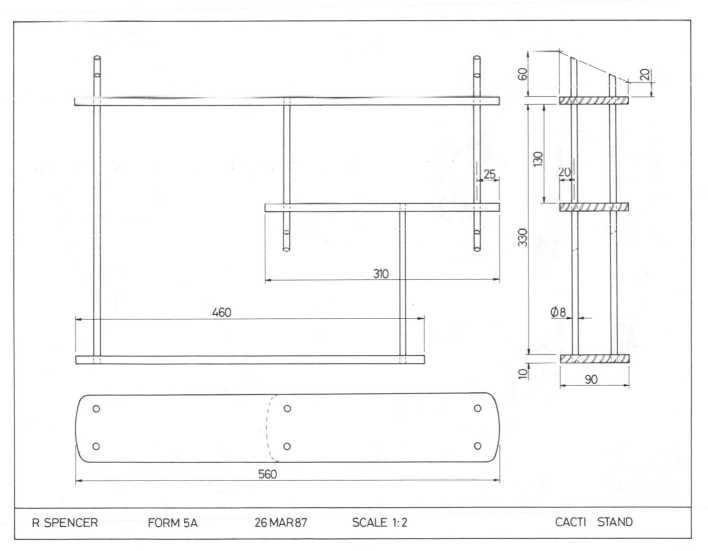

| R SPENCER | FORM 5A | 26 MAR 87 | SCALE 1:2 | CACTI STAND |

Lamp stand

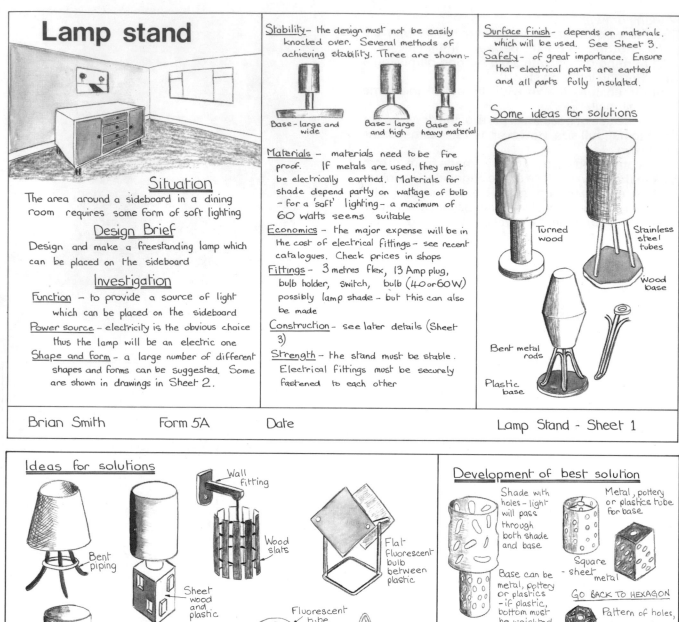

Situation

The area around a sideboard in a dining room requires some form of soft lighting

Design Brief

Design and make a freestanding lamp which can be placed on the sideboard

Investigation

Function – to provide a source of light which can be placed on the sideboard

Power source – electricity is the obvious choice thus the lamp will be an electric one

Shape and form – a large number of different shapes and forms can be suggested. Some are shown in drawings in Sheet 2.

Stability – the design must not be easily knocked over. Several methods of achieving stability. Three are shown:–

Base – large and wide

Base – large and high

Base of heavy material

Materials – materials need to be fire proof. If metals are used, they must be electrically earthed. Materials for shade depend partly on wattage of bulb – for a 'soft' lighting – a maximum of 60 watts seems suitable

Economics – the major expense will be in the cost of electrical fittings – see recent catalogues. Check prices in shops

Fittings – 3 metres flex, 13 Amp plug, bulb holder, switch, bulb (40 or 60W) possibly lamp shade – but this can also be made

Construction – see later details (Sheet 3)

Strength – the stand must be stable. Electrical fittings must be securely fastened to each other

---

Surface finish – depends on materials, which will be used. See Sheet 3.

Safety – of great importance. Ensure that electrical parts are earthed and all parts fully insulated.

Some ideas for solutions

Turned wood

Stainless steel tubes

Wood base

Bent metal rods

Plastic base

Brian Smith   Form 5A   Date   Lamp Stand – Sheet 1

Ideas for solutions

Bent piping

Wall fitting

Wood slats

Flat fluorescent bulb between plastic

Sheet wood and plastic

Metal plate in triangle mounted on circular base

Fluorescent tube

Bulb slung in cradle

ditto

Copper plate with cut-out shapes

DEVELOP

Bulbs mounted in bent plastic sheet

Turned wood

Sheet plastic

Development of best solution

Shade with holes – light will pass through both shade and base

Metal, pottery or plastics tube for base

Square – sheet metal

Base can be metal, pottery or plastics – if plastic, bottom must be weighted

GO BACK TO HEXAGON

Pattern of holes, or engraved, or pieces glued – prefer holes

GO BACK TO ORIGINAL

pattern of triangles

6 pieces brazed together

Better

Bend to hexagon

THUS   each 70

130

Brian Smith   Form 5A   Date   Lamp Stand – Sheet 2

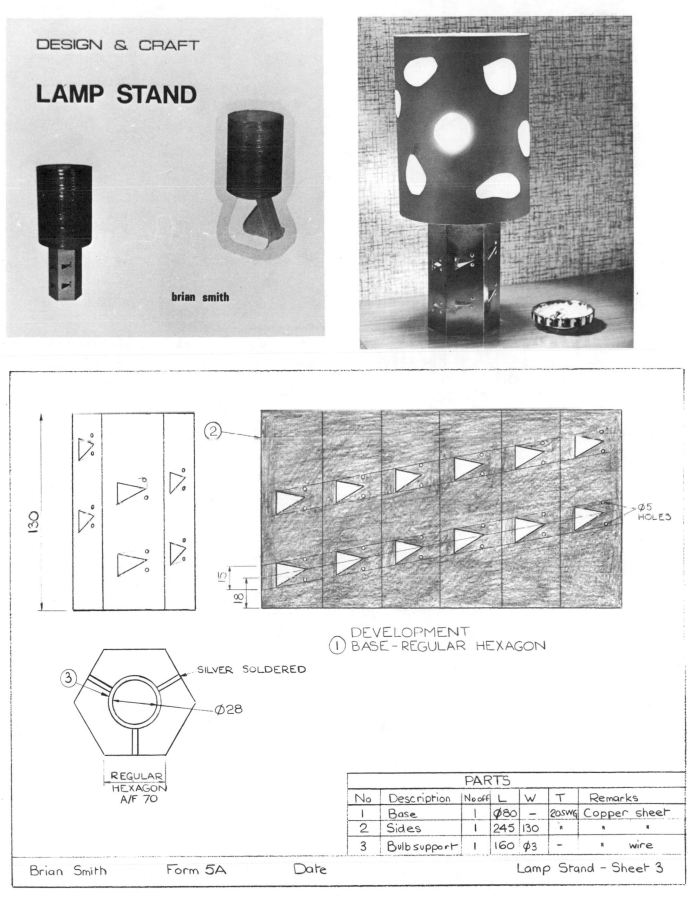

DESIGN & CRAFT

LAMP STAND

brian smith

130

15
18

② ... Ø5 HOLES

DEVELOPMENT
① BASE – REGULAR HEXAGON

③ SILVER SOLDERED

Ø28

REGULAR
HEXAGON
A/F 70

PARTS						
No	Description	No off	L	W	T	Remarks
1	Base	1	Ø80	–	20swg	Copper sheet
2	Sides	1	245	130	"	" "
3	Bulb support	1	160	Ø3	–	" wire

Brian Smith   Form 5A   Date   Lamp Stand – Sheet 3

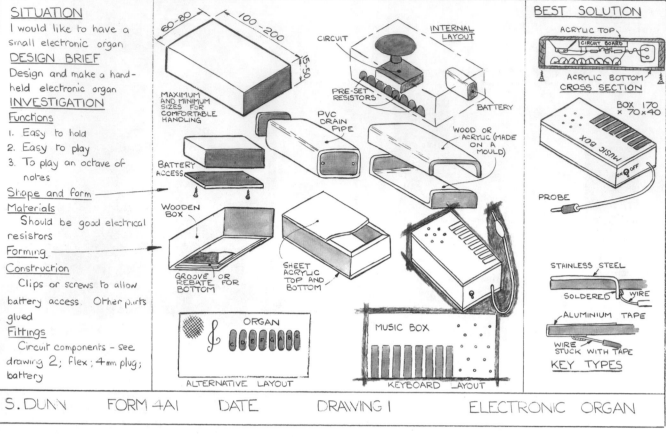

SITUATION
I would like to have a small electronic organ
DESIGN BRIEF
Design and make a hand-held electronic organ
INVESTIGATION
Functions
1. Easy to hold
2. Easy to play
3. To play an octave of notes

Shape and form
Materials
   Should be good electrical resistors
Forming
Construction
   Clips or screws to allow battery access. Other parts glued
Fittings
   Circuit components – see drawing 2; flex; 4mm plug; battery

60-80
100-200
15-50
MAXIMUM AND MINIMUM SIZES FOR COMFORTABLE HANDLING

CIRCUIT
INTERNAL LAYOUT
PRE-SET RESISTORS
BATTERY
PVC DRAIN PIPE
WOOD OR ACRYLIC (MADE ON A MOULD)

BATTERY ACCESS
WOODEN BOX
GROOVE OR REBATE FOR BOTTOM
SHEET ACRYLIC TOP AND BOTTOM

ORGAN
C D E F G A B C
ALTERNATIVE LAYOUT

MUSIC BOX
KEYBOARD LAYOUT

BEST SOLUTION
ACRYLIC TOP
CIRCUIT BOARD
ACRYLIC BOTTOM
CROSS SECTION
BOX 170 × 70 × 40
MUSIC BOX
ON OFF
PROBE

STAINLESS STEEL
SOLDERED WIRE
ALUMINIUM TAPE
WIRE STUCK WITH TAPE
KEY TYPES

S. DUNN   FORM 4A1   DATE   DRAWING 1   ELECTRONIC ORGAN

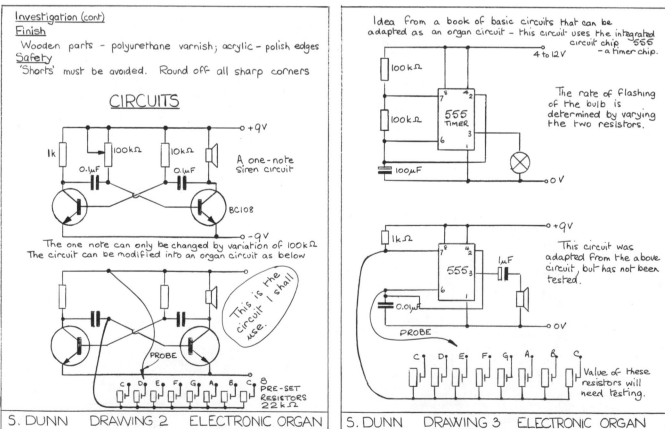

Investigation (cont)
Finish
   Wooden parts – polyurethane varnish; acrylic – polish edges
Safety
   'Shorts' must be avoided. Round off all sharp corners

CIRCUITS

+9V
1k
100kΩ
10kΩ
0.1μF
0.1μF
-9V
BC108
A one-note siren circuit

The one note can only be changed by variation of 100kΩ
The circuit can be modified into an organ circuit as below

PROBE
C D E F G A B C
PRE-SET RESISTORS 22kΩ

This is the circuit I shall use.

S. DUNN   DRAWING 2   ELECTRONIC ORGAN

Idea from a book of basic circuits that can be adapted as an organ circuit – this circuit uses the integrated circuit chip 555 – a timer chip.

100kΩ
100kΩ
555 TIMER
100μF
4 to 12V
0V

The rate of flashing of the bulb is determined by varying the two resistors.

1kΩ
555
1μF
0.01μF
PROBE
+9V
0V

This circuit was adapted from the above circuit, but has not been tested.

C D E F G A B C
Value of these resistors will need testing.

S. DUNN   DRAWING 3   ELECTRONIC ORGAN

Electronic organ

A simple ergonomic sketch to show the sizes related to handling has been included.

The drawings are in pencil or crayon, shaded with colour wash or crayon colours. The best solution is outlined strongly with crayonned lines.

Various details are included in the best solution column to show how the electronics relate to the box designed to hold them.

Note the use of dry-transfer lettering on the completed design.

Notes have been drawn freehand in pencil using lower-case lettering. Two arrows, from Shape and Form and from Forming, indicate that these parts of the investigation are completely covered in the solution drawings.

Notes on drawings are in 4 mm capitals. The title is in 6 mm capitals.

The working drawing is a three-view orthographic drawing of the box and its parts. Two of the views are sectioned to show clearly the internal layouts. Part associated with the circuitry are colour-washed to differentiate them from the container.

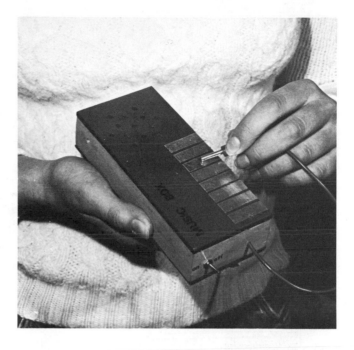

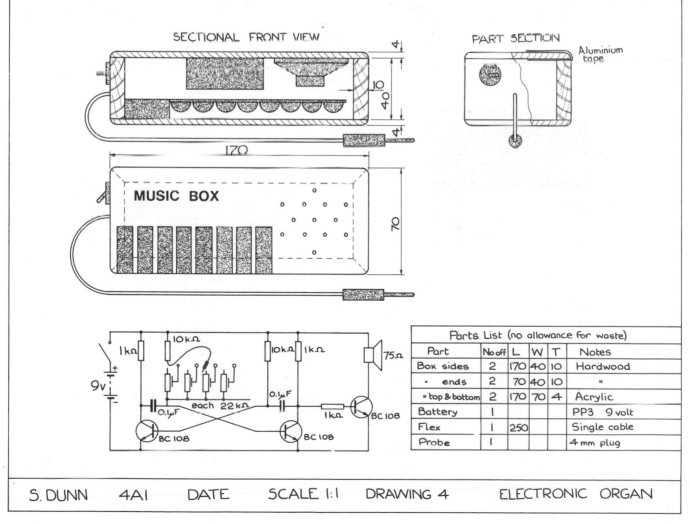

SECTIONAL FRONT VIEW

PART SECTION

Aluminium tape

170

40

10

4

4

MUSIC BOX

70

1kΩ 10kΩ 10kΩ 1kΩ 75Ω

9v

each 22kΩ

0.1μF

0.1μF

0.1μF

1kΩ

BC 108

BC 108

BC 108

Parts List (no allowance for waste)				
Part	No off	L	W	T	Notes
Box sides	2	170	40	10	Hardwood
„ ends	2	70	40	10	„
„ top & bottom	2	170	70	4	Acrylic
Battery	1				PP3 9 volt
Flex	1	250			Single cable
Probe	1				4 mm plug

S. DUNN   4A1   DATE   SCALE 1:1   DRAWING 4   ELECTRONIC ORGAN

Stool

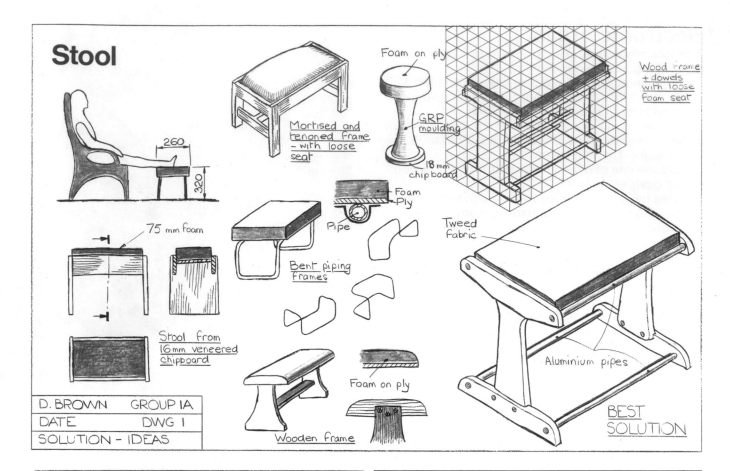

260

320

75 mm foam

Stool from 16 mm veneered chipboard

Mortised and tenoned frame – with loose seat

Foam on ply

GRP moulding

18 mm chipboard

Wood Frame + dowels with loose foam seat

Foam Ply

Pipe

Bent piping frames

Foam on ply

Wooden frame

Tweed Fabric

Aluminium pipes

BEST SOLUTION

D. BROWN	GROUP 1A
DATE	DWG 1
SOLUTION – IDEAS	

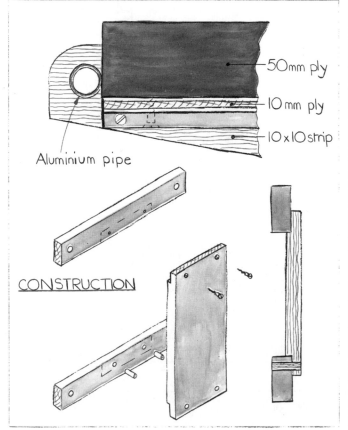

50mm ply

10 mm ply

10 x 10 strip

Aluminium pipe

CONSTRUCTION

SITUATION

My parents wish to 'put their feet up' when watching television.

DESIGN BRIEF

Design a suitable footstool.

INVESTIGATION

Function – to provide an upholstered surface at the right height – 320 mm. Upholstery to be about 260 mm wide.

Shape and form – a length of 420 mm will give a 'Golden mean' of 260:420. Framed construction. Frame parts shaped. Rectangular block upholstery.

Materials – various dark-coloured hardwoods were considered for the wooden parts – afrormosia, teak, iroko, but teak was chosen, even though it is very expensive. Dowels from wood were considered for the cylindrical rods, but aluminium pipe was chosen in the belief that it would form a pleasing contrast to the dark colours in the teak. Polyurethane foam block covered with a rough tweed furnishing material was selected for the loose seat.

Economics – all the materials will be expensive and their costs will have to be worked out from up-to-date catalogues. This is a present for my parents, so the expense will be well worth while. Probably a full term's work.

Shaping – all shaped edges will be bow-sawed, filed and sanded.

Construction – uprights will be glued and screwed to the top rails. Uprights will be glued and dowelled to the bottom rails. The Ø20 mm aluminium pipes will be glued with an epoxy resin glue to the end frames.

Strength – will be more than sufficient.

Finish – two coats of clear polyurethane varnish to both wooden and aluminium parts. The rough tweed surfaces of the upholstery will form a pleasing contrast to the smooth varnished surfaces of the stool.

Special factor – holes must be bored in the plywood of the loose seat to allow air to escape from the foam as it is sat upon.

Safety – remove all sharp corners.

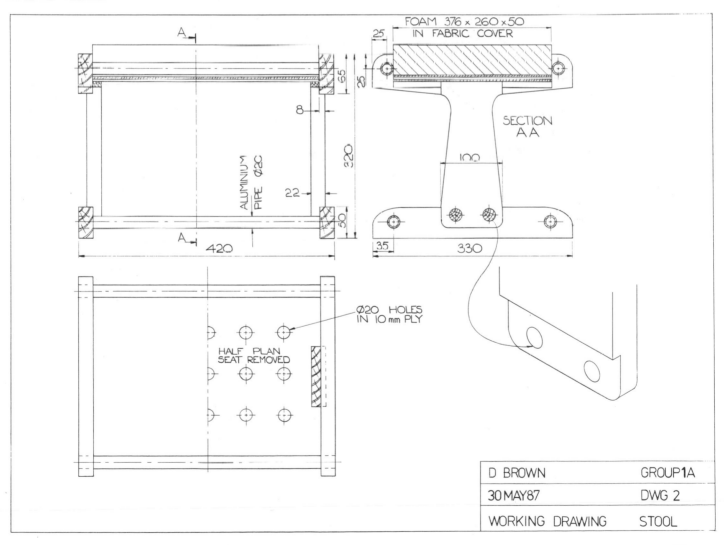

A

ALUMINIUM PIPE Ø20

65

8

320

22

50

A

420

FOAM 376 × 260 × 50
IN FABRIC COVER

25

25

SECTION
A A

100

35

330

Ø20 HOLES
IN 10 mm PLY

HALF PLAN
SEAT REMOVED

D BROWN	GROUP 1A
30 MAY 87	DWG 2
WORKING DRAWING	STOOL

27

Drawing table

Situation
A girl taking a course leading to an art examination needs a table at which to practice.

Brief
Design a lightweight knock-down table suitable for the girl's art work.

Investigation
Function Sizes found by measurement—approximately 1200 mm by 600 mm, 750 mm high.

Top must be waterproof to allow washing of paints, glues etc. from the surface.

Must be robust yet light in weight and easily 'knocked down' for storage.

Shape and form The final idea is to support a boxed top on two framed ends with rails between. Simple radius curves are to be worked on the end frame members.

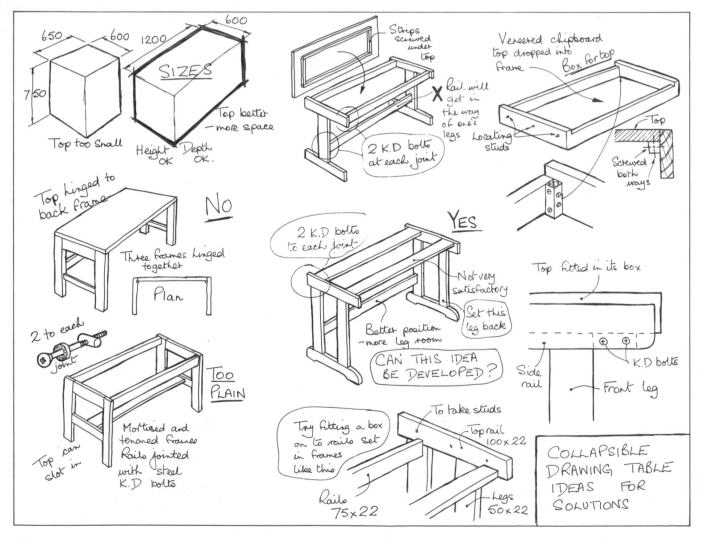

COLLAPSIBLE DRAWING TABLE IDEAS FOR SOLUTIONS

Top is to be a double square. Ends to be in proportions near to a golden mean. Rails will be carefully proportioned so as to avoid over-heavy or over-thin appearance.

Strength Chipboard top is adequately strong. Framed ends are held to rails by steel KD bolts.

Materials Framework—mahogany. Top—vinyl-coated chipboard.

Economics The design will possibly take two terms of workshop time to make. Cost—must check with recent catalogues.

Shaping Curves on frame members.

Jointing Top screwed via 15 mm strips to its box. Box jointed with similar strips. End frames mortised and tenoned. Long rails joined to end frames with 50 mm steel bolts and collars in steel dowels.

Fittings 12 steel bolts; 12 steel dowels; 12 collars for bolts; 6 brass dowels for locating top to frames.

Surface finish Top requires no finish, being vinyl. Framework to be given three coats of matt polyurethane clear varnish.

Note
The solutions drawings are in ball-point pen work. Working drawings are inked.

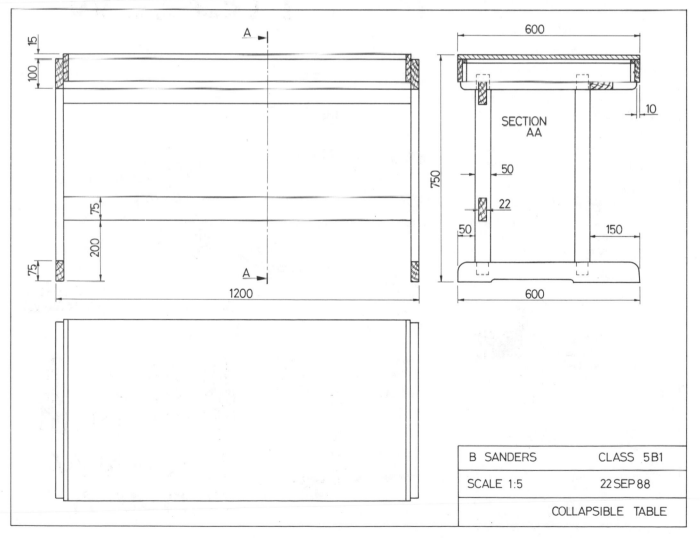

B SANDERS	CLASS 5B1
SCALE 1:5	22 SEP 88
	COLLAPSIBLE TABLE

Windvane

Investigation
Function
1. To be seen easily from the bedroom window.
2. To indicate wind direction.
3. To be maintenance-free.
4. Must be capable of being fixed to a roof.

Shape and form Many and varied. Choose bird and arrow for windvane.

Materials Windvane and letters from sheet steel 2 mm thick. Bearings carbon tool steel and ball bearing. Frame of mild steel.

Economics Check costs against recent catalogues. Probably at least a term's workshop lessons required.

Shaping and forming Vane and direction letters shaped by drilling and filing.

Jointing Vane, arrows and letters riveted. Rotating parts turned on the lathe. Ball bearing and rotating parts packed with grease to stop entry of rain and water.

Fittings Ball bearing. Rivets.

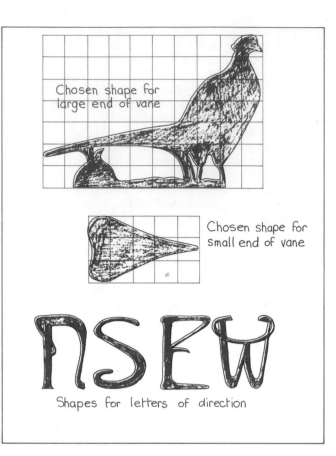

Chosen shape for large end of vane

Chosen shape for small end of vane

Shapes for letters of direction

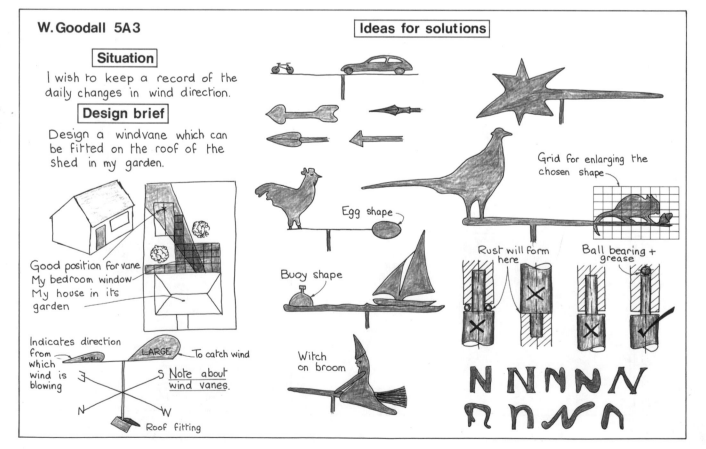

W. Goodall 5A3

Ideas for solutions

Situation

I wish to keep a record of the daily changes in wind direction.

Design brief

Design a windvane which can be fitted on the roof of the shed in my garden.

Good position for vane
My bedroom window
My house in its garden

Indicates direction from which wind is blowing

SMALL   LARGE   To catch wind

N   S   E   W   Note about wind vanes.

Roof fitting

Egg shape

Buoy shape

Witch on broom

Grid for enlarging the chosen shape

Rust will form here

Ball bearing + grease

Strength   Must withstand gale-strength winds.
Surface finish   All parts painted. Red oxide primer followed by three coats of matt top-coat.
Special factors   Vane must be located correctly according to compass points. Stem must be upright if the vane is to work correctly and easily. Must be in a position where wind is not deflected by nearby features.
Safety   Ensure the fitting to the roof is secure to avoid danger of the windvane falling away from the roof.
The drawings   All drawings are in ball-point pen with colour and crayon shading.

The working drawing is a single partial view, with the main upright and the south arm 'broken'. This was necessary to ensure the whole fitting could be drawn to a reasonable scale (1:2) yet fit on an A3 sheet.

Note

A photograph of a full-size model made to test whether the arrow of the windvane would work well is included on page 110.

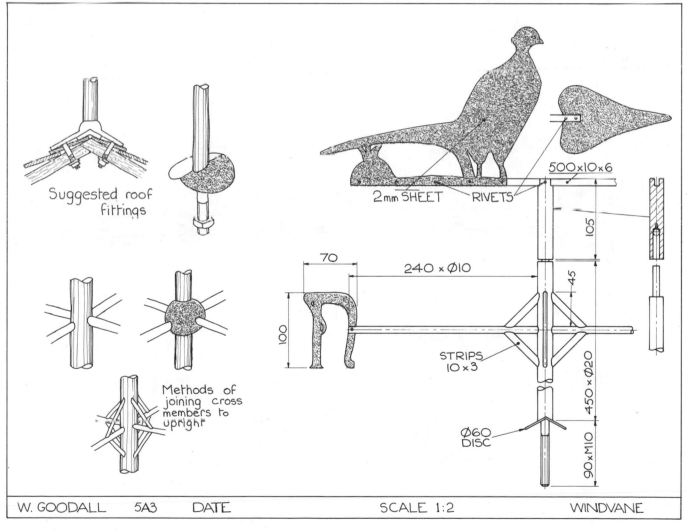

31

Sculpture

Situation
A decorative item is required on a sideboard.

Design brief
Design a free-standing piece of sculpture.

Investigation
Function To attract attention and to give visual pleasure. Should be at least 300 mm tall.
Shape and form Geometrical or from nature. Tall in relation to width. Idea for the best solution makes use of movement caused by magnetic attraction.
Materials Colourless acrylic sheet chosen. Also a length of white acrylic rod.
Economics Much time spent, because a second sculpture had to be made. Check cost of acrylic. Economy of line, shape and form satisfactory.
Jointing Tensol No. 12 for jointing the acrylic.
Fittings Short length of chain. Roller bearings. Magnet.
Strength Tensol glue lines are quite strong enough.
Surface finish Sides of acrylic polished. Edges left sanded.
Special factors Much time spent in arranging positions of rollers to ensure that the magnetic rod returns to vertical.
Safety No problems.

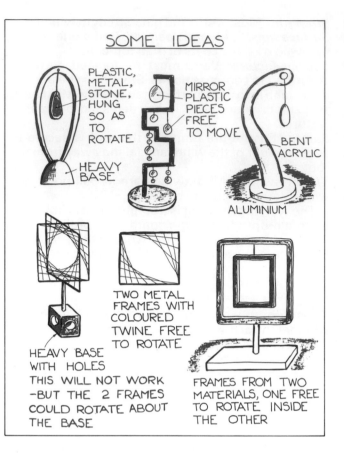

SOME IDEAS

PLASTIC, METAL, STONE, HUNG SO AS TO ROTATE
HEAVY BASE

MIRROR PLASTIC PIECES FREE TO MOVE

BENT ACRYLIC
ALUMINIUM

HEAVY BASE WITH HOLES THIS WILL NOT WORK —BUT THE 2 FRAMES COULD ROTATE ABOUT THE BASE

TWO METAL FRAMES WITH COLOURED TWINE FREE TO ROTATE

FRAMES FROM TWO MATERIALS, ONE FREE TO ROTATE INSIDE THE OTHER

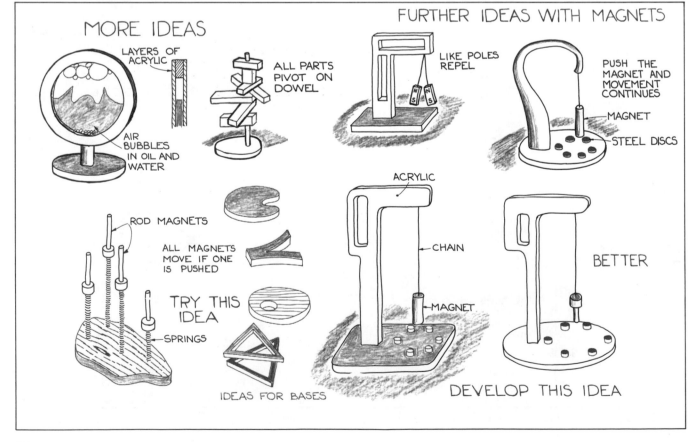

MORE IDEAS

FURTHER IDEAS WITH MAGNETS

LAYERS OF ACRYLIC

AIR BUBBLES IN OIL AND WATER

ALL PARTS PIVOT ON DOWEL

LIKE POLES REPEL

PUSH THE MAGNET AND MOVEMENT CONTINUES
MAGNET
STEEL DISCS

ROD MAGNETS

ALL MAGNETS MOVE IF ONE IS PUSHED

TRY THIS IDEA

SPRINGS

IDEAS FOR BASES

ACRYLIC

CHAIN

MAGNET

DEVELOP THIS IDEA

BETTER

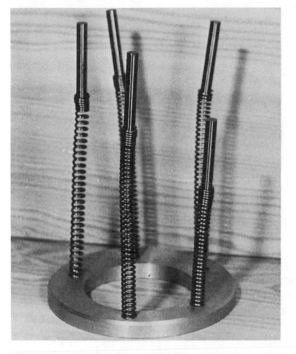

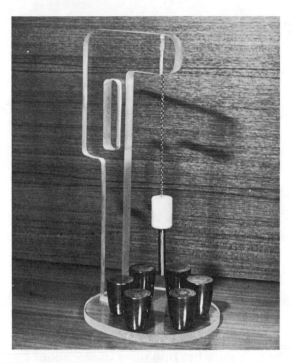

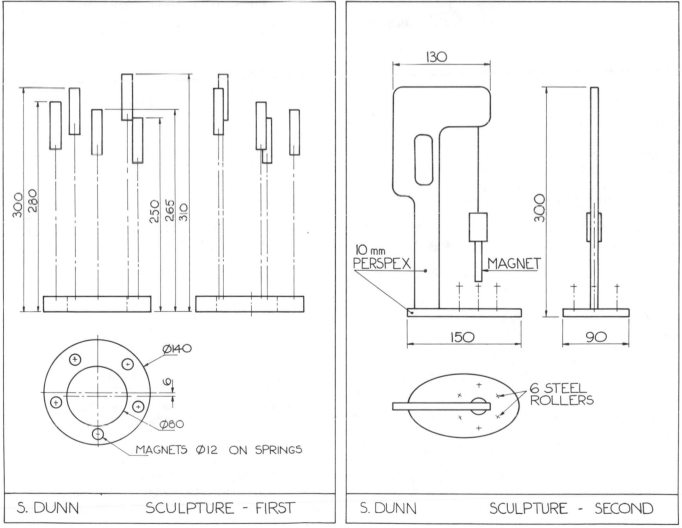

300
280
250
265
310

Ø140
6
Ø80
MAGNETS Ø12 ON SPRINGS

S. DUNN   SCULPTURE - FIRST

130
300
10 mm PERSPEX
MAGNET
150
90
6 STEEL ROLLERS

S. DUNN   SCULPTURE - SECOND

SECTION 2

The Design Process

Situation

All designing is concerned with finding solutions to problems caused by situations from the environments in which people live. These situations give rise to needs which designs attempt to satisfy. If a design fully satisfies the needs caused by a situation, it can be said to be successful.

Some examples of situations
1. 'I need to talk to Jean.'
   'I want to hear what Brian has to say about our holiday.'
   'I must thank Uncle Harry for his birthday present.'
Situation—People have a desire to communicate with each other.
   From this situation such services as postal and telephone systems have been designed.
2. 'I must go to school.'
   'We would like a summer holiday in Switzerland.'
   'I want to visit Aunt Anne, but she lives thirty kilometres away.'
Situation—People need means of transport.
   From this situation a variety of methods of personal transport have been designed—buses, trains, cars, aeroplanes, ships and so on.
3. An infant is bored and restless. This is a situation. To meet this situation a range of toys have been designed.
4. When people visit me at my home they always have difficulty in finding my house.
Situation—My house cannot be easily identified.
   From this situation it is obvious that the house requires some means of identification.
5. A friend with permanently paralysed legs cannot travel to the library to obtain books.
Situation—A man with paralysed legs requires some means of transport which he can control by himself.
   From this situation many types of invalid chairs and vehicles have been designed.
6. My father always leaves his do-it-yourself tools in inconvenient places about the house.
Situation—There is no place where my father's tools can be stored.
   From such a situation some form of storage needs to be designed.

What you must do
1. Before commencing work on a design, write a clear statement of the situation for which your design is being made.
2. While investigating problems relating to your design keep thinking back to the situation you are attempting to satisfy.
3. When you have completed a design ask yourself the question:
   'Does my design satisfy the situation?'

Other situations
Some design situations arise from existing designs. Some examples:
1. *Situation*—That kettle is dangerous. When filled with boiling water its handle is too hot to hold.
2. *Situation*—When I sit in this chair for any length of time my back begins to ache.
3. *Situation*—If I read a book under that light my eyes begin to feel painful after about an hour.
4. *Situation*—It is almost impossible to work at that table. It is too high.
   In meeting the design demands of such situations, the existing design may need to be modified, altered or changed, or a new design produced.

Exercises

1. Find five design situations selected from your own home:
   (a) from the kitchen;
   (b) from the sitting-room;
   (c) from the bathroom;
   (d) from the entrance door or hall;
   (e) from a bedroom.
   Write clear statements for each of the design situations you have found.

2. Find five designs in your home which you consider do not meet the situations for which they were made. Write clear statements giving the design situation for the five articles.

3. Some newspaper and magazine articles bring out clearly the needs for new designs to meet certain situations. Find such an article, cut it out, paste it to a sheet of writing paper and add a clear statement of the design situation covering the needs brought up in the article.

4. Write the design brief from which the video cassette case shown in the photograph could have been designed.

Design brief

A design brief is a statement setting out clearly what is to be designed. A design brief arises from a design situation. The purpose of the brief is to select and state exactly how the needs arising from the situation are to be met.

Some examples of design briefs
Taking some of the situations from page 34 and stating the design briefs arising from them:
1. *Situation*—My house cannot be easily identified.
Brief—The house name is LONGCROFT. Design a house name-plate which can be attached to the brickwork at the front of the house. The name should be clearly readable from the pavement.
2. *Situation*—My father always leaves his do-it-yourself tools in inconvenient places about the house.
Brief—Design a tool box which will hold all my father's tools and which can be carried from place to place around the home.
3. *Situation*—That kettle is dangerous. When filled with boiling water its handle is too hot to be held.
Brief—Design a new handle which can be fitted in place of the existing handle.
4. *Situation*—When I sit in this chair for any length of time my back begins to ache.
Brief—Design a new chair in which I can sit without discomfort.

The wording of a design brief requires careful consideration. A wrongly worded brief may result in a design which does not satisfy the needs of the design situation. The aim of the brief is to give an instruction which can be carried out by those de-signing a solution to the brief.

Alternative briefs
The needs of most design situations can be met in a variety of ways and thus several briefs can be written in answer to the needs of any design situation. Two examples:
1. *Situation*—I have hundreds of books which, at the moment, are piled in a corner of my bedroom.
Brief—(a) Design a free-standing, open-fronted bookrack to contain all the books.
Brief—(b) Design a set of wall shelves to hold all the books.
Brief—(c) Design a box in which the books can be stored.
Brief—(d) Design a bookcase with glass doors in which the books can be placed.
2. *Situation*—When writing at my desk I need some form of lighting to illuminate the paper.
Brief—(a) Design a table lamp which can be stood on the desk.
Brief—(b) Design a wall lamp which can be fitted to a wall near the desk.
Brief—(c) Design a lamp which can be fitted to the ceiling above the desk.

Amendments to a brief
While investigating problems relating to a design brief, you may find some amendment of the brief to be necessary. Providing approval for such amendment is given, such changes are quite acceptable. After all, a design brief can be regarded as the starting instruction from which a design is developed. If it is found that the brief cannot be followed because of difficulties thrown up during an investigation, then modifications of the brief may be desirable. For example, if the brief had asked for wall shelving to store books and it was subsequently found that no wall was suitable for some reason then it might well be desirable to amend the brief to ask for shelves which can be stood on the floor.

Exercises

1. *Situation*—A sports centre is to be built 20 metres from a road. A form of identification for the centre is needed. The identification must be seen by anyone travelling along the road by car.
   Write two different briefs for this given situation.
2. Chairs are made for very many different purposes—easy, lounge, dining, picnic, desk—to state a few. Write design briefs which state quite clearly the type of chair to be designed for five different circumstances.
3. Some form of boundary to a garden is required. Write two design briefs which state clearly the form which the boundary is to take.

Exercises

The ten photographs on this page and on page 37 opposite suggest situations in a home from which design briefs could be stated.

Examine each of the photographs and:

1. state the design situation in each case;
2. from each of the ten situations you have stated write two design briefs.

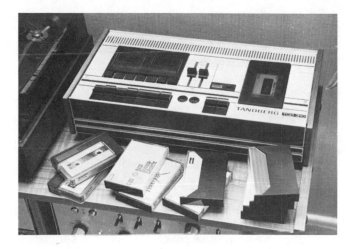 

Investigation

You are about to design an article which you will be making. You will have stated the design situation and from it written, or have been given, a design brief. Now you should carefully investigate all the conditions which will enable you to make a good design. Solving problems is easier if you follow a logical sequence of investigation into all the details involved. As you proceed, write notes and make drawings. It is easy to forget details. If you make notes or draw the details as you come across them, they will not be forgotten and you can refer back to the notes and drawings you have made as the investigation proceeds.

The following sequence is suggested

1. Function and ergonomics
State the functions which you hope your design will achieve. In particular study the relationships of your design to the human beings who may use it. Find the essential functional dimensions.

2. Shape and form
Consider the variety of shapes, proportions, colours, textures, forms and so on which may relate to your design.

3. Materials
What materials are available for making the design? Which are the best materials? Why are you making the choice you have made?

4. Economics
Work out the cost of your design in terms both of money and of time taken. Think about economical use of line and space.

5. Shaping
What methods of shaping can be used for making the design? How will they affect final shape and form?

6. Jointing
How will the design be made? Will it be jointed, moulded or cast? Is it necessary to join parts of the design? If it is, study the methods of jointing which can be used. Are the joints to be permanent, temporary or movable?

7. Fittings
Some fittings may have to be purchased. Study the choice of suitable fittings available. Look around shops to find types and prices.

8. Strength
Is great strength necessary? It may be of value to carry out tests on the materials, jointing methods and fittings to be used.

9. Surface finish
What factors will govern any surface finish for your design? What finishes will satisfy the correct functioning of the article you are making?

10. Special factors
There may be some special factors which have to be considered.

11. Safety
Look at any hazards peculiar to your design from a safety angle.

Design investigation chart
Although it has been suggested that the investigation follows a sequence, each stage of the sequence is related to previous stages. The diagram shows the inter-relationship between parts of the investigation. Numbers show the sequence stage. Lines and arrows show the need for checking back and the inter-relationship between later and earlier stages. For example, when thinking about the strength of your design, you will have to go back to the function, to the materials used, to shaping methods, to jointing methods if any, to fittings and so on. The investigation is a sequence procedure but also requires checks backwards and forwards within the sequence.

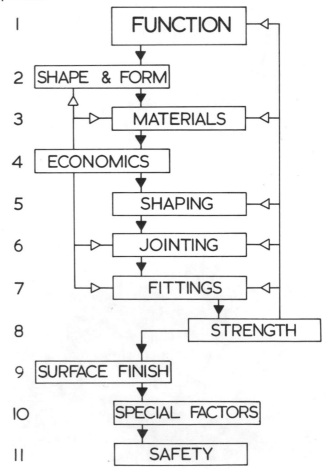

Function and ergonomics

Function

If a design is to be successful it must be completely suitable for the purposes for which it is being made. When the design has been made it should function properly and should satisfy all that is demanded of it. What you are making should meet the requirements of the design brief under all the circumstances which may arise within the design situation. Just 'looking good' is not necessarily good design. The design must also function properly.

Three factors to consider

1. Make a list of what you consider are the functions of your design. What are the purposes for which it is being made? What is required from the article you are making?
2. You must remember that people will be using your design. A study of humans within their environment is therefore a necessary part of function. This study is known as *ergonomics*.
3. One very important aspect of function is the need for functional sizes to be correct. 'Is it the correct size?' is a question you must always be asking. Functional sizes are closely linked to ergonomics.

How to list the functions

1. You will soon discover that the making of this list is possibly the most difficult part of designing. It is, however, very necessary. As you work through the steps of the investigation you should check back from time to time to see whether the investigation is satisfying the list of functions you make.
2. Be prepared to be inquisitive and very critical. Be prepared to ask yourself, your classmates, friends, parents, teachers and other questions about your design. These questions will contain the words: How? Why? Where? When? Who? Write down the answers.
3. List both sensible and highly improbable requirements. Then select those which are most suited to your design.
4. Read the pages on ergonomics in this book. Do any of the situations shown affect the functions of your design?
5. Make notes of functional sizes. Use a ruler. Keep a 2-metre measuring tape in your pocket. Such tapes are fairly cheap and easy to purchase.

An example of bad functioning

A boy makes a very fine-looking milk bottle container for his mother as a birthday present. Unfortunately he did not measure milk bottle sizes nor did he make any attempt to discover his mother's usual maximum milk order. As a result his mother could not place milk bottles in the container. So the carefully made container was never used. What a disappointment for both the boy and his mother! If he had thought of the essential functions for a milk bottle container these disappointments could have been avoided.

Examples of function lists

1. *What are the functions of a wooden toy?*
(a) Must appeal to the child's age and ability.
(b) Should provide interests—movement, colour, noise, feel, shape.
(c) Requires to be safe in use and sufficiently strong to resist rough treatment.
(d) Must be easy to store.
(e) The more versatile the toy is, the more it will be used.

2. *State some functions of a screwdriver*
(a) To insert, drive home and unscrew screws.
(b) A large twisting force must be exerted on the screw head.
(c) The tool should be comfortable to use.
(d) The blade must grip the screw head securely.
(e) The tool must not become distorted when in use.

3. *List some functions of a plant stand*
(a) The roots must be held firmly within the soil.
(b) Watering of the plants must be easy.
(c) The stand should preferably be waterproof.
(d) Plants must be held quite firmly and not be easily knocked over.
(e) The stand and its plants should be easy to keep clean.

Exercises

1. List as many functions as you can in connection with each of the following articles:
(a) a ball-point pen,
(b) a coffee table,
(c) a coat rack,
(d) an egg cups holder, remembering salt and shells,
(e) a firm's trade symbol,
(f) a telephone.

2. Make a pair of lists comparing what you consider to be the functions of
(a) a cheap car,   (b) an expensive limousine.

3. Newly designed products are often on sale. Sketch two examples of such newly designed products and those which they replace. Give reasons why you think the newly designed products function better than the older designs.

Ergonomics

Ergonomics can be defined as the study of man in relation to his environment. When considering function on the last page, it was stated that it must be remembered people will be using your designs. You must bear in mind all the time you are designing that no design has ever been made or ever will be made for any purpose other than for use by human beings. Therefore the shapes and sizes of human beings, the manner in which they behave, move, use their senses, act and react must be carefully considered in relation to the correct functioning of any design.

Ergonomic human being
Humans are capable of a great range of complex movements. They can crawl, walk, jog, run, lie down, sit, sprawl and kneel. They can reach forwards, sideways, upwards, can grip or grasp and perform complicated actions with hand-held tools. They require a degree of comfort and warmth for maximum efficient functioning. Human beings have only two legs, so balance is important. Height, weight, sitting and lying positions, width, reach and hand sizes give a range of functional dimensions vital to much design work. Some or all of the senses of hearing, vision, smell, taste and touch must be satisfied in relation to many designs.

The ego of human beings will demand stimulation and satisfaction. They have a very strong sense of what is right as far as they individually are concerned and will often make considerable efforts to achieve results which satisfy their personal egos. Much of modern design work aims at pleasing in this sense. Examples can be seen in the designs of furniture, houses, house fittings, cars and motor cycles. The constantly changing fashions in clothes stimulate and satisfy many people. The design of advertisement material often deliberately sets out to stimulate self-satisfaction.

All human beings change during their lifetimes. The child is smaller and of different proportions to the adult. The senses of children are very keen and are used to learn methods of meeting the challenge of their environment. As the child becomes adult, maximum size and strength are reached and under the influence of the environment the adult uses the senses to gain fuller feelings of achievement. In old age the adult becomes usually slightly smaller, certainly less agile, with senses somewhat dulled. In old age more warmth and comfort are desired and many may require special attention because of infirmities. At each stage of life the ergonomic problems relating to design are distinctly different.

The senses

Touch (and feel)
We often make contact with the articles we make. This means that attention must be given to:
(a) sharp edges should be removed or protected;
(b) protection must be provided for very hot or very cold parts;
(c) the skin must be allowed full ventilation;
(d) special attention must be given to the design of hand-held articles or parts.

Vision
Communication by visual means is of the greatest importance. Therefore the design of letters, words, symbols and pictures form the basis of graphical design. Colours can affect a person's mood. Thus red is a warm colour and also spells out danger. Blue spells out cold.

Hearing
If noise is too loud it can be unbearable. Constant squeaks or knocks can be very irritating. Does your design need silencing?

Smell
Unpleasant smells can annoy particularly in a confined area. Pleasant smells can be exciting or stimulating.

Taste
Humans have four main tastes—sweet, sour, bitter, salty. Smell is related to taste.

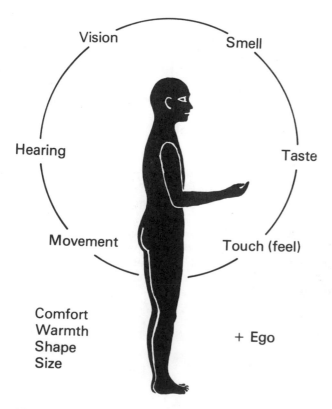

Vision

Smell

Hearing

Taste

Movement

Touch (feel)

Comfort
Warmth
Shape
Size

+ Ego

Movement

Human beings are always moving. Even when sitting 'still', as for example when reading a book or watching television, you will be making small movements such as moving legs and feet, blowing your nose, turning to speak to someone. It is natural to move in certain ways, although we sometimes indulge in unnatural movement such as trying to run sideways, standing on one's head, trying to play a guitar behind one's back.

Natural movements

To succeed in design work you should note natural movements and apply your observations to the articles you make. There are limitations to natural movement which you should also observe. How does this affect design? Let us look at some examples.
1. Can you turn a screwdriver through a complete revolution in one movement?
2. Can you touch all parts of your back?
3. Your body must be in balance when moving. When cycling both you and your bicycle lean inwards at corners. Why is this so? Have you ever run downhill so fast that you felt as if you were about to fall on your face?
4. The design of chairs and tables must allow for leg movement.
5. The sizes of articles you design must be based on natural movement. Sitting low, reaching too high, lying uncomfortably, etc. may be due to non-ergonomic dimensions.

Unnatural movements

If your design calls for unnatural movements then you have made mistakes and should re-design. Good design must take account of natural movement and ergonomic dimensions.

Movement and dimensions

With reference to the drawings on this page, answer the following questions:
1. At what maximum height should a bookshelf be placed to enable books to be easily reached without the need to use a chair or a step ladder?
2. The height of a kitchen sink is of great importance to a housewife. State a good height. What various actions take place at a kitchen sink which involve having to step sideways or backwards to retain balance?
3. When sitting at a table to eat a meal many movements are involved. The height of table and chair are important if these movements are to be carried out comfortably. Find good heights and write them down. Space for leg movement is necessary—by how much should the table top overlap the legs? The seat and back of the chair should be of a shape to allow movement backwards and forwards yet be comfortable. Make notes on the good design of dining chair seats and backs.
4. Old people often need to lever themselves from an easy chair because their movements become painful as age increases. The design of an old person's chair must take account of this. Make notes on the dimensions and design of a chair for an old person who suffers from arthritis.
5. When resting after a hard day's work, we all like to be comfortable yet must be allowed to make small movements while lounging. What details should you observe when designing a chair and stool intended to allow a person to rest? Find and state critical dimensions for the chair and stool.

Maximum comfortable reaching height

Height of sink unit

Eating at a table

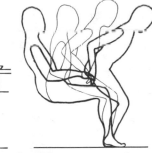
An old person may have to lift himself or herself from an easy chair

Comfortable seating and lounging position

Ergonomics—a typist's chair

This example is given to show how ergonomics affect the function and design of a common piece of furniture.

What must a typist do?
A typist working in an office will make a large number of quite complicated movements during a working day. The typist's chair must be designed to take account of these movements and allow maximum seating comfort and efficiency.
1. A typist may need to write at a desk.
2. Typing is often carried out at the same desk.
3. Papers will be taken or placed at each end of the desk.
4. Filing cabinets, cupboards and drawers will be used, preferably while still seated.
5. The telephone will need answering.
   Note that this list could form a similar list stating the functions of the chair. Compare the two lists.

Functions
1. To allow comfortable seating in a writing position.
2. To allow a comfortable typing position.
3. Allow movement to both ends of a desk.
4. To allow filing cabinets, etc. to be reached with ease.
5. To allow easy access to a telephone.

A good typist's chair

Movement
1. Typists come in all shapes and sizes. The seat must therefore be adjustable for height. This adjustment allows the correct typing position to be found for any typist. See drawings.
2. The chair back is adjustable in three directions.
(a) Height in relation to seat—maximum support in the arch of the back.
(b) Angle in relation to the seat. User can tilt backwards or forwards as desired.
(c) Back swivels vertically so as to automatically adjust itself to the seated person.
3. Seat swivels in a full circle about its base to allow easy movement from end to end of desk, to cabinets behind or telephone to one side.
4. Castors on the feet allow chair to be moved from place to place within an office without standing.
5. Wide span of a four or five footed base allows good balance to be maintained.

Touch (feel)
The seat should be soft yet firm to give adequate support. The upholstery should be covered with a material which allows the skin to be well ventilated without causing undue perspiration. The seat front must be rounded to avoid pressure points forming behind the knees. Back-rest upholstery and shaping should be based on the same principles.

Ergonomic dimensions
The seat height, angle and height of back in relation to the seat are adjustable. The seat should be sufficiently large to give full support to a seated person and not too deep from front to back to cause discomfort. The back rest must also be of a size adequate to give full support to the arch of the back.

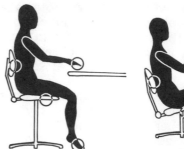

Too high. Discomfort points ringed   Too low. Discomfort points ringed

Just right. No discomfort points

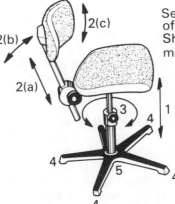

Seat and back rest of adequate size. Shaped to give maximum comfort

Ergonomic details of typing chair

Ergonomics—touch and feel

Articles which will come into contact with parts of the body should be designed so as to 'feel' comfortable. The sense of touch is usually assumed to be in the fingers and palms of the hand, but other parts of our bodies are also sensitive to touch. Look at some examples.

1. Shoes of the wrong size or of the wrong materials can be a source of acute discomfort, even pain.

2. Many motorists complain about PVC(vinyl)-coated car seats. On long journeys such seats cause sweating along the back, thighs and bottom.

The following details should be considered

1. Sizes and shapes. Does It fit?
2. The parts of the body which will make contact.
3. Proper ventilation. Will it cause sweating?
4. Avoid sharp edges. Remove or protect.
5. Insulate against heat and cold.
6. Is the weight right? Not too heavy or too light.

Hand-held designs
Look at the drawings on this page.

Door handles
Write down reasons why you consider one of the handles to be superior to the other from an ergonomic point of view.

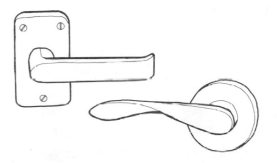

Cutting-out scissors
Note how the thumb, the three fingers and the index finger fit. Pick up a pair of scissors. Have they been designed ergonomically? Compare modern cutting-out scissors with those shown. If you are left-handed, can you use the scissors shown?

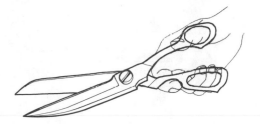

Pruning secateurs
Examine secateurs of this type. Pick them up. Are they comfortable to use? Do the blades open wide enough? What makes this particular pair of secateurs ergonomically so well designed?

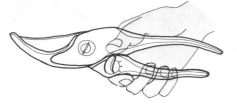

Stapler
Designed to fit the hand, mainly the palm. Is the stapler too heavy? In this example the whole body weight could be put on to the lever—is this necessary?

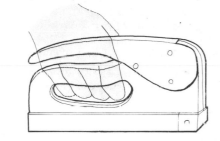

Hand size
In the examples given hand size and shape is important. Place your own hand on to a sheet of paper and draw around it. Measure essential sizes of your hand.

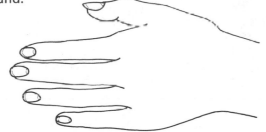

Exercises

1. Design a handle for a portable television set.

2. Explain why magazines tend to be of a common size.

3. Draw a side-view of a kettle pouring boiling water. Explain:
(a) why the handle does not become too hot to hold;
(b) how the kettle balances in the hand.

4. Sketch or design a pair of headphones that can be in use for a long time without causing discomfort. Explain the details of the design which allow for such comfort.

Ergonomics—vision—lighting

Much more attention is given to good and effective lighting at the present day than in the past. More care is taken over the design of lighting fittings, to the position of the source of illumination and to the amount of illumination needed. Why is this so?

Factors affecting lighting
1. The amount of illumination required.
2. The position of the source of illumination.
3. The areas which should be illuminated.
4. The distance from the source of illumination.
5. How the light is controlled.
6. The appearance of the source of light.

1. Illumination required
The level of intensity of the light varies with the situation. Some examples:
when reading—good lighting;
when writing—good lighting;
when dining—medium, perhaps diffused lighting;
when cooking—good overall lighting.
A lounge can be illuminated generally with diffused lighting but reading and writing lights should be available.

The source of light can give different effects.
Red lighting is warm and comforting. Blue light gives a feeling of coolness. Tungsten bulbs (commonly used) give a reddish light. Fluorescent tubes usually give a blue light but can be coated to give a pink or yellow light.
Reflected light can be a good source of illumination. White surfaces will reflect 75% of light; dark green may reflect only 5% of light. Some design work makes good use of such differences in reflected light.

2. Position of lighting
Never allow a bright light to shine in your eyes. Look at the drawings. The positions of the source of light for reading and writing are such that the book and page are well illuminated yet the light source does not shine into the eyes of reader or writer. In the case of the dining-table lighting, the source of light is over the table yet is diffused so that it does not irritate the diners.

3. Areas to be illuminated
Related to the source of light and the shading which it receives. Varies with the activity being carried on in the area which is illuminated.

4. Distance from source of illumination
The intensity of the illumination varies inversely with the square of the distance from the source. Thus a spot 2 metres from a light source is lit with an intensity only ¼ of the intensity on a spot at 1 metre from the light. At 3 metres the intensity is only ⅑ compared with 1 metre distant.
Note $\frac{1}{4} = \frac{1}{2}^2$; $\frac{1}{9} = \frac{1}{3}^2$

5. Controls
The lighting can be controlled by switches or by dimmers. It may be controlled manually, remotely or automatically. All three types of control are in fairly common use today.

6. Appearance
Direct lighting usually needs some form of decorative cover, shade or directing device. Diffused lighting can be obtained by the use of semi-opaque plastic sheets, ground glass screens, special ceiling tiles or by shades completely surrounding the light source.

Exercises

1. Make a list of the factors which should be considered when designing lighting for a fish tank.

2. List the factors governing the position and strength of lighting required when watching television.

3. Explain how you could illuminate the water in a swimming pool.

Lighting for reading

Lighting for writing

Lighting for a dining table. Medium diffused

Ergonomics—human scale models

The three outlines given on this page are intended to assist you with ergonomic problems you may wish to solve in your design work.

To use the outlines trace each separate part of the figure on to cardboard or stiff paper. Remember to mark the pin-hole positions accurately. Then cut out the parts with scissors. To use the model outlines you have made either pin the parts together or paste them in the positions you require on to paper.

For most design work, the smallest figure is probably of the most value to you, but the larger figures will also be of value for solving some ergonomic problems. You will already have noted that this type of figure has been used in this book in connection with ergonomics.

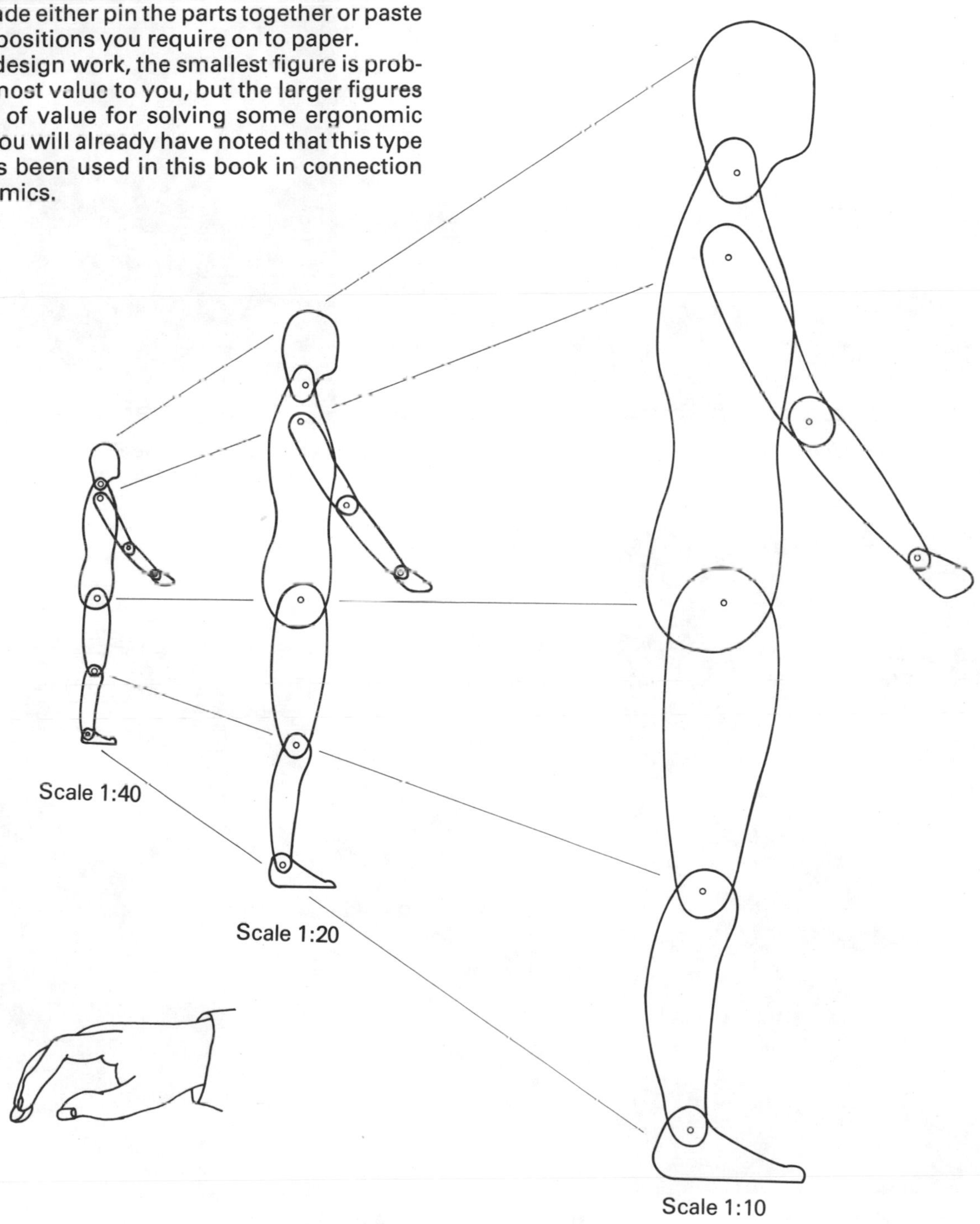

Scale 1:40

Scale 1:20

Scale 1:10

Part of the 'Sanka' range of lighting fittings incorporating 'Perspex'

The handles of these Stanley secateurs are made from glass-filled nylon

Push horse made from wood

'Alkathene'—ICI's polythene used for toys and play chairs

Shape

Proportions

An important aspect of design is proportion. Overall proportions and the proportions of parts of a design must be considered. If the proportions of a design are poor, it will look wrong. If a design functions well and is suited to its purposes, then its dimensions will be good and its proportions will be good. This is because designs are based upon that well proportioned shape—the human figure. Careful measurement of the various parts of the human body show that a proportion, known as the golden mean frequently occurs. In design work golden mean proportions can often be exploited. Builders of ancient Greek architecture, architects of the European Renaissance, together with European painters of the same period all made great use of the golden mean of proportions. The terms 'Golden Section' or 'Golden Ratio' refer to the same proportions. Some believed these proportions to be perfect and endowed with almost magical properties, even calling them the Divine Proportions. Modern design can also be based partly on golden mean proportions.

Golden mean proportions

Look at the rectangles A to K. Which rectangles do you think are the most pleasing in appearance? Ask a number of people to choose which rectangles they think are the most pleasing. Try it with your classmates. The larger the number of people you ask to join in this experiment the better will be the result. The chances are that two of the rectangles will prove to be the most popular. This is because two of the rectangles have been drawn to golden mean proportions.

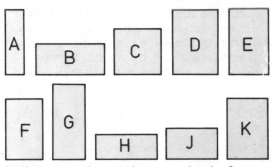

Which rectangles are the most pleasing?

Two methods of obtaining this proportion are shown.

Geometrical method

Draw a triangle ABC in which AB = twice AC. With C as centre, draw a compass arc of radius CA to give D on BC. With centre B and radius BD, draw a compass arc BE. The resulting rectangle ABEF is in golden mean proportions.

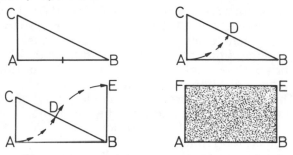

Golden mean rectangle: geometric construction

Arithmetical method

Leonardo Fibonacci, a great 13th-century mathematician, devised a number series—1, 1, 2, 3, 5, 8, 13, 21, 34, 55 and so on—in which each number in the series is the addition of the previous two. Take any adjacent pair in the series and that pair gives an approximation of golden mean proportions. The higher the pair of numbers, the nearer to the perfect golden mean will be obtained.

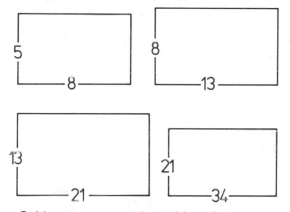

Golden mean rectangles: arithmetical

Some applications to furniture design are shown.

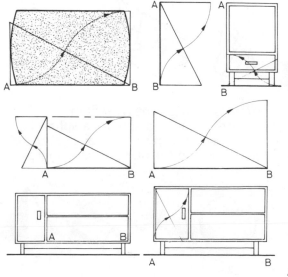

Form

A plane surface is a two dimensional (2D) shape. Three dimensional (3D) shapes can be referred to as forms. Such forms have the third dimension of depth in addition to length and width. Lines which do not outline a shape or form can be two or three dimensional when they are bent or curved.

The shapes and forms you include in your design should, as far as is possible, be functional. They should arise out of the purposes for which the design is being made.

Shapes and forms can be sub-divided into two main categories—geometrical and free. Some are compositions of both geometrical and free.

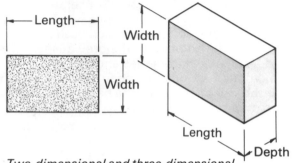

Two-dimensional and three-dimensional shapes and forms

Three-dimensional geometrical line forms
The drawings show—a cylinder, a rectangular prism (or cuboid), a hexagonal pyramid, a hyperboloid, a rectangular prism braced on all four sides and a triangular prism.

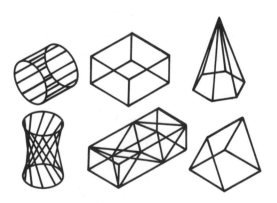

Three-dimensional geometrical forms
Those illustrated are—a sphere, a spheroid, a half cylinder, a square pyramid, a hyperboloid, a triangular prism, and an oblique octagonal pyramid.

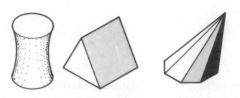

Two-dimensional geometrical shapes
Those shown are—a dot, a circle, an ellipse, a square, a rectangle, a regular pentagon, a regular hexagon, a regular octagon, a straight line and a curved line composed of a semi-circle added to a semi-ellipse.

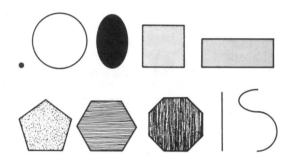

Three-dimensional forms from planes
Shown are—a semi-cylinder, a triangular prism and four rectangles arranged around a line.

Free shapes or forms
A variety of free shapes and forms are shown. Some of these are derived from natural objects. Such natural objects are excellent sources upon which shapes and forms can be based. Some examples are—stones, leaves, fruit, nuts, trees, streams.

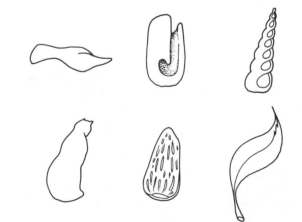

Arrangements of shapes and forms

In the examples of arrangements given on this page and on page 48, free use has been made of the golden mean of proportion.

Patterns
Two- or three-dimensional patterns are achieved by the repetition of lines, shapes, forms, surfaces, textures or colours. The drawings show patterns achieved by curved lines; by contrasting grainy surfaces with clear surfaces; by the arrangement of different textures and sizes of circles; by arranging rectangles within a rectangle; by a composition of identical cylinders; by an arrangement of leaf-like shapes.

Harmonising shape and form
Similar or identical shapes or forms can be employed. Illustrated are—a well designed page of print composed of a variety of rectangles; three rectangles with radiused corners; a fibre-glass table of harmonising curves; a beaker designed around circles; a cabinet composed of all flat surfaces; a lamp shade of all circular parts. Even harmonising shapes may require contrasts in texture, colour or shade of surfaces to enhance the harmony of the parts.

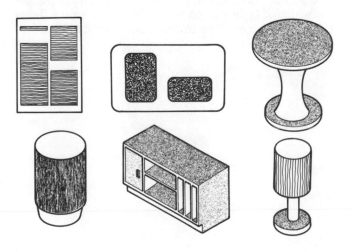

Families or sets
Many designs depend upon families or sets of identical or similar articles. Those shown are a composition of similar cylinders; a form made by a book-like arrangement; a cruet set for salt, pepper and mustard. Other examples would be sets of crockery, sets of cutlery, sets of matching books.

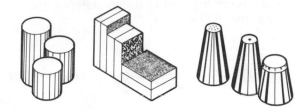

Shapes made by spaces
Many shapes and forms depend upon cutting away parts of surfaces or of structures. The examples show—initials cut from a piece of metal sheet; six circles cut from a rectangle of wood; three semi-circular pieces cut out and bent back on to the parent material; a 'see through' concrete wall brick.

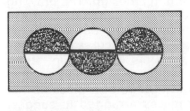 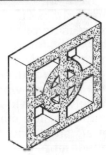

Contrasting shapes and forms
Combinations of contrasting shapes and forms can enhance design work. Such contrasts must be carefully arranged to look well. Good proportions between the parts are essential. The illustration shows a circle within a rectangle; a square within a circle; two rectangles within an ellipse; straight lines within a rectangle; strips of contrasting textures or contrasting colours; the natural shape of a tree contrasted with the geometrical forms of a house.

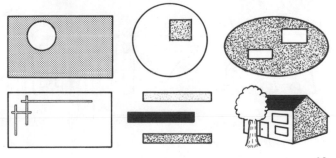

Focal points

Shapes and forms arranged around focal points may play an important part in some design work. A series of rectangles 'pointing' to a focal circle; an arrow 'leading' to a focal point; three quadrilaterals suggesting a focus; an obelisk arranged at a focal point in a housing scheme. Such focal points are of obvious design interest in much switching work in electrical installations.

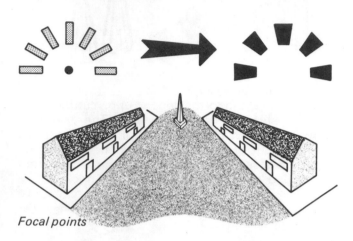

Focal points

Movement

Lines, shapes and forms can be arranged to give the impression of movement in a design. The drawing shows the following. A line arranged to show movement not only along its own length but also by the outline it produces as a whole; the curve of the edge of a piece of wood; a couple of pieces of string loosely intertwined; a sequence of kicking a ball in diagrams; the curve of an edge of a piece of material; small identical pieces arranged to suggest movement.

Movement

What affects these arrangements?

Texture
Soft, smooth surfaces not only look soft and smooth, but are usually friendly and pleasing to touch and stroke. Rough, sharp surfaces, while being less friendly to the touch, may produce interesting visual effects. Most materials have their own peculiarities of surface texture. Think about, touch and compare the surface textures of woods, metals, plastics, cloths, furs, glass, bricks, concrete, paintwork, linoleum, carpets, cork, soap, various papers.

Colours
Colour plays a very important role in design work generally. Much thought should be given to the selection of the colours you wish to employ. Reds, for example, tend to make a design look warm, more comfortable, more friendly. Blues have the reverse effect—tending to produce a colder, more frigid, unfriendly appearance than do reds. Some colours are neutral and can be used as backgrounds or in conjunction with other colours—greys, some browns, some greens, white are the most obvious of the more neutral colours. The various shades of each colour need careful choice—a pastel green, for example, will produce an entirely different effect to a dark green. Some dark colours will given an appearance of heaviness. Light colours will give an appearance of lightness of weight. Some colours produce a feeling of spaciousness. For example, a room with white walls and ceiling may appear considerably larger than will the same room finished with dark colours.

Shadow
The position of lighting in connection with shape and form needs consideration. The interplay of light and shadow can accentuate shape, form, pattern and surface textures. If your design is to incorporate a source of lighting, some desirable design effects can be produced with translucent plastic sheet.

Personal taste

Environmental influences and the personal experiences resulting from them have a profound influence on people's likes and dislikes. Abstract designs can perhaps be best appreciated by those who have undergone experiences similar to the designer. Others may not be able to understand or appreciate a particular design because of a lack of similarity of experience.

Look at the three shapes illustrated. Does the left-hand shape give you a free feeling as compared with the centre shape which may make you feel restricted or squashed? What does the right-hand drawing convey to you? A wood knot, a spider's web, a tunnel, a well, a falling bomb, looking up from inside a glass dome? A circular electrical radiator guard? Or what?

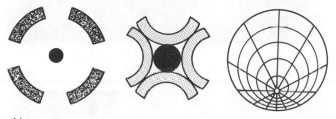

Abstracts

Hand made hall table—sapele and sycamore

Production processes

Compare the two designs shown in the photographs. The table with drawers was made by hand by a craftsman. The chairs were mass-produced in a factory. The craftsman was a highly skilled cabinet maker employing a wide range of highly developed skills such as sawing, planing, jointing, veneering, inlaying, polishing. The machine process workers at the factory were performing simple, highly specialised single skills. The hand-made table contains 32 parts held together with 36 joints. Each of the mass-produced chairs contains only two parts clipped to each other. This comparison shows how production processes can affect the shape and form of designs.

Standardised parts

Standardised parts can be used to produce many designs. A house brick is a standardised part which is used to produce the huge variety of buildings seen in many countries throughout the world. Two examples of standardised parts in craft designs are shown. In the first, four pipes of the same diameter are joined to each other to make a pencil holder. In the second, three short pieces of square tube make an interesting neck pendant.

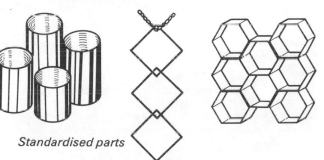

Standardised parts

Chairs made by Sanka Oy—ICI acrylic sheet on stainless steel tubing

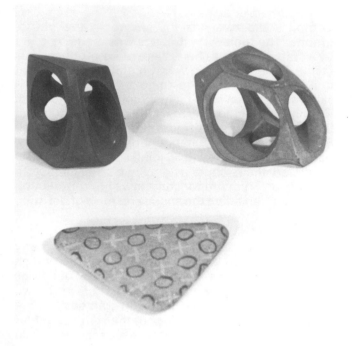

Forms made from fired potter's clay

Form carved from a block of teak

3D shapes made from paper cut-outs

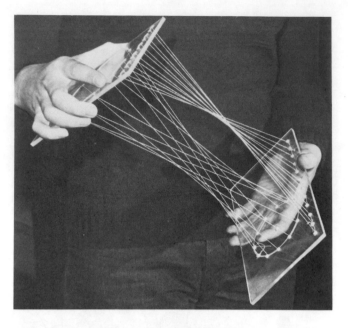

Elastic strings in Perspex rectangles

Geometrical shapes arranged from paper cut-outs

Child's construction kit

New ideas for shapes and forms

From natural objects
Sketch part of a natural object—in this case the branch of a tree joining its trunk. Develop the idea by amending its form in further sketches.

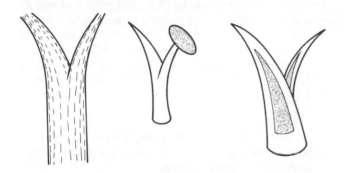

From letters
Open a book. Put your finger down anywhere. Take any two letters covered by your finger. Then amend the letters to find a new form.

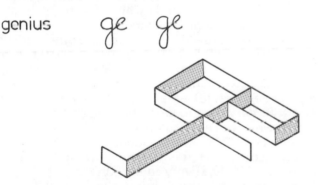

Develop by adding
Draw a basic shape—say a square. Develop a new shape in stages by adding to the basic shape.

Develop by subtracting
Draw a basic shape—in this example a square again. Develop a new shape in stages by taking parts from the basic shape.

Using a module
Draw a basic shape. Try to develop that shape as a modular standardised part. In the example given a three-part flower-container has been designed.

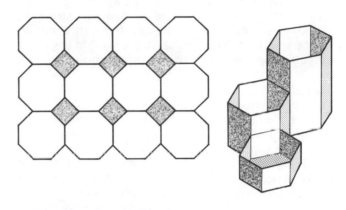

Scribbles
Draw a scribble of freely drawn lines crossing each other. Look at the shapes formed by the intersecting lines. Select different shapes so produced.

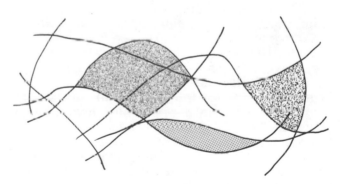

Using a projector or an enlarger
Place a glass slide on a table. Sprinkle some rubbish on to its surface. Sellotape the rubbish in place. Now project the slide on to a screen. Some interesting shapes may show up.

From one's thoughts
Close your eyes and handle some object. Now try drawing the pictures which form in your thoughts.

Tracing paper
Trace parts of drawings or photographs from books, newspapers or magazines. Assemble your tracings to try to develop new shapes.

Choosing materials

Pages 134 to 154 give more information about materials. In the following short descriptions the properties of the materials are comparative within each group. Thus a wood classed as strong will be stronger than wood classed as average strength, but not as strong as most metals. The figure following the name of the material is the weight in grams per cubic centimetre of an average sample.

Woods

Woods are chosen for design work in preference to other materials for their colour, grain, beauty and availability. Woods are generally in abundant supply, comparatively cheap and easily worked. Their variability of colour and grain makes them one of the most beautiful of craft materials. A disadvantage is that woods will shrink and expand causing warping, splitting and twisting. However, by good selection of woods and well designed constructions, this problem can be overcome. Manufactured boards do not shrink and so remain flat and free from splits. Nearly all woods when seasoned have a density less than water (which is 1 gram per cubic centimetre). Durability is the ability to resist decay.

Some hardwoods

Afrormosia (0.75)—Strong, hard and stiff. Average workability. Very durable. Brown. Straight grain. Some interlocking of grain.

Ash (0.7)—Strong, tough and elastic. Sometimes tough to work. Not durable. Light brown. Distinct, straight grain.

Balsa (0.1)—Weak. Soft and easily damaged. Very easy to work. Perishable. White. Straight, indistinct grain. Silky surface lustre.

Beech (0.75)—Hard, tough and stiff. Average to tough workability. Not durable. Pale brown. Straight grain. Ray flecks on quarter sawn faces.

Mahogany (*African*) (0.55)—Average strength. Fairly stiff. Works well, but sometimes coarse. Resists splitting. Moderate durability. Reddish. Interlocking, straight grain.

Oak (*English*) (0.7)—Strong, tough and resilient. Average to difficult workability. Very durable. Yellow-brown. Distinct ray flashes on quarter sawn faces.

Teak (0.7)—Strong, but not elastic. Average hardness. Works well, extremely durable. Golden brown. Straight grain.

Some softwoods

Redwood (0.5)—Average hardness and toughness. Easily worked. Not durable. Pale reddish-brown. Fairly distinct, straight grain. Sapwood light coloured.

Spruce (0.4)—Tough for its weight. Imported spruce better quality than home grown. Very easy to work.

White to pale pink. Straight but not very distinct grain. Lustrous silky surface.

Western Red Cedar (0.35)—Soft and of low strength. Very easily worked. Very durable. Pinkish to brown. Indistinct straight grain.

Metals

Metals are chosen in design work for their strength, toughness, hardness and resistance to wear and corrosion. A vast range of different alloys of metals are made. Metals are generally heavier than woods and, because of their better strength values, can be employed in smaller sections than can woods. Metals are good conductors of electricity, some better than others. Metals can be purchased in sheets, rods, bars and pipes in a good range of sizes.

Some metals

Black mild steel (8)—Straight from hot rolling. Medium workability. Hard and tough. Hardens when worked. Rusts. Cheap.

Bright mild steel (8)—Straight from cold rolling. Already work-hardened. Tough, hard and strong. Average workability. Rusts. Cheap, but more expensive than black.

Carbon tool steel (8)—Tough, hard and strong. Hard to work. Can be hardened by heat treatment. Rusts. More expensive than mild steels.

Stainless steel (8)—Various types. Some can be hardened. Tough and strong. High resistance to corrosion. Expensive. Bright silver polished surfaces. Work well, but some types are hard.

High speed steel (8)—Many types. Very hard, tough and stiff. Very hard to work, but will grind. Will not soften when run hot. Expensive.

Aluminium (2.7)—Soft, ductile and malleable. Easily worked. Hardens when worked. Resists corrosion. White, silvery colour. Cheap.

Duralumin (2.9)—Tough but easily worked. Not so resistant to corrosion as aluminium. White silvery colour. Good, lightweight construction material. More expensive than aluminium. Good electrical conductance.

Copper (9)—Ductile and malleable. Hardens when worked. Easily worked. Excellent conductor of electricity and of heat. Red in colour. Tarnishes but does not corrode.

Brass (8.8)—Tougher and harder than copper. Many different brasses. Machines well. Works well. Good anti-corrosive properties. Yellow.

Zinc (7)—Soft. Work hardens. Very resistant to corrosion. Silver-white in colour.

Lead (11.3)—Soft, little strength. Very malleable. Dense and heavy. Dull silver colour. Good sound insulator.

Silver (10.5)—First-class electrical conductivity. Soft and malleable. Work hardens. Expensive. Tarnishes but very anti-corrosive.

Gold (19.3)—Does not tarnish. Extremely anti-corrosive. Extremely expensive. Yellow.

Plastics

Plastics are chosen for designs because of particular advantages certain plastics have over other materials. They tend to be somewhat more expensive as craft materials than woods. Usually they do not need any special applied finishes and can be obtained in a good range of colours. Many are good electrical insulators. Some are transparent or translucent. Some can be easily moulded into quite intricate shapes.

Some elastomers

Rubber—Common natural material. Very elastic.
Isoprene—Synthetic natural rubber. Better elasticity than natural rubber.
Neoprene—Good resistance to oils. Good resistance to permeability by gases.
Butyl—Excellent resistance to tearing and flexing. Excellent resistance to gas permeability.
Silicon rubbers—Excellent chemical and oil resistance at high and low temperatures. Moulding rubber.

Some thermoplastics

Polythene—Waxy surface. Waterproof. Good electrical resistivity. Can be obtained as a powder for hot dip coating.
Polypropylene—Rigid. Good chemical resistance. Unique flexing property. Can be hot-air welded.
Polyvinyl chloride—Rigid or flexible types. Water and chemical proof. Excellent electrical resistivity.
Acrylics—Rigid and hard, but brittle. Flexible at 90°C to 150°C. Transparent clear acrylic available.

Polyurethane foam—Flexible for upholstery. Rigid for sculpture. Fire hazard. Very easily worked.
Polystyrene foam—White, rigid, very light in weight.

Some thermosetting plastics

Polyester resin—The resin of fibre glass. Several types. Hard but brittle unless reinforced. Sets hard at room temperature when 'catalyst' is added.
Epoxy resin—Expensive. Sets hard at room temperature when hardener added. Adheres firmly to most materials. Does not shrink on setting. Very tough and strong when reinforced.

Other materials

Clay—Hard but brittle when fired in a kiln. Clay 'slip' easily cast. Plastic 'cold clays' set hard at room temperatures when mixed according to maker's instructions.
Concrete—Mixture of cement and sand. Very hard, but brittle unless reinforced. When reinforced tough and strong. Cheap.
Glass—Sheet glass brittle. Glass fibre tough, and excellent reinforcement for thermosetting resins.
Leather—Expensive. Good appearance. Smooth outside or suede inside surfaces.
Plasticine—Good modelling material. Can be reworked time after time. Very easily moulded into shape with fingers, tools or wooden spatula.
Plaster of Paris—Quick setting white plaster. Heat generated as it sets. Good material for moulds. Brittle, but can be reinforced with rag.

CHOOSING MATERIALS – A SUMMARY

WOODS		METALS		PLASTICS		
SOFTWOODS	**HARDWOODS**	**FERROUS**	**NON-FERROUS**	**THERMOPLASTIC**	**THERMOSETTING**	**ELASTOMERS**
BC Pine	Afrormosia	Dead mild steel	Aluminium	Acrylics	Urea formaldehyde	Butyl
Larch.	Ash	Medium mild steel	Aluminium alloys	Cellulosics	Phenol formaldehyde	Isoprene
Redwood	Balsa	High carbon steel	Brass	Nylon	Melamine	Neoprene
Spruce	Beech	Stainless steel	Bronze	Polyester film	Epoxy resin	Rubber
Western red cedar	Box	High speed steel	Copper	Polypropylene	Polyester resins	Silicones
Yew	Chestnut	Tinplate	Cupronickel	Polystyrene		Styrene butadiene
	Elm		Lead	Polystyrene foam		
	Iroko		Nickel silver	Polythene		Urethane
	Jelotung		Tin	Polyurethane foam		
	Mahogany		Zinc	PTFE		
	Oak		Precious metals			
	Sapele		Silver			
	Sycamore		Gold			
	Teak		Platinum			

OTHER MATERIALS

Clays	Glass fibre
Concrete	Leather
Fabrics	Plaster of Paris
Glass	Plasticine

Economics

The economics of hand-made craft work can be considered under three headings.
1. Cost of materials and the cost of material for making additional equipment such as moulds.
2. Time required for making.
3. The economical use of line and space.

Cost of materials

The cost of the materials and fittings used for making school craft designs by hand is usually the total cost for making the design. Items such as equipment and tools are usually already in existence—as in a school workshop—and can be ignored. Some special tools may have to be purchased and an allowance for the cost of items such as sandpaper, emery cloth, polishes, varnishes and paints will have to be considered. The costs of the labour involved in making the design can be ignored.

Note the differences between the economic considerations involved in a design made by a pupil in school when compared with an industrially made design for sale to the public.

School made design
Cost of materials, fittings and finishes.

Industrially made design
Cost of overheads—buildings, power supply, heating, lighting.
Cost of equipment—machines, equipment, tools.
Cost of labour—labour involved in making, administration, sales staff.
Cost of transport—vehicles, parcel and postal charges.
Cost of materials, fittings and finishes
All these costs have to be carefully considered if an industrially made design is to be sold profitably to the public.

Costing materials

Metals
Metals are most often sold by weight—at so much per kilogram. Some metal sections such as pipings, rods and extruded aluminium sections are sold by length—at so much per 'metre run'.

Woods
Woods may be sold by area—so much per square metre; by length—per 'metre run'; by standard board sizes; by weight.

Hardwood boards are sold by area; plywoods, blockboards, chipboards and other boards are most often sold in standard board sizes—a common standard size is 2440 mm by 1220 mm; veneered and edged chipboards are often sold in standard board sizes; dowels, mouldings, small sections such as squares or strips and many standard softwood sections are sold by length—so much per 'metre run'. Some scarce hardwoods are sold by weight—rosewood, box, ebony, lignum vitae are examples.

Plastics
A variety of methods are used for costing plastics, the most common being to sell by weight—so much per kilogram. However, some sheet material is sold by area and some pipings and extruded sections are sold by length.

Fittings
Fittings are priced singly, in pairs, in tens, hundreds or in packets containing measured weights such as 500 grams. Many small fittings such as nails, screws, bolts can be purchased in sealed plastic packets which may contain any convenient number of the fittings.

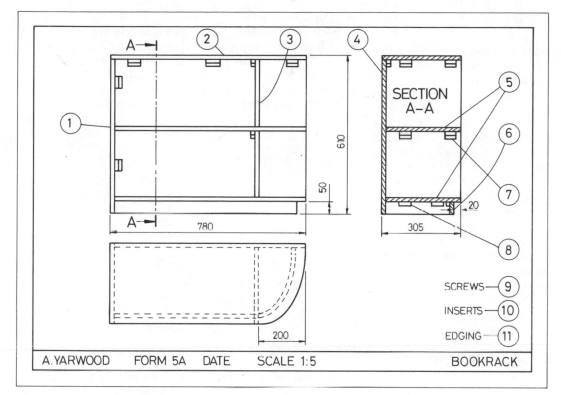

Working drawing of a bookrack

Part No	Material	Dimensions	Pieces off	Cost	Approx price
1	Vinyl coated	595×305×16	1	£6 per	1.35
2	chipboard	780×305×16	1	sq metre	1.45
3	" " "	258×290×16	2	"	90
4	" " "	765×605×16	1	"	2.75
5	" " "	765×290×16	2	"	2.70
6	" " "	900×50×16	1	"	30
7	Double joint blocks		9	8p each	72
8	Single " "		5	6p "	30
9	Screws	50 gauge 10	22	£3 per 100	66
10	Nylon inserts		22	£2 " "	44
11	Vinyl edging	2500 mm	1	30p per m	75
				Total - £12.32	

Costing chart for the bookrack

Costing a bookrack

The bookrack in the photograph is made from a vinyl-coated chipboard—Target Panel. The construction involves knock-down fittings—brass-plated screws in nylon inserts and two types of joint block (see Jointing, page 76). A working drawing and a costing chart are shown. Note the drawing below. Target Panel is sold in standard board sizes, one of which is 2440 mm by 610 mm. Maximum use has been made of this standard board to economise in the use of material. The vinyl coated chipboard requires no finish.

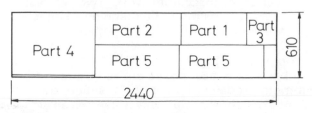

Maximum use of a standard board

Time

To the worker outside school 'time is money'. The pupil working on a craft design at school can ignore his labour costs. The pupil should, however, be conscious of the time involved in making the design because of the limitations of school timetabling. How many lessons per week can be spent in the school workshops? Can the workshops be used after school hours? Can some of the work be carried out at home? In the light of such considerations, it will be an advantage if a production sequence for the realisation of the design can be written. A time allocation for each part of the sequence should be suggested. The timing can be adjusted as the work proceeds. Such a production sequence will allow economies of time because each stage has been thought about in advance. Such planning is an essential feature of economics.

Production sequence for the bookrack
1. Mark parts 1 to 5 on Target Panel boards—1 hour.
2. Saw and plane parts 1 to 5 to size—2 hours.
3. Shape parts 2 and 5—1 hour.
4. Iron edging strip to fronts of 2 and 5 and to ends of 2 and 4—40 minutes.
5. Mark, bore and countersink all screw holes—1 hour.
6. Mark and bore screw insert holes—40 minutes.
7. Screw halves of double joint blocks in position to 1, 3, 4 and 5—2 hours.
8. Screw 1 and 3 to 5—30 minutes.
9. Screw second halves of joint blocks in position and bolt the pairs together—1 hour.
10. Saw and plane 6 to size. Cut saw kerfs for rounding it to shape—2 hours.
11. Screw 6 to rack with single joint blocks—1 hour.

Time-reducing aids

Much time can be saved by the sensible use of aids such as templates (sometimes spelt templets) and jigs. Not only will time be saved, but greater accuracy will be gained by working with these aids. The greater accuracy achieved can also be regarded as an economy because less time will be necessary for the correction of inaccurate work. Two templates and two jigs such as might be made by a handcraft worker are shown.

Development template
A number of identical boxes are to be made from sheet metal. A development of the shape is accurately cut from sheet metal. This is used as an aid for marking the other developments.

Wood template
Four wooden legs of the same shape are required. A template from plywood, hardboard or cardboard is cut to the required shape. The four legs are then drawn on to the wood with pencil markings around the template. Note the economical use of wood by alternating the position of the four legs.

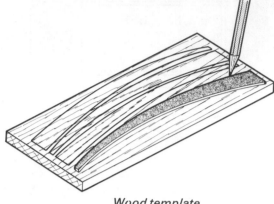

Wood template

Drilling jig
This jig, made from steel, locates the positions of three holes to be drilled at one end of a bar. The hole centres can be marked by punching through the holes in the jig with a centre punch.

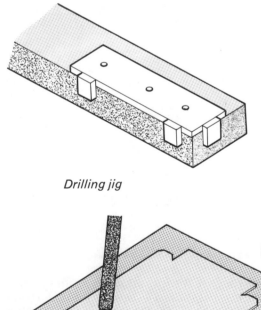

Drilling jig

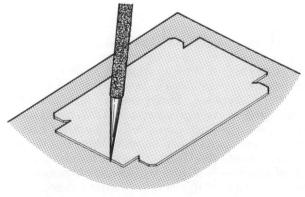

Development template

Dowel jig
This jig, made from steel, is held to the piece of wood with a G cramp while the drill for the dowel holes is passed through the holes in the jig.

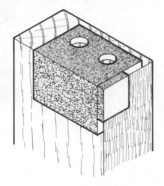

Dowel jig

Industrial jigs
Jigs are in common use in industry to speed up manufacturing processes. An example of a quick hold-and-release jig worked by pneumatics is shown. The work piece is automatically locked in position ready for tooling when the air supply is switched on. The work piece is as rapidly released.

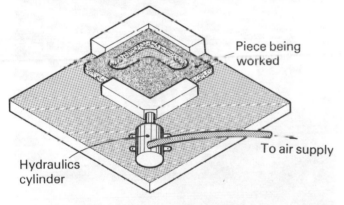

Piece being worked

To air supply

Hydraulics cylinder

Industrial jig

Hand production compared with mass production
The two graphs compare the costs of producing hand-made articles with the cost of producing the same article using mass-production methods. Fixed overhead costs such as buildings, power supplies, heating, lighting, sales and administrative staff salaries and transport have not been shown in the graphs. The costs of the materials for each chair have been assumed to be equal. Labour costs for each hand-made chair will be considerably greater than for each mass-produced chair because of the greater length of time taken to make a chair by hand than by machine. After the initial very high costs per mass-produced chair due to the high costs of introducing machinery, the production costs per chair decrease rapidly. This means that it is cheaper to produce a few chairs by hand, but cheaper to produce a large number of chairs using mass-production methods.

Economic use of line and form

Do not try to embellish and decorate your designs merely for the sake of decoration. When designing your craft work consider all its lines, all its shapes, all its forms with care. Each part of your design should have a purpose—either to fulfil the function imposed by the design brief or to produce good shape and form. Be economical in the use of shape and form. This may not only produce a better design but save time.

Exercises

1. On page 56 a comparison was made between a design made by a pupil at school and an industrially produced design. It could be said that the actual cost of a design made by a pupil is much greater than the cost of the same design made by an industrial concern. What costs have been ignored when considering the economics of a pupil-made design?

2. Write a short essay explaining why mass-produced products are often cheaper than hand-made products.

3. Despite the relative cheapness of mass-produced articles, there will always be a demand for hand-made articles. Why is this so?

4. On page 117 there is a working drawing of a design for a tiled table. Write a production sequence for this tiled table. Add the approximate times you think each stage of the sequence will occupy.

5. On page 118 is shown a drawing of a coat rack. Work out the costs of the materials needed to make the coat rack. Obtain the latest materials costs from current catalogues.

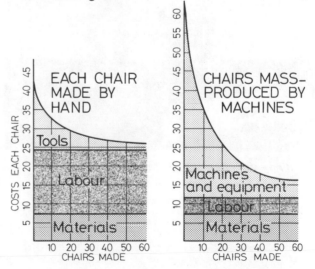

Graphs comparing hand and industrial production

Addition—Aerolite urea—formaldehyde glue for boat building

Reduction—salt and pepper pots turned from blocks of ash

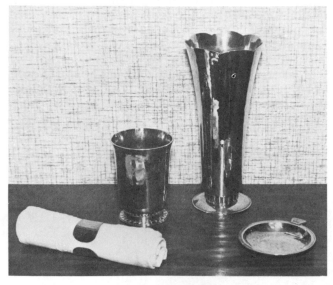

Moulding—four items of beaten copper work

Casting—entrance to Civic Centre at Hampstead

Shaping and forming

During the designing process the question arises —'How can the design be made?' The methods employed for obtaining the shapes and forms required in craft designs can be divided into four groups—addition, reduction, moulding and casting.

Addition

The most frequently used method is by adding parts to each other by some form of jointing. Addition methods are of sufficient importance to warrant a whole section of this book—pages 67 to 81. Addition methods include wood jointing; joining by gluing; metal jointing by soldering; brazing and welding; nuts, bolts, rivets; clips and tapes; the intertwining of cane as in basketry. Numerous other examples could be given.

Addition methods have advantages such as the following.
1. Small parts, easily handled, can be added to each other to form large structures. Example—a house.
2. There is no limit to the combinations which are possible.
3. Worn or broken parts may be replaceable. Example—a car.

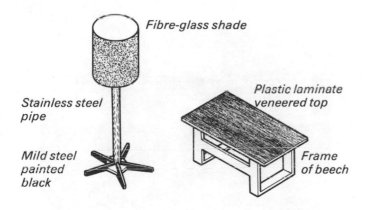

Fibre-glass shade

Stainless steel pipe

Mild steel painted black

Plastic laminate veneered top

Frame of beech

Reduction

The second most important method is by the removal of parts from an existing shape or form. A vast range of hand and machine tools have been developed for this purpose. Some reducing is carried out to enable parts to be added to each other, but there are many examples of shapes and forms produced completely by reduction. Two examples are illustrated—an abstract shape made of wood, the idea having been developed from a bone, and a salad-serving fork made from acrylic sheet.

Moulding

Moulding is taken to include methods by which materials are pushed or forced into a mould, laid on to a mould, folded or bent. Heating of the material or of the mould may or may not be necessary according to the materials and to the method employed. Some examples of moulding are—bending strip-metal around jigs, pipe bending, laminating wooden forms, steam bending of wood, fibre-glass moulding, beaten metalwork. Two examples are shown in drawings—an egg and toast rack made from veneers laminated around a former, and a fibre-glass canoe made by laying-up on moulds.

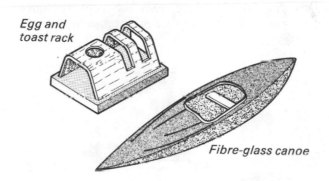

Egg and toast rack

Fibre-glass canoe

Casting

Casting usually involves the pouring of a liquid or a paste into a previously prepared mould. Some castings are made from powders. Heating of the materials involved may or may not be necessary. Pressure may sometimes be involved. Quite intricate shapes can be speedily made once the mould has been prepared. Examples are—castings such as in car engines, bronze casting in sculptures, wax casting as for candles, cement casting as in large buildings, casting in Plaster of Paris, casting in plastics.

Wooden abstract

Salad fork made of acrylic sheet

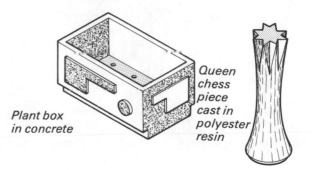

Plant box in concrete

Queen chess piece cast in polyester resin

Addition

Very complicated constructions can be made by adding parts or components to each other. Designs such as the Concorde supersonic aeroplane are produced by adding some half a million parts together. The parts are made from a vast array of different materials. In craft work addition methods are often used to produce designs. Two examples of craft design are shown in photographs. The design for a carrier bag was made from two pieces of paper, cut to shape and glued together. The wall bookrack contains twelve pieces of melamine-veneered chipboard, twelve corner knock-down fittings, sixteen adjustable shelf supports, four screw and socket knock-down fittings, two hinges, a door handle, two lengths of melamine pre-glued edging strip and four wall plates.

The advantages of addition methods are:

1. The best materials for each part of the design can be selected. For example—stool frame made from wood, seat made from rubber webbing, polyether foam, furnishing fabric, two different adhesives, one for stool joints, the second for joining the fabric to the seat.

2. Parts can be replaced when broken or worn—tyres from a car, brake shoes from a bicycle, transistor from a television set, glass from a window.

3. Some designs incorporating parts made in a workshop with ready-made fittings can be made. An example is a table lamp which requires a length of flex, a switch and a bulb holder.

4. Very large constructions are possible while using easily handled components. Examples can be found in buildings, in bridge construction, in roads and railways, apart from craftwork.

If you decide your design is to be made by addition methods you should turn to the section on Jointing (pages 67 to 81).

You will need to answer the following:

1. Is the jointing method to be permanent, temporary or movable?

2. Are the addition methods to involve cold or hot joints? Cold joints include:
  (a) using adhesives
  (b) woodwork jointing
  (c) nuts, bolts, rivets.

Hot joints include:
  (d) soft soldered
  (e) hard soldered—silver or brazed
  (f) welded.

Hot joints are permanent.

Addition—a wall bookrack made from veneered chipboard

Addition—a shopping bag for records made from coloured paper

Reducing

The reducing or cutting away of material to obtain a required shape or form is performed with a large range of tooling equipment, both hand and machine.

Some reducing is usually required when shaping parts which need jointing or adding to each other. Reducing materials to shape is thus one of the major operations carried out in craft work, either to produce a final shape or form or to prepare parts which will be jointed or added to each other.

Metals are harder and more difficult to work with hand tools than are plastics and many plastics are formed by moulding or casting. Two details arise from these factors.

1. Machining plays a more important part in the shaping of metals than when working wood in craft designs.
2. Except for drilling, the machining of plastics is often limited to materials such as nylon and acrylics in craft work.

Other details affecting the reduction of wood to shape and form are.

1. Wood cannot be cast to shape so is more frequently reduced by tooling than are metals, some of which can be cast using craft room equipment.

2. Wood machinery tends to be dangerous in use. Thus the working of wood by circular saws, band-saws and planing machines is restricted to people who have reached school-leaving age.

Most of the reduction of plastics is carried out with woodwork or metalwork hand tools. When machining nylon and acrylics a negative or zero top rake is necessary and the cutting edge should be well lubricated with a copious flow of water.

The drawings on this page show the results of the shaping of metals and of woods with power machinery. Power drills such as a pillar drill will produce accurate circular holes in woods, metals or plastics. Lathes will produce circular, cylindrical or conical shapes and can also machine flat surfaces. A shaping machine will form many of the shapes required in metal as will also a milling machine. Wood machine saws such as circular saws and band saws can be used to produce shapes quite apart from their more usual function of sawing wood to size.

Two other machines of value for reducing materials to shape are metal grinders and sanding discs fitted to hand power drills. Hard metals will probably have to be shaped by carborundum grinding wheels. Wood can often be shaped by a coarse sanding disc fitted to a hand power drill, but the wood being worked must be held quite securely in a vice or by cramps.

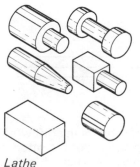

Drilling machine

Drilling machine

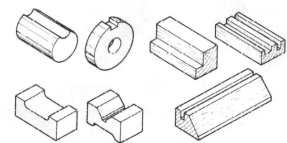

Shaping machine   *Wood circular saw*

Lathe   *Wood-working lathe*

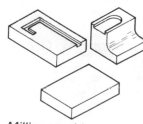

Milling machine

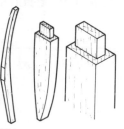

Wood bandsaw

Moulding

In craft work the term moulding can be taken to cover those methods involving beating or bending metals to shape, the bending and laminating of woods and the various methods by which plastics can be moulded.

Metals

The forcing of sheet metals on moulds as is employed for making articles such as car bodies is not used in craft work. In craft work when it is necessary to mould sheet metal, it is beaten to shape on 'stakes' using mallets and hammers. Metals can also be heated and forged to shape with hammers on anvils. Pipe bending machines and a variety of strip-metal bending jigs are also available for moulding metal. Some shapes can be produced by bending metal in a vice after heating. Sometimes cold bending is practised.

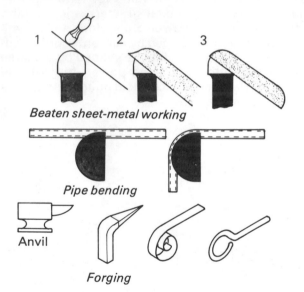

Beaten sheet-metal working

Pipe bending

Anvil

Forging

Plastics

Several methods are practised for the moulding of plastics.

Vacuum moulding involves sucking heated thermoplastic sheet plastic on to a mould.

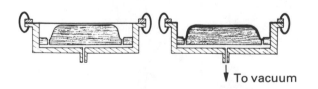

To vacuum

Woods

Woods are not easily moulded to shape. Two methods are available to the craft worker. In the first, shapes are built up on moulds with thin laminations or layers of wood glued to each other. The assembly laminations are held on the mould under pressure until the glue sets. The resulting laminated forms are very strong and flexible. A second method involves the heating of wood in steam chests to nearly the boiling point of water. The steamed timber is then quite pliable. While hot it is forced on to a mould and held in position until cold and dry.

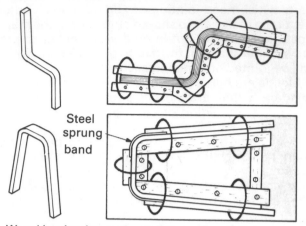

Steel sprung band

Wood laminating and wood steam-bending

Blow moulding is the reverse of vacuum moulding. In blow moulding air is blown between a flat surface and heated thermoplastic sheet which is held firmly to the edges of the flat surface.

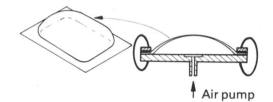

Air pump

Fibre-glass mouldings are 'laid up' on moulds by working glass fibre and polyester resin in laminations on the mould. Fibre-glass moulding is a cold process, no heat being involved.

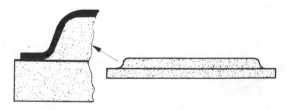

One difficulty in the use of moulds in craft work is that the expense of making the mould is often not worth while when making only one article. Moulding such as vacuum moulding of plastic sheet, steam bending of wood or the laying of a glass-fibre moulding is only truly economical when several identical articles are required or when the mould can be cheaply and speedily made.

Casting

The term casting covers a variety of methods for producing shapes and forms by pouring liquids or by packing powders into moulds and then allowing them to set hard. The liquids for casting may be either hot—as in the case of casting molten metals—or cold—as when casting polyester resins. For the small number of methods involving powders (sintering) heat is usually necessary and for some sintering procedures pressure will also be required.

Casting metals

In craft work metal casting is usually restricted to aluminium or lead. This is because these metals can be melted at relatively low temperatures. Sand casting is the most common method. A pattern of the required shape is necessary for forming the mould which is made in casting sand. Such patterns are often made from wood. The drawings show a pattern for an aluminium base for a photographic enlarger and a section through the base after it has been cast in a casting box.

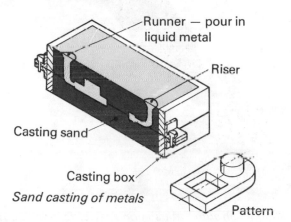

Sand casting of metals

Lost-wax casting is practised in craft work for making small and delicate metal castings such as the brooch shown. A pattern of the required form is made from wax. The pattern is coated with a special casting plaster which is allowed to set hard. After melting the wax from the plaster mould, molten metal can be poured into the hollow so formed. Lost-wax casting produces precise copies of the wax pattern.

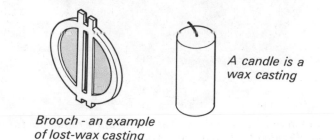

Brooch - an example of lost-wax casting

A candle is a wax casting

Concrete casting

Some craft shapes and forms can be cast in concrete. Many different materials can be used for making the moulds. One problem when casting in cement is the heaviness of the resulting casting. Concrete castings may need reinforcing by embedding strips or rods or wires of mild steel within the concrete.

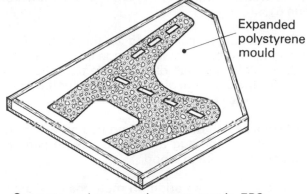

Concrete end to a garden seat cast in EPS

Casting in plastics

Polyester resins can be cast by pouring. Granules can be cast by heating the powders or granules in moulds in ovens.

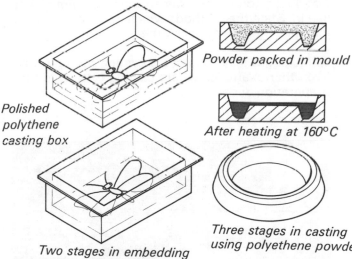

Polished polythene casting box

Powder packed in mould

After heating at 160°C

Two stages in embedding with polyester resin

Three stages in casting using polyethene powder

Plaster

Plaster of Paris is a valuable casting material being easy to mix, pour and cast and because it sets very rapidly. It is most often used for the casting of moulds into which other materials can be cast (such as clays), or on which other materials can be laid (as in fibre-glass work). Plaster of Paris can also be used for castings. The surfaces of plaster casts are very precise imitations of the surfaces of the moulds into which the plaster is poured. They can be reinforced with strips of butter muslin or rags worked into the plaster as it sets.

Exercises

1. Make freehand sketches and add notes to show how the five-sided base for the lamp stand shown on page 61 can be joined to the stainless steel tube.

2. Make freehand sketches showing a construction for the wooden frame of the small table shown on page 61.

3. The shaped pieces added to the sides of the concrete plant box shown on page 61 are cast with the box. Make a sketch of a suitable pair of casting boxes for the concrete plant box—one for the inside of the box, the second for the outside.

4. Make a sketch of a pair of moulds on which the curved part of the egg and toast rack on page 61 could be laminated in wood.

5. Make a list of ten addition methods of shaping and forming.

6. List ten articles which could have been made by moulding. Against each article state the method by which the moulding was made.

7. Write down fifteen materials which have in some way been added together to make the house you live in. State the methods which have been used to join the materials to each other.

8. Making a jelly employs a casting method. Give five other examples where casting is used in food preparation or cooking.

9. List ten examples where parts of an article can be replaced or renewed when broken or worn. Do not include those already given on page 60.

10. Sketch freehand a development for the shopping bag shown in a photograph on page 62.

11. How could the various parts of the bookrack, shown in a photograph on page 62, be joined to each other? Make a freehand drawing of suitable methods for joining the shelves to the right-hand upright end of the bookrack. (See pages 69 to 87.)

12. Two examples of wood laminating and steam bending are given in an illustration on page 64. Make freehand sketches of two further examples of wooden parts of designs which would be shaped by either of these two methods.

Addition—an automatic steering device for a sailing yacht

Moulding—fruit bowl vacuum-formed from acrylic sheet

Moulding—bowl which has been blow-moulded from acrylic sheet within its own wooden surround

Jointing

In this section we will be dealing mainly with the methods of jointing which are available for metals, woods and plastics. Many other materials will need to be jointed when making designs. Some examples are: fabrics, canes, glass, clays, papers. Some references will be made to these other materials but only to a limited extent.

It should be noted that some of the problems related to the jointing of materials in the three groups are different. For example, wood is stronger along the 'grain' than across it; wood cannot be heated above about the boiling point of water when being joined; each metal and each plastic possess the same strength in all directions; some metals can be heated to very high temperatures for jointing; some plastics will not accept glues because they are practically inert chemically.

Despite these differences, the designer should select the best material most suitable for the design. Once the material has been selected then methods of jointing can be considered. The pages which follow should help in the selection of the most suitable jointing method.

Three groups of joints

1. Permanent
These are jointing methods which are expected to last throughout the life of a design without movement taking place between the parts of the join. The joints will be fixed, incapable of movement and a strong bond will be expected between the parts of each join.

2. Temporary
A temporary joint can be taken apart either with the use of screwdrivers or spanners or by being pulled apart. Temporary joints are not necessarily any less strong than permanent joints. 'Knock-down' jointing methods are included in this group.

3. Movable
Although the parts may be fixed to each other either permanently or temporarily, movement between the parts can occur. These movements may be sliding, rotating, bending, flexing or movement along arcs.

Methods of jointing

1. Glues (Adhesvies)
Animal and vegetable glues, which in the past were very popular, have now largely been replaced by synthetic glues, many of which are polymers ('plastics'). Although animal and vegetable glues were strong, they could only be used with a very limited range of materials. Being organic, they were damaged by dampness, heat and fungal attack. At the present time modern synthetic (polymer) glues can be obtained for a wide range of materials and purposes.

Good, adequate, permanent joints can be obtained by gluing together the parts of many designs. It is important, however, to make quite sure the best adhesive is selected for the purpose. Of equal importance is the need to ensure the adhesive is used in the correct manner. Read instructions on the containers.

2. Joints formed by heat
Some of the jointing methods used with plastics and metals require heat. When heat-jointing plastics, temperature control is important—too cold and the join will not make; too hot and the plastic is damaged. When heat-jointing metals, other metals are melted into the joint. Heating the metals to the required temperature is carried out by soldering irons, brazing torches, arc-welding equipment or oxy-acetylene welding equipment.

Plastics
Welding by hot air or by heated rollers. Temperatures from 90°C to 160°C depending upon the plastic.

Metals
Soft solder (lead and tin). Low temperature—200°C to 250°C. Good conductor of electricity. Large surfaces need to be soldered if strength of join is necessary.
Silver solder (silver and copper)—Various mixtures melting up to 800°C. Much stronger than soft solder.
Brazing (brass) Temperatures up to 850°C. Stronger than silver solder.
Electric arc welding (various welding rods)—Temperatures up to 1500°C. For metal above 1 mm thick. Very strong.
Oxy-acetylene welding (various welding rods)—Mainly for sheet metal. Very strong.
Aluminium solder (aluminium alloys)—Temperatures up to 600°C. Strong and successful if instructions are carefully followed.

3. Fittings
Hinges, knock-down fittings, stays and other such fittings form an important group of jointing methods.

4. Fabrication
Designs are fabricated when their various parts are assembled from a number of pieces. These parts may be glued, jointed by the many methods shown later in this book using common jointing techniques, heat, knock-down fittings and so on.

5. Intertwined joints

Such joints are formed by knotting or weaving. A reef knot between ropes is an intertwined joint. A dog basket and a shopping basket are made with intertwined joints. A knitted piece of clothing consists of intertwined joints.

6. Smoothing joints

A cup handle is joined to the body of a cup by smoothing the handle on to the body while the clay is still in a plastic state. When the cup is fired in a kiln the join becomes permanent. Smoothing joints are common when working in clay or in Plasticine.

Jointing fabrics with Velcro

Knock-down jointing combined with permanent jointing

Knock-down jointing combined with movable parts jointing

An example of many different types of jointing

Jointing by gluing

Note the following
When using modern synthetic (plastic) adhesives some important details must be observed.
1. Select the best adhesive for the material and the purpose. Do not use any adhesive for all purposes.
2. Follow all instructions on packets or containers.
3. Clean and dry all surfaces which are to be glued.
4. The larger the surfaces glued together the stronger the joint will be.
5. With many modern glues, setting times will be affected by temperature. On cold days setting times will be increased.

Some plastics cannot be glued
Polythene, polypropylene and nylon cannot usually be glued. Polythene and polypropylene can be jointed by heat-welding. Nylon requires physical jointing—screws, rivets, locking devices, etc.

Type	Use for these materials	Comments	Clean off waste glue with
PVA Evostik W Croid Polystik	Wood, paper, expanded polystyrene, leather, fabrics.	Poor water resistance. Cheap. Very easy to obtain.	Water.
CONTACT Evostik Bostik	Laminated plastic, rubber, leather, fabrics to wood, polyurethane foam.	Joint made on impact. Not particularly strong but valuable for large areas.	Petrol.
UREA FORMALDEHYDE Aerolite 300 Cascamite	Wood. Laminated plastics to wood. Chipboard.	Good water resistance. Strong.	Water.
LATEX Copydex	Rubber, paper, leather, fabrics.	Waterproof. Elastic and flexible.	Rubs off with fingers.
EPOXY Araldite Plastic padding	Wood, metals, acrylics, polystyrene, polyester, melamine, glass, ceramics, bakelite.	Glues nearly all materials—does not shrink on setting. Waterproof.	Difficult to remove. White spirit.
ACRYLIC Tensol	Acrylics (e.g. Perspex).	Good water and oil resistance.	
POLYESTER RESIN	The resin of fibre-glass —metals, wood, polyurethane foam.	Good water resistance.	Acetone.
POLYSTYRENE	Polystyrene Kits (e.g. Airfix).	Dissolves expanded polystyrene.	
PVC CEMENT Vinyl or beach ball glue	PVC (Vinyl).	Slow setting.	
BLU-TACK Bostik	Hanging posters, cards, etc. Useful for temporary tacking joints.	Temporary joining device. Use straight from pack.	Not needed.
SILICONE RUBBER Bath sealers	Metals, glass, ceramics.	Flexible sealer. Hot water and corrosion proof. Insulator.	White spirit.

Metal jointing—permanent

Before commencing permanent jointing in metal ask yourself the following questions.

1. Are you certain you require the joints to be permanent?
2. Can the shape you need be obtained by bending?
3. Is strength or appearance the main consideration?
4. Do you need inside or outside surfaces to be clear of obstructions at corners?
5. When making designs in tubing, is it better to join or to use a pipe bender and bend?

Selection of suitable methods

A selection of permanent jointing methods for box shapes, dividing partitions and frames are shown. Select the method best suited to your design. Permanent joints include the following.

Gluing—For craft work epoxy resin is the most suitable. Many industrial glues not commonly available for craft users.

Riveting—Of value for joining dissimilar metals.

Soft soldering—For thin sheet metals. Laps needed to spread jointing area.

Hard soldering—Mainly for non-ferrous metals such as copper and brass.

Brazing—Mainly for steels.

Welding—Very strong. Mainly for steels.

Divisions

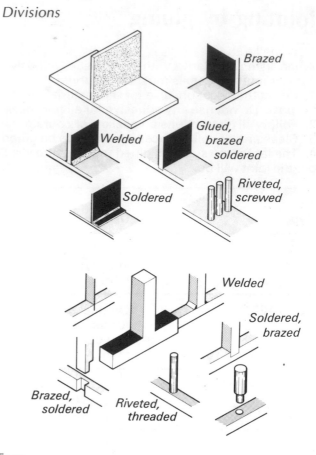

Box

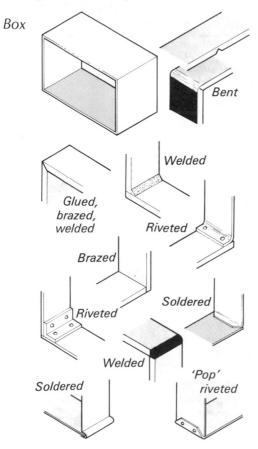

Frame

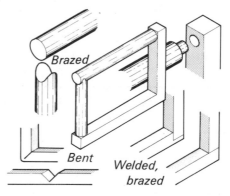

End to end or edge to edge

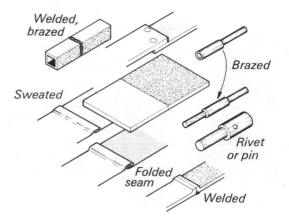

70

Metal jointing—temporary

Note

1. Generally sheet metal requires the use of self-tapping screws for temporary jointing. Thicker metals require bolts or nuts and bolts.
2. In order to screw parts to each other, a generous overlap is required when working in thin sheet metal.
3. Square and round section 'knock-down' kits can be purchased. You should consider whether it is worth-while purchasing such kits.
4. It is difficult to avoid overlaps when temporarily joining metal end to end or edge to edge.

Frames

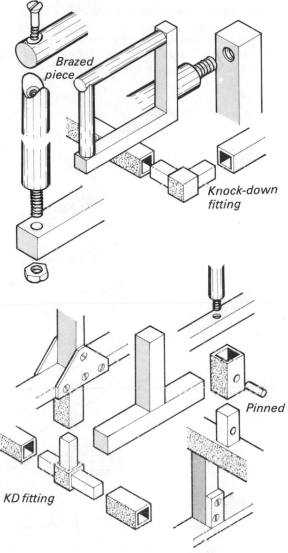

Brazed piece

Knock-down fitting

Box

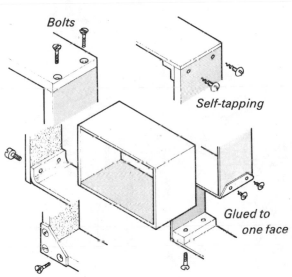

Bolts

Self-tapping

Glued to one face

KD fitting

Pinned

End to end or edge to edge

Divisions

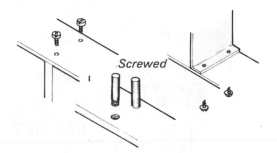

Screwed

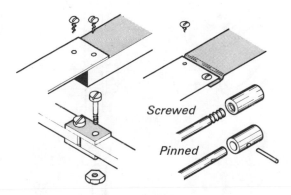

Screwed

Pinned

71

Metal jointing—movable

Movable joints in metal will be based upon
1. How many axes of movement are required.
2. The speed or frequency of the movement.
3. Whether the movement must be stopped and clamped in fixed position on occasion.

4. How the joint is to be assembled.

In an arc
The two most common methods involve either a pivot or springy pieces of metal. Hinges can be attached in a variety of ways, only two of which are shown. Springy pieces of metal can be obtained from piano wire or steel packing-case strip.

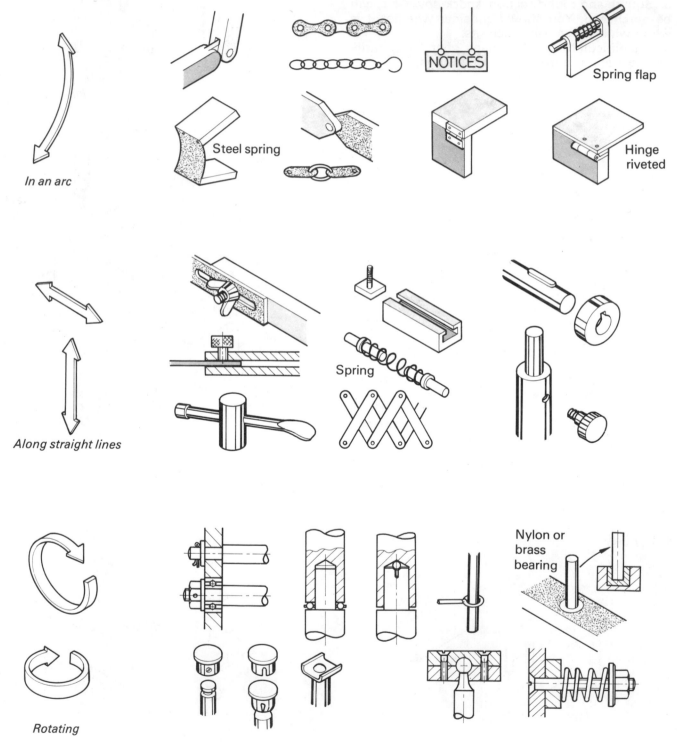

In an arc

Steel spring

Spring flap

Hinge riveted

NOTICES

Along straight lines

Spring

Rotating

Nylon or brass bearing

Along straight lines
How quickly do you require the movement to be made? If the movement is fast, it may be necessary to insert bearing materials such as brass or nylon.

Rotating
How easy does the rotation have to be? Is it to be fast or slow? Can wear be tolerated? Ball bearings are expensive so should possibly be avoided in craft work. Oil impregnated sintered iron bearings are cheaper and nylon bearings can be made by cutting to shape and drilling.

Multi-directional movements
These jointing methods allow movements in more than one direction in the same component.

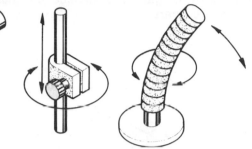

Multi-directional movements

Exercises—General

1. Acrylic sheet is soft and pliable at a temperature between 165°C and 175°C. In this condition the sheet may be bent and sharp angles obtained. When cooled the acrylic sheet will retain its new shape. Slow cooling minimises stress in the material. A jig has to be designed on which acrylic sheet up to 400mm wide and 6mm thick can be bent to any desired angle up to 90°. The jig may be made in any suitable material or combination of materials.

Write a design analysis for the jig listing the problems to be faced and suggest methods of overcoming them.

London

2. To enliven a corner of a paved area you are to design a garden box to be made in wood with a metal or glass-fibre liner. The approximate sizes are 600 × 250mm if rectangular or 600mm if circular. Flowering plants, already brought on in pots, will be transplanted into it.

Oxford

3. The most common modern materials used in school workshops are
(a) fibre glass—reinforced plastic,
(b) acrylic resin—perspex.

Write notes on one of these materials and its use, including safety precautions. Also make a freehand drawing of a job which you have made or seen made in a school workshop, using one of these materials. Annotate the drawing to make clear that you are aware of technical, aesthetic or functional requirements of the piece of work.

Oxford and Cambridge

4. Design a free-standing mirror which will be used on the flat surface of a storage chest constructed of either teak-veneered chipboard with natural teak drawer pulls or white plastic laminate veneered chipboard with anodised aluminium drawer pulls. The mirror should not exceed 300mm in any dimension and provision should be made for the mirror to be held at any desired angle to the horizontal. It should be easily dismantled to facilitate packaging.

Welsh

5. Design and make a standard lamp to illuminate a dark corner of a foyer. It could stand behind an easy chair. Electrical fittings are to be purchased, but you are expected to design and make the shade.

Oxford

6. Design and make a storage unit for holding a limited selection of daily papers and a few magazines. The unit is for use by people in the foyer and may well be seen in conjunction with the scene suggested in question 5.

Oxford

7. *Either* (a) Name the ferrous alloys used for making the following parts of an engineer's vice
   (i) jaw plates
   (ii) body
   (iii) screw and tommy bar.
Describe the production of *one* of these alloys from pig iron.
Or (b) A garden bench is to be made of teak, an easy chair of oak and a kitchen stool of pine. Briefly list the major characteristics of each of these materials and state why each is particularly suited for its intended use. Describe the final stages of cleaning up, preparation for and application of a suitable protective finish to *one* of these seats.

London

Wood jointing—permanent

Box

Methods of making permanent corner joints of box-like constructions are shown. Three groups of wooden materials are involved—'solid' wood, chipboard and other manufactured boards.

Some of the constructions involve nails and screws. Some form of gluing is advised for such nailed or screwed corners.

Chipboard

Glued joints in chipboard are as strong as the chipboard itself. Provided glues are either PVA or urea formaldehyde, and the joints are held under pressure until the glue sets, nails or screws are not necessary.

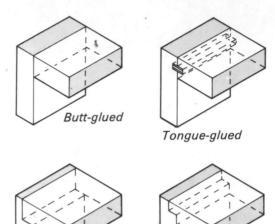

Butt-glued

Tongue-glued

Rebated-glued

Double rebated-glued

'Solid' wood

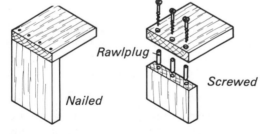

Rawlplug

Nailed

Screwed

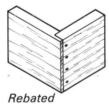

Rebated

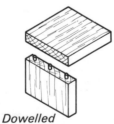

Dowelled

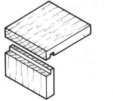

Grooved

Housed

Manufactured boards

Strips of wood are required to strengthen corner joints made in thin manufactured boards such as plywoods and hardboards. Such joints are sufficiently strong if glued under pressure until the glue sets, although nails or screws may be necessary to apply the pressure. Thicker boards can be screwed from inside the strips.

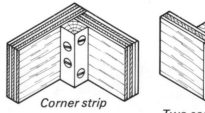

Corner strip

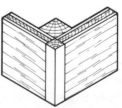

Two corner strips

Rebated strip

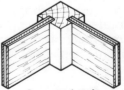

Grooved strip

Wood jointing—permanent

Divisions

Methods for jointing dividers such as shelves or partitions within box-like constructions are shown on this page.

Methods for jointing backs and bottoms are also shown. Plywoods or hardboards are suitable for bottoms and backs.

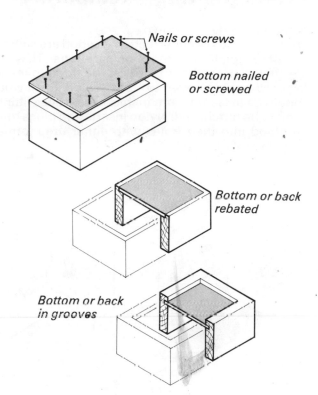

Nails or screws

Bottom nailed or screwed

Bottom or back rebated

Bottom or back in grooves

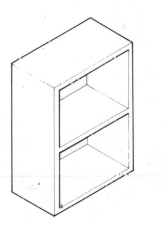

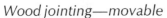

Nailed

Screwed — Rawlplug

Housing

Stopped housing

Corner strip

Dowelled

Wood jointing—movable

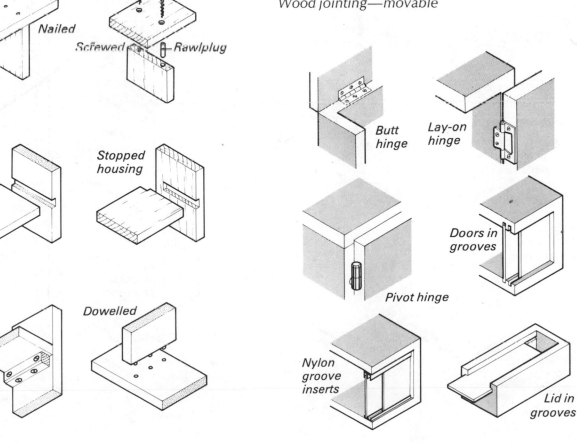

Butt hinge

Lay-on hinge

Pivot hinge

Doors in grooves

Nylon groove inserts

Lid in grooves

75

Wood jointing—temporary

Temporary—knock-down
These methods of construction in wood are suitable for either jointing corners or partitions. They are designed for chipboard, but can be fitted to manufactured board or even to 'solid' wood. Such wood should be at least 15mm in thickness. These fittings need to be purchased. Nylon inserts and plugs must be glued into their holes with either urea formaldehyde or PVA glue.

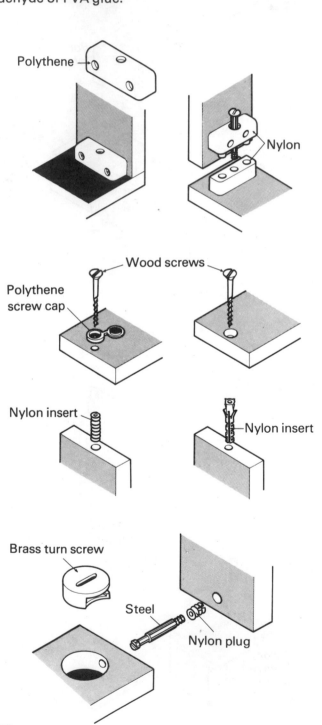

Polythene

Nylon

Wood screws

Polythene screw cap

Nylon insert

Nylon insert

Brass turn screw

Steel

Nylon plug

Frame constructions—permanent

Two-dimensional frames are usually made from 'solid' wood. This use of 'solid' wood ensures rigidity in framing constructions. The joints shown should be glued, preferably under cramping pressure.

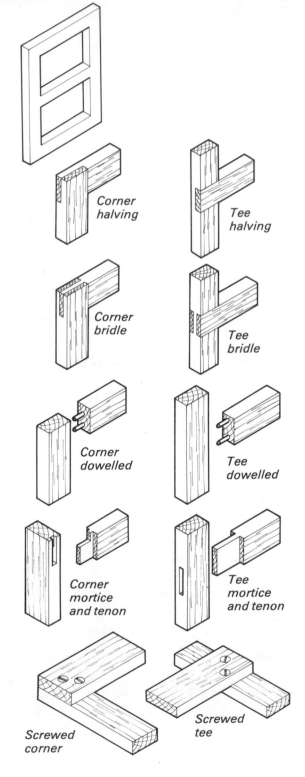

Corner halving

Tee halving

Corner bridle

Tee bridle

Corner dowelled

Tee dowelled

Corner mortice and tenon

Tee mortice and tenon

Screwed corner

Screwed tee

76

Wood jointing

Three-dimensional frames—permanent
Three-dimensional frames can be constructed by glueing and screwing flat frames to each other. If this is not suitable, the three common forms of 3D frame jointing are shown. Each requires to be glued, preferably under cramping pressure.

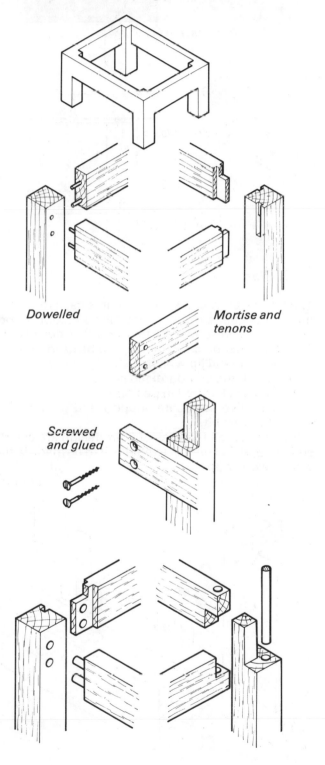

Dowelled

Mortise and tenons

Screwed and glued

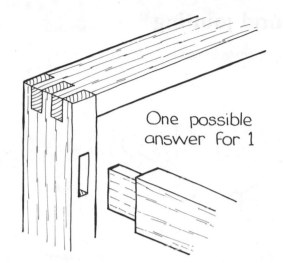

One possible answer for 1

Exercises

Six 3D frames of different designs are shown. These frames are suitable for table or stool designs.
(i) Draw freehand sketches showing the methods by which the parts of each frame could be jointed. Use as many different jointing methods as possible.
(II) Draw freehand three more frames of different designs to those given. The frames you draw should also be suitable for stool or table designs.

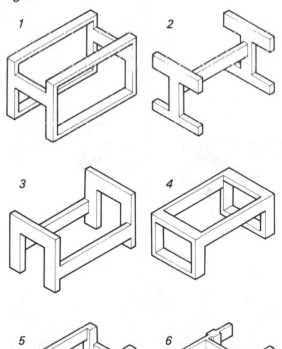

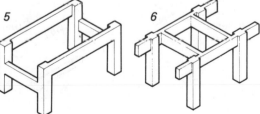

Wood jointing

Frame constructions—movable

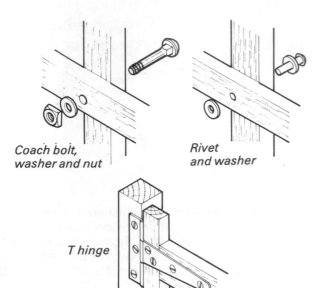

Coach bolt, washer and nut

Rivet and washer

T hinge

Temporary—knock-down

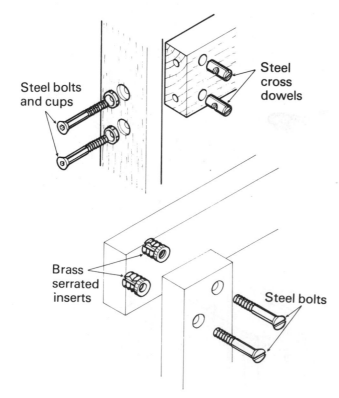

Steel bolts and cups

Steel cross dowels

Brass serrated inserts

Steel bolts

Jointing tops to frames

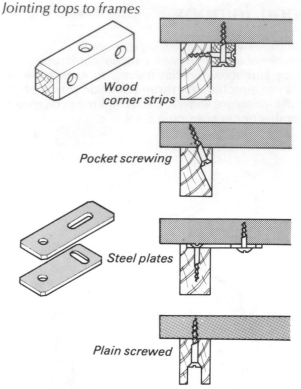

Wood corner strips

Pocket screwing

Steel plates

Plain screwed

Exercise—general

The figure below shows dowel joints used to make a number of chairs from standaridised section wood, 35 × 20. Each joint requires two Ø18 dowels. To speed production a drilling jig is to be used.

Design a metal jig which
   (a) will fit the standardised section
   (b) can be clamped in position
   (c) will give adequate support and guidance to the twist bit.

Ensure that all features of your design are clearly shown. Give full details to enable it to be made in the school workshop.

London

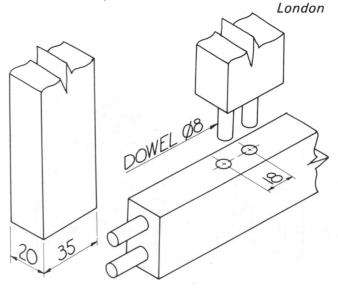

DOWEL Ø8

20   35

8

Plastic jointing—permanent

Note

Permanent joints in plastics may be achieved by
1. *Gluing*—The adhesive used must be appropriate for the particular plastic being jointed. Not all plastics can be glued and some plastics need special glues. See page 69.
2. *Welding*—Some plastics are suitable for welding. Others cannot be welded. See page 69.
3. *Heat bending*—While not a jointing method, it should be noted that some plastics can be formed into shape by bending after heating.
4. *Riveting*—Soft rivets should be used to avoid damage to the plastics being jointed.
5. *Heat shrinking*—Some permanent joints in plastics can be formed by heat shrinking. It must be remembered, however, that most plastics will disintegrate under the action of high temperatures.

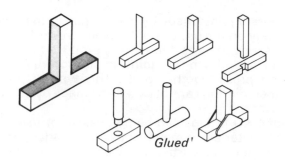

Glued

End to end

Box

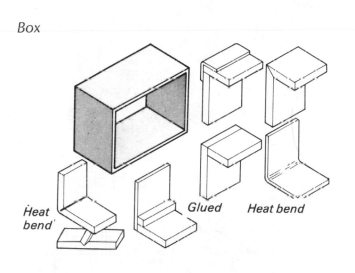

Heat bend   *Glued*   *Heat bend*

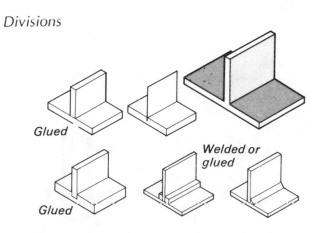

Glued

Taped

Glued

Glued

Rivet

Frame

Divisions

Glued

Welded or glued

Glued

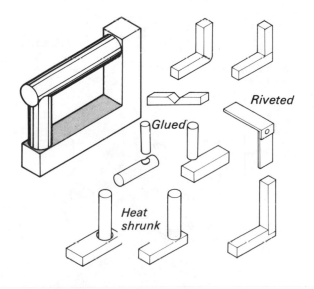

Glued

Riveted

Heat shrunk

79

Plastic jointing—temporary

Temporary joints made by hand in plastic materials often rely on the use of self-tapping screws, bolts or other screwed parts. Industrially produced temporary or knock-down (KD) joints in plastics frequently rely on press-together parts. This type of press-together jointing cannot usually be made by hand in craft work.

Some KD fittings can be purchased for use with plastic materials. It may be possible to adapt some fittings, such as curtain track parts for jointing in craft work.

Frames

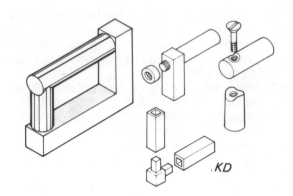

.KD

Box

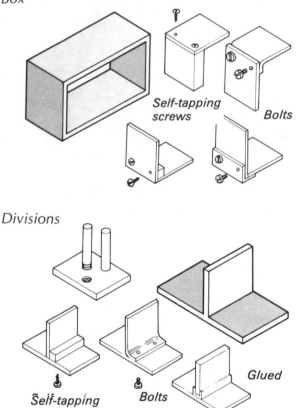

Self-tapping screws

Bolts

Divisions

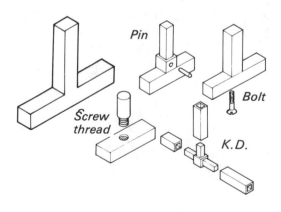

Self-tapping screws

Bolts

Glued

Pin

Screw thread

Bolt

K.D.

Others

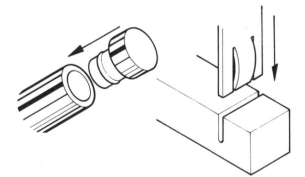

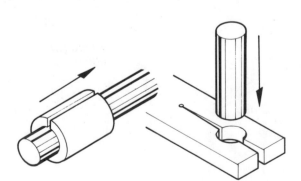

Plastic jointing—movable

Examples of jointing methods to obtain movement between parts are given on this page.

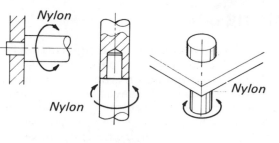

Nylon

Nylon

Nylon

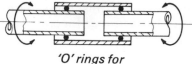

'O' rings for watertight joint

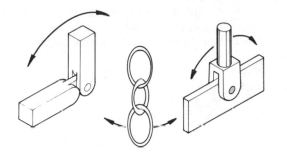

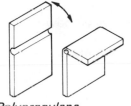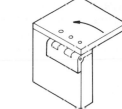

Polypropylene

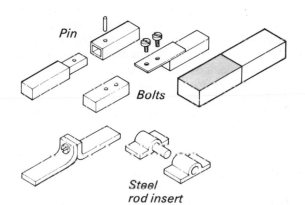

Pin

Bolts

Steel rod insert

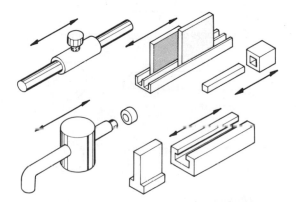

Exercise

Salad servers both of which are of the basic form shown schematically in the figure below, may be made of wood, metal or plastics.

(a) Give an exact specification of the material from which you would make the servers.
(b) Name the method by which you would make them.
(c) Describe in detail the finishing and polishing operations which you would adopt following the shaping process.

London

PROJECTION ⊕ ◁▭ DIMENSIONS IN MILLIMETRES (mm)

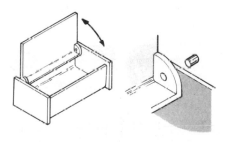

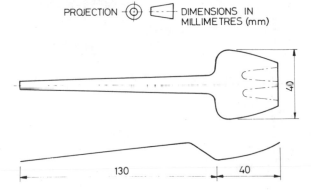

130   40

47

Fittings

All the parts required in craft designs do not have to be made by hand. Some parts may need to be purchased from shops or ordered from suppliers. Time and money can be saved by purchasing such 'fittings' rather than attempting making them in a workshop. An enormous range and variety of fittings are sold for craft work. Only those in common use are shown in this book. Firms which specialise in supplying fittings for craft work publish catalogues of their products.

Woodscrews

Woodscrews are most often made from steel. Brass and aluminium screws are made for use where resistance to corrosion is an important aspect of a design. Woodscrews may be coated with other metals—brass, chromium, cadmium, zinc or copper or may be enamelled. Coated screws are selected both for their resistance to corrosion and for their appearance. Woodscrews are made in lengths from 5 mm up to 300 mm. The gauge number of a screw indicates its diameter. Common gauges for craft design are 2, 4, 6, 8 and 10.

Ordering screws

When ordering woodscrews the following details will be required: number of screws; type of head; length; gauge; metal; coated (if required).
Countersunk—General purposes.
Round head—Fixing sheet materials to wood.
Raised head—Screwing fittings to wood.
Pozidriv—Fast driving; twin-start thread.
Coach screw—Spanner had. Heavy woodwor.
Screw caps—Often used when fixing mirrors.

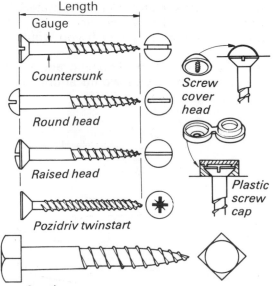

Bolts, nuts and washers

Bolts are most often made from steel. Small bolts for instrument making and electrical work are made from brass. Steel bolts are often finished 'blue'. They may be zinc or cadmium plated for anti-corrosion resistance. Bolts employed for craft work are often made with metric threads, designated M6, M8, etc., the figure denoting the thread diameter in millimetres. If designated M6 × 0.8, M8 × 1, etc., the second number denotes the thread pitch in millimetres.
Socket bolt—Hexagon socket for Alan key.
Castle nut—Split pin makes secure lock nut.
Cheese head—Small bolts. Screwdriver slot.
Washer and nut—May work loose. Washer protects surfaces.
Round head—Small bolts. A common type of bolt.
Lock nuts—The two nuts lock firmly on thread.
Countersunk head—Small bolts. Screwdriver slot.
Spring washer—A locking washer.
Coach bolt—Square nut. Heavy woodwork.
Hexagon bolt—Spanner head.
Wing nut—Removable with fingers.

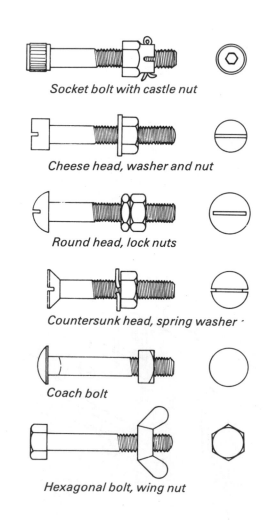

Socket bolt with castle nut

Cheese head, washer and nut

Round head, lock nuts

Countersunk head, spring washer

Coach bolt

Hexagonal bolt, wing nut

Wood nails

For speedy, yet strong construction work in wood, wood nails are unsurpassed. Probably the most common of all wood-jointing methods.

Oval nail—General purposes. Line up oval with grain. 12 mm long and upwards. Bright steel.

Wire nail—Most common nail. General construction. 25 mm to 300 mm in length. Steel, aluminium or copper.

Panel pin—Bright steel. A thin nail. Light woodwork. 12 mm to 50 mm lengths.

Veneer pin—Bright steel. Very thin. Valuable when model-making in wood; 10 mm to 20 mm long.

Tack—Blued steel, also copper or aluminium. General upholstery.

Staple—Steel. Fabric and wire netting to wood.

Masonry nail—Hardened blued steel. Wood to walls.

Clout—Fabrics to wood. Steel galvanised. Also aluminium.

Rivets

Rivets are designed for jointing sheet materials —metals, leathers, plastics, etc.—to each other. Riveted joints are made by forcing one end of the rivet on to the sheet material. The force is applied by hammering, or with purpose made pliers, guns or stamps.

Round head—Soft steel, copper or aluminium. Steel rivets for steel, others for non-ferrous metals or for plastics. Hammered end formed with a punch.

Countersunk—Same as round head except the end is hammered flush with sheet surface.

Pop rivet—Purpose-made rivet for use with a special gun or pliers. Will speedily join most materials.

Leather eyelet—For soft materials such as leather. Rivet made with special punch pliers.

Bifurcated—Another rivet for soft materials.

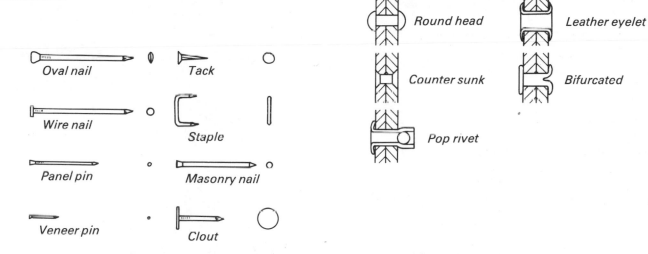

Oval nail Tack

Wire nail Staple

Panel pin Masonry nail

Veneer pin Clout

Round head Leather eyelet

Counter sunk Bifurcated

Pop rivet

Hinges

Hinges designed for operating wooden doors or box lids can be fitted to woods, metals or plastics. In place of woodscrews, the hinges can be fixed with rivets or with bolts if used on materials other than wood. There is a good range of varieties of hinges available for wooden doors or lids. The four shown here are those which can also be most easily adapted for metal or plastic work.

Butt—The most common door or box lid hinge. Made from steel, brass or nylon in a range of different lengths.

Lift-off—A development of the butt hinge. The hinge shown will enable a door opening on the left to be lifted free. Right-hand hinges would be needed for a right-hand door.

Pivot—Brass-plated steel. That illustrated is designed for use with chipboard. The hinges fit into nylon inserts.

Piano—Lightweight. Steel, brass or nylon. Made in lengths up to 2 metres.

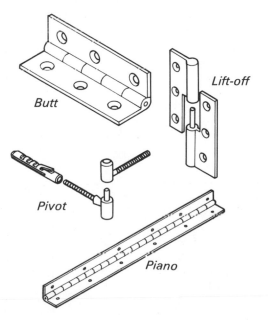

Butt Lift-off

Pivot Piano

Self-tapping screws

Self-tapping screws are made from hardened steel. These screws are designed to cut their own threads in a pilot hole into which the screw is driven. Used for joining sheet metal parts to each other, they can be found in many modern poducts made from sheet metal—motor car bodies, washing machine cases, refrigerator bodies and so on. Some are designed for self tapping into deeper holes—see bottom right-hand screw of the four illustrated. Self-tapping screws can be regarded as knock-down fittings. The parts held together by the screws can be speedily taken apart (knocked-down) for repair or replacement and then as speedily reassembled.

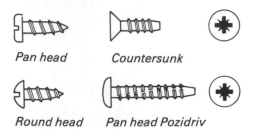

Pan head   Countersunk

Round head   Pan head Pozidriv

Self-tapping screws

Knock-down fittings for wood

Some of the more common knock-down fittings have already been described on page 76 under 'Jointing'. Here are three more.
Confirmat chipboard screws—A hard steel screw especially designed for making strong box corners between 16mm thick chipboard parts. The box can be quickly knocked down by unscrewing.

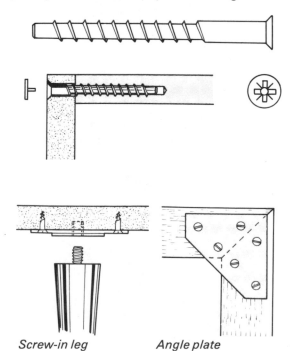

Screw-in leg   Angle plate

Screw-in leg—A two-part fitting. One part with a bolt is screwed to the top of the leg. The second part with a tapped hole is screwed under the table top.
Angle plate—A steel plate which makes a strong corner frame joint. Quickly knocked down by removal of the screws.

Wall plugs

Some of your craft work may need to be screwed against a wall. If the wall is made from bricks or from breeze blocks, a hole is bored into the wall with a masonry drill in a power drill. The hole is plugged with a wall plug. Four types of wall plug are shown. Mirror plates, or wall plates, are screwed to the back of your design. The design can then be fitted to the wall by screwing through the wall or mirror plates into the wall plug. If the wall is made from plaster board either cavity anchors or Rawlnuts can be used in place of wall plugs.

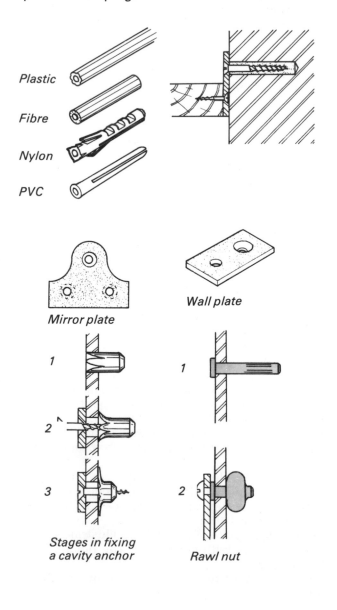

Plastic

Fibre

Nylon

PVC

Mirror plate   Wall plate

Stages in fixing
a cavity anchor   Rawl nut

Catches

Catches for securing doors and box lids are made from metal or plastic materials. They are intended to be screwed or bolted in position.

Magnetic—Nylon case, sintered iron magnets. Steel catch holds against magnets.

Spring—Nylon rollers in steel springs engage in catch.

Ball—Ball bearing under spring pressure in a brass case.

Bolt—Many types.

Toggle—Box catch. Clamps lid securely to box case.

Hasp and staple—A padlock slipped through staple closed inside hasp guards against pilfering.

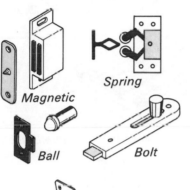

Magnetic
Spring
Ball
Bolt

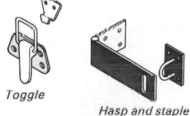

Toggle
Hasp and staple

Lighting fittings

The fittings shown are for connecting into a circuit from a mains supply. Because of the dangers involved when including mains circuits in your designs, check all wiring before connecting to the mains. Another different range of fittings are available for connecting to a 12 volt supply such as from a car battery or from a transformer, itself connected to mains.

Pygmy bulb—15 to 25 watts. Bayonet fitting.

Common bulb—25 to 150 watts. Above 150 watts with screw fitting instead of bayonet type.

Spot bulb—60 to 150 watts. Above 150w—screw fitting. Silver reflector inside bulb produces spot or floodlighting effect.

Hanging bulb socket—Connected to flex. Bayonet or screw fitting.

Lamp stand sockets—Either made to screw on to a brass fitting itself screwed to the top of a stand or a cheaper version screwed direct to stand.

Fuses—Usually fitted in plug. Cartridge fuses; 3 and 13 amps are common sizes.

Terminal connectors—Ends of wires to various parts of a circuit held in sockets by screws. Can be purchased in strips containing many terminal points.

Flex switch—Connected in or at end of flex leading to an electrical appliance.

13 amp plug—Connects a circuit to the mains by plugging into mains outlet socket.

Adhesive insulating tape—When joining wires, knot the two ends together, then preferably solder joint. Finally cover with insulating tape.

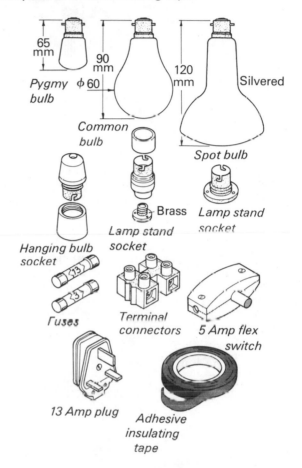

65 mm
Pygmy bulb φ 60
90 mm
Common bulb
120 mm Silvered
Spot bulb
Brass Lamp stand socket
Hanging bulb socket Lamp stand socket
Fuses Terminal connectors 5 Amp flex switch
13 Amp plug Adhesive insulating tape

Mirror clips

Two clips are shown for holding a mirror to a wooden panel made from plywood or chipboard. Usually plated brass.

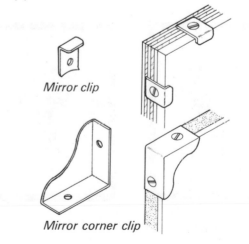

Mirror clip
Mirror corner clip

Sliding door tracks
Plastic tracks which can be either screwed direct to the inside of a cabinet or sunk into grooves. Suitable for glass, wooden or plastic doors.

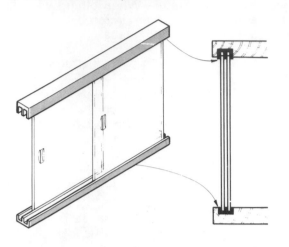

Pirelli webbing
A webbing made from rubber and rayon for the springing of seats and backs of chairs, beds, and settees. The webbing can be fixed to a wooden framework either with tacks or with purpose-made Pirelli webbing clips. The clips are closed over the ends of the webbing and held in sloping grooves cut in the framework.

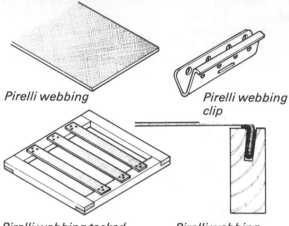

Pirelli webbing

Pirelli webbing clip

Pirelli webbing tacked to frame

Pirelli webbing held by clip

Hooks
Many different shapes of hooks can be obtained. Four are shown. These are for driving into wood. They can be purchased with bolts and nuts for use with metals and plastics.

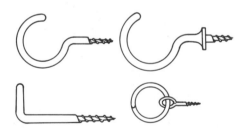

Dexion angle strips form a corner

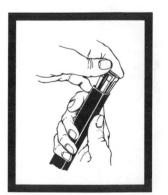

Dexion—'Speedframe' fittings

Exercises—general

1. (a) Screws are frequently used to join materials. State one advantage and one disadvantage of using metal woodscrews for wood to wood joints, and metal machine screws for metal to metal joints.

(b) Sketch two different screw head shapes and two different screw head styles to accept screwdrivers.

(c) State two advantages of using self-tapping screws in sheet metal or plastics.

(d) By means of a sectional view show how the appropriate screw holds together either two pieces of wood or two pieces of metal.

London

2. Different types of fastenings are given below. In the spaces provided, give examples of situations where the fastening could be best used, and also a reason for your choice.

Welsh

Type of Fastening	Typical Use	Reason for Choice
Self tapping screws		
Countersunk head rivets		
Pop rivets		
Electric spot welding		
Soft solder		

3. When pupils are preparing drawings for Design and Craft lessons in the design office of a school, each requires the following instruments and equipment:

A pair of compasses to draw circles up to 300 mm in diameter
A pair of spring bow compasses to draw circles up to 50 mm in diameter
A 60° set square
A 45° set square
A protractor
A rubber
Two pencils
A 300 mm rule.

Design a stand or tray in which the above equipment can be stored so that it can be placed on a pupil's drawing table, or placed on or in a stand nearby. Show by sketches and notes how 20 of the trays/ stands you have designed could be quickly and economically made.

4. The keeping of livestock involves the woodworker. It is necessary to know something of (a) the requirements of the particular livestock, (b) woodwork constructions, and (c) timber preservation. Write under these three headings in relation to a design for housing some animals or birds in which you are interested.

Oxford and Cambridge

5. Although vehicular traffic is generally prohibited from a precinct, the occasions arise when a light van or small truck will be required to obtain access.

Design some form of simple bollard which can be lowered or removed by a responsible council employee, but which under normal circumstances will allow easy access for prams, wheelchairs, etc., while restricting the entry of cars.

Oxford

6. You are to design a wall cupboard in which all the tools shown in the photograph below can be stored. The tools have been arranged in the photograph as they are expected to be placed in the cupboard. Each tool is to be individually racked so that it can be placed in its own special holder within the cupboard. Some of the tools can be racked on the insides of the doors if thought necessary.

On the drawing paper provided draw a vertical line at 200 mm from the right-hand border.

Make *all* the following drawings:

(a) In the space to the right of the line:

(i) A *freehand* sketch showing a design for the cupboard without its tool racks.

(ii) *Freehand* sketches showing methods by which the following tools can be individually racked within the cupboard:

The handsaw; The five firmer chisels; The two hammers.

(b) In the space to the left of the line:

Using your freehand sketches as a guide draw accurately with instruments, to a scale of 1:5, the following views of the cupboard you have designed:

(i) A front view which includes the three racks you have sketched to hold the handsaw, the chisels and the hammers.

(ii) A sectional end view.

Fully dimension the two views.

WMEB

Strength

When designing craft work, consideration must be given to the strength of the completed design. The following problems will have to be considered and satisfactory and answers to them provided if the design is to function properly.

1. Is the design sufficiently strong for its function?
2. Are the materials chosen the most suitable as regards their strength?
3. Is the construction of the design suitable for withstanding the strains which will be imposed?
4. Is overall weight of the design in relationship to its strength satisfactory?
5. Has the most economical use of materials been considered in relationship to the strength of the design?

What is meant by strength?

When using the term 'strength' in connection with designing, we are concerned with judging how best to deal with the results produced by the following forces:

1. *Tension*—Forces which are tending to stretch.
2. *Compression*—Forces which are tending to shorten.
3. *Shear*—Tendency to fracture or to cut.
4. *Bending*—Tendency to produce bowing.
5. *Flexing*—Tendency to flex or spring.
6. *Splitting*—Forces which are tending to cause separation along a line of cleavage.

Forces producing tension

Forces producing compression

Forces causing shear

Forces causing bending

Forces causing flexing

Strength and design

How are the problems resulting from these forces to be overcome?

1. Materials should be chosen with due regard to their strength properties.
2. The position and direction of parts within a design must be considered.
3. The sizes of all parts should be selected in relation to the strength of the part.
4. The methods of jointing the parts together should be considered. The first consideration will be whether the jointing is to be permanent, temporary or movable.
5. The methods of construction involving easily fractured materials such as glass, cement and chipboards should be given special attention.
6. Constructional methods will differ considerably between different materials depending upon their relative strengths.

Remedies

The drawings 1 to 8 show the results of forces applied to materials in various directions. Each drawing also shows a suggested remedy.

1. The bending of thin sheet material across the width can be prevented by adding stiffening strips. Lightness of weight and economy of material achieved with sufficient strength.

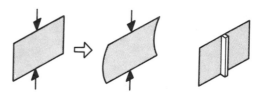

2. The bowing and flexing of a lightweight box frame can be prevented by adding a stiffening sheet. The all sheet construction will still be considerably lighter in weight than a solid of the same volume, yet be sufficiently strong and also be cheaper to make.

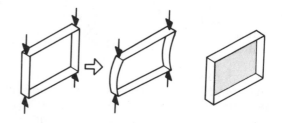

3. The bowing of sheet material along its length can be prevented by adding stiffening strips. Lighter weight than the equivalent solid sheet, yet as strong and making economical use of material.

4. Bowing of a beam along its length can be eliminated by turning the beam edgeways to the fore.

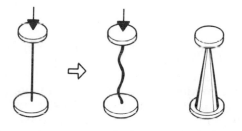

5. The distortion of the lightweight vertical caused by compressive forces can be prevented by amending the shape of the vertical member.

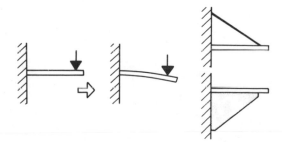

6. The flexing resulting from weights placed on a horizontal arm or shelf can be prevented either by adding a thin tension support from above, or by adding a bracket below. The bracket will resist compressive forces.

7. The splitting of wood caused by forces acting on short grains can be prevented by selecting wood with grain running along the length of the piece.

8. Splitting of wood caused by forces acting along the grain can be prevented by selecting wood with the grain at right angles to the forces causing the splitting.

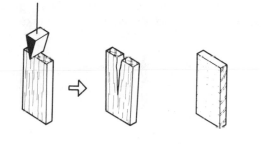

A one-kilogram hammer supported on a strip of drawing paper

Strength and different materials

The constructions necessary to obtain sufficient strength in a design will vary when different materials are used to solve the same design brief.

Field gates

Examine the drawings A, B, C and D of field gates. If the gate is made as at A, its own weight will cause the right-hand side of the gate to sag as at B. This will effectively prevent the gate from being opened. The design will obviously not function properly.

One remedy could be to add a diagonal across the gate to hold the forces causing the sagging.

If the gate is made from steel piping as at C with its parts welded together, a spring steel tension wire will prevent the sag. The tension wire is light in weight.

If the gate is made of wood as at D, a supporting bar across the other diagonal prevents the sagging. The stiffness of the wood allows the bar to take the compression resulting from the weight of the gate.

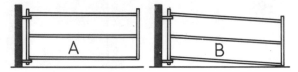

Garden seat

Compare the garden seats A and B. The frame of A is made from lengths of 50 mm square steel tubing welded together to form a rigid frame to which wooden seat and back strips are bolted. The welded joints are as strong as the steel itself and no additional support for the frame is necessary. The wooden seat frame B is made from strips of hardwood jointed together with mortise and tenon joints. The joints would quickly shear when the seat is sat upon unless additional supports under the seat are added to the frame to give the necessary strength to the design.

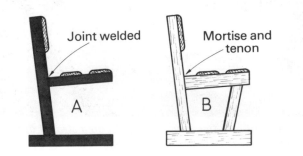

Strengthening sheet shelves

Drawings A, B, C and D show different materials used for making a shelf in a given design situation. To economise in both material and in weight, the shelf has been made as thin as possible in each case. The steel shelf A is made rigid and strong by edge bending as shown. Plastic shelving, B, of thicker sheet—plastic sheet as thin as steel sheet would bow across the width—is made with a simpler form of edge bending. The plywood shelf, C, is made rigid with strips joined under front and back edges. The concrete shelf at D, while being thicker, is reinforced with steel rods positioned when the shelf was cast. Concrete is more brittle than the other materials, hence it needs to be thicker as well as reinforced.

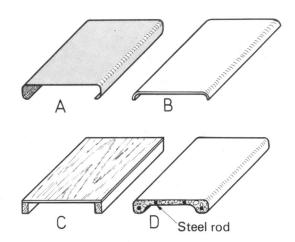

Sizes of members in a design—Table designs

We expect to see variations in the proportions of parts of a design in relation to the materials from which it is made. This is because we have unconsciously learned to expect steel, for example, to be much stronger than wood. If th proportions of parts of a design in relation to its materials look wrong we will dismiss the design as being poor. Examine the four table designs on page 91. The parts of A are grossly over large whatever the material. The proportions of B would be acceptable if the table were made of wood. The proportions of C would be acceptable if the table were made of steel. The proportions of the members of D are too light for any material.

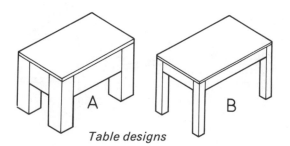

Table designs

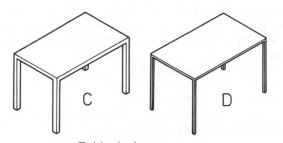

Table designs

Testing materials for strength

A whole range of experiments can be devised to test the strengths of materials. Many quite simple tests can be carried out in a craft room without the need for elaborate equipment. Other tests will require purpose-made testing machines, some of which can be made in a workshop.

Simple tests

Two very simple tests which can be worked with the minimum of equipment are shown. The first is designed to find the thickness of shelf material sufficiently strong to support a load of books in a bookrack without bowing. The second shows up the need for triangulation to obtain strength and rigidity in a frame made from thin material. Other similar simple tests can be devised as the need arises.

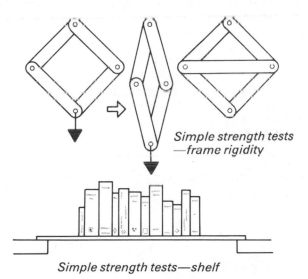

*Simple strength tests
—frame rigidity*

Simple strength tests—shelf

Materials testing

More advanced tests can be carried out using special equipment not suitable for use in a workshop. The drawings show the outline of two tests on wood as recommended by a British Standards booklet on comparison testing for woods. The first compares the bending qualities of woods before breakage occurs, the second compares along-grain shear qualities. Both these tests are devised to compare one wood with another for particular design purposes. Wood is very variable and wide differences will show up if attempts are made to obtain precise figures for any one species. For example, two batches of the same wood grown in different localities could show widely different strength qualities. This problem does not occur to the same extent when testing man-made materials such as metals, plastics, adhesives, glass, etc. Indeed these materials can be made to possess quite clearly defined strength qualities.

Another British Standard test is shown. This is devised to test PVA glues. The test piece, glued as shown, is placed under measured pressure until breakage occurs along the glue line. The measuring device of the machine will record a figure which can be stated as one of the strength values for the particular glue under test.

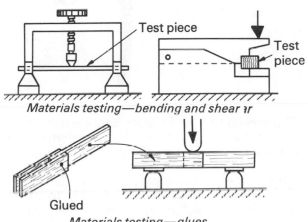

Materials testing—bending and shear ir

Glued

Materials testing—glues

Experimenting with rigid frames

Exercises

1. Drawings of two incomplete shelf brackets are given, one made of wood, the other made of mild steel. Neither of the two brackets is sufficiently strong as shown.

   Show by sketches how additional members can be jointed to each of the brackets to ensure they are sufficiently strong to support a loaded shelf. Your sketches should include the methods of jointing for each of the brackets.

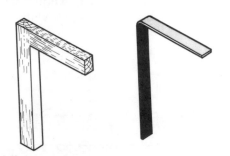

2. The design of a step ladder as shown in a drawing must take into account the problems of the forces causing tension, compression, shear, bowing and flexing of its parts. The design must also ensure that the ladder is sufficiently light in weight to be carried from place to place. Examine a ladder of this type and make sketches and notes on the methods employed to overcome the strength problems involved when a person climbs the ladder.

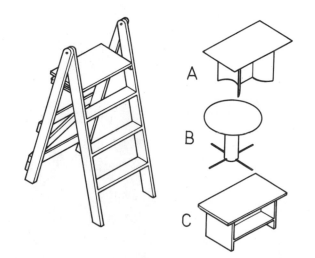

3. Outline designs for three tables are given. A is to be made from plastic sheet; B is to be made from metal; C is to be made from wood. The forms of the designs are dependent on the different strength qualities of the materials from which each will be made. Make sketches and write notes commenting on the reasons for the differences in the designs.

4. The drawing shows a lightweight door to be made for a small cabinet. Make sketches and notes showing the design and construction of suitable doors.
   (i)   Clad both sides with 3 mm plywood
   (ii) Made throughout with aluminium sheet
   (iii) Made from sheet acrylic.
   The doors should be sufficiently strong for the purpose yet light in weight.

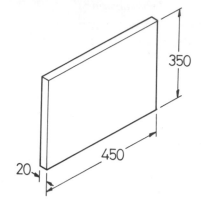

5. A child's swing is an excellent example of a design made to overcome problems created by forces causing tension, compression, shear, bending and flexing. Examine children's swings and make sketches and notes commenting upon the design features of:
   (i) a set of swings as set up in a corporation park;
   (ii) portable swings as used by children in their own gardens.

6. Describe clearly, with the aid of large annotated diagrams, the methods by which you would make a stationery tray as shown in the figure below from *one* of the following:
   (a) aluminium sheet
   (b) plywood
   (c) glass-reinforced plastic
   (d) acrylic sheet.

   London

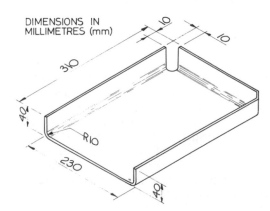

DIMENSIONS IN MILLIMETRES (mm)

The Humber Bridge

Cooling towers at West Burton power station on the River Trent

Suspension tower showing
toughened glass insulators

Surface finishes

The selection of an appropriate surface finish for a piece of craft work is an essential feature of the design process. The choice of an unsuitable finish may indeed prevent a design from fulfilling its function.

Reasons for surface finishes

When choosing a finish it is necessary to ask why the finish is to be applied. Reasons for applying a surface finish are as follows. These reasons do not all apply to all designs.

1. To provide protection against handling, dirt, dust, corrosion and weathering.
2. To allow for easy maintenance so that the surface can be quickly restored to its original condition by dusting, cleaning, washing or polishing.
3. To prevent corrosion such as rusting.
4. To prevent decay such as may occur when woods are used in outdoor work.
5. To provide a pleasing colour.
6. To match or blend with other design features.
7. To provide a surface texture such as hard, soft, sheen, glossy, matt, rough, smooth, patterned.

Materials not requiring a finish

There are many materials which do not require the application of a surface finish. Such materials tend to be more expensive than others, but they do often have the advantage of being corrosion proof, requiring minimal maintenance or presenting surfaces of very high quality.

Metals

Stainless steels, aluminiums, chromium plated metals, zinc plated (galvanised) metals, pre-painted metal parts, cadmium-plated metal fittings.

Woods

Plastic-veneered boards such as vinyl-coated chipboard, melamine-coated chipboard, plastic laminate-coated plywood and blockboard; pre-painted hardboards; aluminium-coated hardboards; veneered and varnished plywoods; building timbers impregnated with anti-decay salts and oils. Some woods in some situations may not need surface finishes—e.g., teak made into garden furniture.

Plastics

Most plastic materials require no finish, the materials themselves having been made to the required colours and surface textures. In some design work, however, it may be necessary to apply a surface finish to plastics such as painting some surfaces of a fibre-glass moulding.

Other materials

Materials such as glass, concrete, rubber parts and so on do not usually require applied finished, although under some design situations a surface finish may be needed for such materials.

Methods of application

When using proprietary finishes it is important that manufacturer's instructions as printed on the containers holding the finish are read and followed.

The commonest method of applying liquid finishes such as paints is with brushes. Other methods include the use of rags and cloths particularly for applying oils and waxes. French polish is best applied with a polishing 'rubber' made from cotton wool wrapped in fine cloth. Some finishes can be applied by spraying using either a spraying machine or spray cans in which the finish is purchased.

Some finishes are glued in position with adhesives—examples are the gluing of leather or plastic sheet, or the gluing of plastic laminate such as Formica to surfaces. The application of decorative transfers can be regarded as a form of surface treatment. Plating with silver, chromium or nickel, etc., is best left to specialist firms, although simple thin silver-plating can be carried out in a craft room.

Some finishes require the application of heat. Examples are the 'bluing' of steel, the polythene coating of metals and the anodising of aluminium.

Surface preparation

The preparation of surfaces to receive finishes must be carried out with care. Failure to prepare such surfaces will frequently lead to the breakdown of the finish. Surfaces must be clean and free from contamination such as dirt, dust, grease, oil or corrosion. Any damaged surfaces must be repaired before finishes are applied.

Surfaces may be prepared mechanically by sanding, emery clothing, grinding or filing; chemically by washing, immersion in cleansing liquids or in some cases dipping in dilute acid. Defects in surfaces should be repaired by filling with fillers such as plaster, putty, epoxy resin fillers, plastic wood, etc. Finishes will usually emphasise and draw attention to badly prepared surfaces.

Finishes for metals

Paints

Paints described as 'oil bound' refer to slow drying paints (four hours or longer) such as are sold for house decoration. These paints are not necessarily 'oil' based. Various chemical liquids other than oils are used in modern paints.

Phosphating paints—E.g., Kurust. Applied to rusty surfaces, chemically seals the corrosion to provide a good painting surface.

Solvent—Methylated spirits.
Red oxide paints—Rust inhibiting. Oil bound or cellulose. Priming paints for steels.
Solvent—White spirit for oil bound. Cellulose 'thinners' for cellulose.
Aluminium paint—Good priming paint.
Solvent—Methylated spirits.
Oil bound paints—Usually need an undercoat and a top coat after priming coat.
Solvent—White spirit.
Cellulose paints—Available as spray paints, but can be brushed. Several thin coats allowing to dry between coats. Fast drying.
Solvent—Cellulose thinners.

Various varnishes
Clear polyurethane or cellulose varnishes. Transparent (or nearly so).
Solvent—White spirit or thinners.

Bluing
Steel dipped in oil after heating to blue colour—provides limited anti-rust finish.

Plastic dip coating
Heat metal to about 300°C (blowlamp or oven) and dip in coloured polythene powder which melts and adheres to the metal.

Anodising
A colour finish for aluminium. An electrical treatment which thickens and colours the natural oxide film of the aluminium.

Finishes for woods

Wax polish
Best applied over sealing coats of French polish or clear cellulose. Soft lustrous finish. Used also for maintenance of furniture polishes.

French Polish
Two types—shellac in methylated spirits or the more modern polyurethane type (e.g., 'Furniglas'). High quality gloss or 'dulled' finish.
Solvent—Methylated spirits or white spirits.

Polyurethane varnish
Clear transparent or tinted translucent in various colours. Hard surface in gloss or matt finishes.
Solvent—White spirit.

Cellulose lacquer
Clear cellulose varnish thinned with thinners. Apply several thin coats by brush or spray. Good sealing for wax polish.
Solvent—Thinners.

Teak oil
Proprietary oil for finishing dark coloured woods—teak, afrormosia, iroko.

Linseed oil
Heat resisting. Takes many days to harden. Darkens wood considerably.

Oil bound paints
For softwoods. Apply primer, undercoat, top coat. If used on hardwoods, open cells must be filled.
Solvent—White spirit.

Knotting
A copal varnish to seal the end grain of knots before applying paint.
Solvent—Methylated spirits.

Polyurethane paints
Can be applied direct to wood. Two coats necessary on bare wood.
Solvent—White spirit.

Cellulose paint
Brush or spray. Several thin coats. Bright colours.
Solvent—Thinners.

Emulsion paints
Good priming paints for wood.
Solvent—Water.

Aluminium paint
Good priming paint for outdoor woodwork.
Solvent—Methylated spirits.

Plastic paints
Fast drying. Available in very small cans. Useful for small areas, lettering and decorative details.
Solvent—White spirit.

Stains
Proprietary types advisable. Various wood and other colours.

Creosote
Wood preservative. Stains brown. Use with care—can damage skin.
Solvent—Petrol.

Preservatives
Proprietary preservatives such as Cuprinol and Solignum. Various colours—red, green, brown. Preserves outdoor work against decay and also against beetle attack.

Finishes for plastics

As mentioned earlier (page 94) most plastics require no surface finish but lettering or decorative features may need to be applied or painted on some designs in plastics. A few notes are given for guidance.

1. Polythene, polypropylene, PVC, polyester film and nylon cannot be easily painted or treated with other applied surface finishes. This is because these plastics have a high resistance to chemical action. This means that surface finishes will not easily adhere to them.

2. Acrylic sheet—a common plastic for craft work—can be painted or finished with acrylic, polyurethane, cellulose or epoxy resin paints.

3. Fibre-glass mouldings will 'take' most finishes satisfactorily.

4. Expanded polystyrene will dissolve if cellulose paint is applied or if it comes into contact with polyester resin. Polyester resin is the resin used for fibre-glass mouldings. Expanded polystyrene can, however, be painted with emulsion paints which then seal the plastic against the action of either cellulose paint or polyester resin.

Colour

Mixing coloured lights

If a beam of white light is passed through a triangular glass prism, the light is *dispersed* into its constituent colours to form a *spectrum*. Seven colours can be distinguished in the spectrum—red, orange, yellow, green, blue, indigo and violet. If a beam of *pure* red light is passed through the prism, there will be no dispersion into other colours, only red passing through. Similarly, if *pure* green, or *pure* blue lights are passed through the prism, only green, or blue will be present. A beam of yellow light, however, disperses into red and green. If both pure red and pure green coloured lights are shone on to a white surface, yellow is produced. The *addition* of green and red produces yellow. Similarly green + blue produces a colour known as *cyan* and red + blue = magenta. Pure red + pure green + pure blue = white.

If, on the other hand, coloured discs of pure red, pure green and pure blue are all placed in front of the source of a white light, one on top of the other, no colour will pass through, the result being black. This is *subtraction* of colours.

From this it will be seen that the primary colours in terms of lighting colours are red, green and blue and that by addition white, cyan and magenta can be produced.

Mixing coloured paints

It is generally recognised that for the purpose of mixing paints, the primary colours are red, yellow and blue and that if yellow and blue are mixed together, the resulting colour is green. This is due to the fact that the paints and pigments we use are not pure colours, but compound ones.

If a pure red coloured light is shone on to a red surface, the surface will show red—the colour red is reflected. The same pure red light shone on to a green surface will show black—the red colour has been absorbed. Similarly pure blue shone on a red surface will also show black, the blue having been absorbed. A pure red light shone on a compound yellow surface (as in a yellow pigment) shows red. A pure green light shone on the same compound yellow shows green. Thus both red and green are reflected. A pure blue light shone on the compound yellow is not reflected, but shows black.

SURFACE FINISHES – A SUMMARY

IS A FINISH NEEDED?	FINISHES FOR METALS	FINISHES FOR WOODS
METALS	PAINTS	Wax polish
Stainless steel	'Oil' paints	French polish
Aluminium	Phosphating	Polyurethane varnish
Chromium plated	Red oxide	Cellulose lacquer
Galvanised	Aluminium	Teak oil
Cadmium plated	Cellulose	Linseed oil
WOODS	VARNISHES	PAINTS
Plastic veneered boards	Polyurethane	'Oil' based
Pre-painted boards	Cellulose	Polyurethane
Impregnated boards	Blueing	Cellulose
Some woods – e.g. teak	Plastic dip coating	Emulsion
Most plastics	Anodising	Plastic
OTHER MATERIALS		Stains
Glass		Creosote
Concrete		Preservatives
Rubbers		

Thus blue pigment (compound blue) plus yellow pigment (compound yellow) will have the following effect:

Compound blue reflects blue and green and absorbs red;

Compound yellow reflects red and green and absorbs blue;

Compound blue plus compound yellow thus reflcts green and absorbs red and blue.

The absorbed colours are *subtracted* from the mixture of pigments.

Colours in the red/yellow area are warm colours —they remind us of the heat from the sun. Colours in the blue/green area are cool colours. They remind us of cold as from ice.

Texture

The appearance of the textures of the surfaces we look at play an important part in forming the visual images we see in our environment. Look at the surface textures of natural items such as stones, earth, leaves, the barks of trees; look at the surface textures of man-made items such as the brickwork of buildings, the surface of a road. The variations of light and shade caused by differences in these surface textures arouse a great deal of visual interest.

The feel of the textures of surfaces is also important. As articles are handled we automatically think 'that's hard' or 'this is soft', 'that's smooth' or 'this is rough'. The feel of an article can give pleasure or may cause dismay.

Deciding on surface texture is thus part of the design process.

Soft, hard, smooth, rough
Surface textures may be roughly grouped into four types:

Soft surface texture Examples—fabrics, carpets, some papers, grass.

Hard surface texture Examples—metals, linoleum, jewellery, gloss paintwork.

Smooth surface texture Examples—polished wood, ice, glazed earthenware, gloss paintwork.

Rough surface texture Examples—concrete, brickwork, Surform tool, glasspaper.

A surface can be hard and smooth—e.g. gloss paintwork, or rough in appearance yet soft to touch —e.g., a fluffy wool blanket.

Metals
The surface texture of metals is generally hard, but the smoothness or roughness of the texture depends on the surface treatment the metal has received—straight from a machine, ground, emery clothed, polished, etc.

Woods
The surface texture of woods will vary considerably between species. The surfaces of softwoods are smooth, because of the lack of cells in the formation of softwoods. Most hardwood surfaces show open cells and these give hardwoods their particular grain formation and texture. Woods can generally be regarded as being softer in texture than are metals.

Plastics
The surface texture of plastics will vary from the waxy texture of polythene, the hard smoothness of acrylics to the roughness of the side of a fibre-glass moulding not in contact with the mould. Some plastics are made with specific surface texture finishes—e.g., fibre-glass surfaces depend entirely on the moulds in which the mouldings are laid; imitation surface textures such as leather or wood grain can be embossed on to pvc sheet—'vinyl' leather or 'vinyl' wood grain.

Texture finishes
Surface textures may be either natural, applied or imitation.

Natural Examples—untreated wood, or wood finished in such a way that its surface texture is unchanged; leather; fabrics; concrete.

Applied Examples—machining a surface such as the knurling process; adding veneers such as leather or plastic to woods; painting and other surface finishes. Note that many surface finishes can be obtained in glossy, matt, eggshell or dull textures.

Imitation Examples—'Vinyl' leather, 'vinyl' wood grain, wallpaper to look like brickwork or stonework.

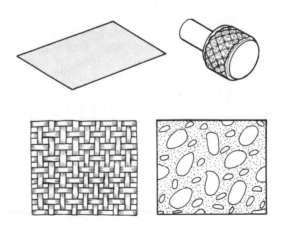

Special factors

There are factors, not considered elsewhere in this book, which may affect some of the design problems you will wish to solve.

Water

Even when designs are intended to be kept permanently indoors, the effects of the water in the atmosphere must be assessed. In centrally heated rooms there is always some moisture in the air—at least about 5% by volume. In unheated rooms this can rise to as much as 15% or more. The presence of this water can be the cause of decay, rusting, tarnishing, discoloration and even the complete disintegration of a design.

Decay

All organic materials will eventually decay if the conditions for fungal and bacterial growth are suitable. Wood is an organic material and is thus liable to attack by wood-rotting fungi. Such fungi cannot commence germinating unless the moisture content of the wood is greater than about 20% by weight for any appreciable length of time.

The major protection against wood rotting is to ensure that only seasoned wood is used (see pages 134 to 139). If a design is intended for outside use, some protection against fungal attack may be thought necessary—such as coating with creosote or making with timbers impregnated with anti-fungal chemicals.

The construction of designs to be situated in the open should be such that water will not accumulate in any part of the design and so cause the wood in that area to become soaked.

Some woods will resist decay better than others —page 134 to 139. Such woods are said to be more durable.

Rusting

Most ferrous metals—those containing iron—are prone to rust in the presence of the water and the oxygen in the atmosphere. Some ferrous metals —stainless steels are examples—are specifically made for their non-rusting properties—see pages 143 to 148. Mild steel, a widely used ferrous alloy, needs protection against the rusting of its surfaces by painting or by the application of other forms of surface finish. You may have to balance the advantages of using more expensive non-rusting materials against the expense of maintaining the painted surfaces of mild steel. It may not be possible to apply a surface finish to some parts of some designs, in which case a non-rusting material may have to be chosen for those parts.

Tarnishing

Some metals become tarnished in the presence of moisture, oxygen and impurities in the atmosphere. Work made from metals such as brass, copper or silver will need to be regularly polished with metal polish to remove such tarnishing. The application of thin, clear lacquer varnishes or wax polishes can eliminate this need for maintenance polishing.

Discoloration

Some materials tend to discolour after prolonged exposure to strong sunlight or as a result of the action of impurities in the atmosphere. A few dark-coloured woods tend to become lighter in colour. Some light-coloured woods tend to become darker. Some plastics tend to fade under the action of sunlight. If designs are to be placed in situations where this discoloration may occur, the materials will need to be selected with some care, or special attention given to protective surface finishes.

Wear

Is the design being made to last for a long period of time or is it one which may be discarded after a day or two, even after an hour or so?

The problem of wear will need to be considered in both cases. The designing of a carrier bag for carrying goods purchased in a shop to your home does not demand a hard-wearing material or a permanent constructional method. The designing of a spindle for a bicycle wheel demands a material which will not wear out during the life of the bicycle and that the wheel is securely held on the spindle. The choice of the best available material and best constructional method suited to the length of time the design will have to last are essential features of these two designs.

Details such as hardness, toughness, durability, resilience and resistance to abrasion of materials and constructions will need to be considered. Durability of surface finish in relation to wearing qualities will also need consideration.

Damage

Ask the following questions relating to any particular design:

Does the design need to be damage proof? Should special attention be paid to those parts of the design which may cause damage—such as sharp corners and sharp edges? Is the design to be in a situation in which its construction must be sufficiently strong to resist damage either caused deliberately, as by vandalism, or by accident? Does the physical balance of the design need to be such that it is stable and not easily knocked over? Should the design be securely held against a wall or on to a floor? If so, the design of the fastenings must be considered.

Storage

If the design is to contain storage compartments, the sizes and shapes and suitability of these compartments will need to be considered in relation to the items to be stored. The design itself may need to be stored and this may affect shape, materials and construction. Some examples are—sports equipment; craft tools; clothing; games; toys. Problems of storage can affect many aspects of a design. In the storage of some items consideration might be given to the possibilities of interlocking devices, or to modular systems based on given shapes and sizes.

Insulation

The most common insulation problem will be concerned with electric circuits, although insulation against heat, cold or noise may have to be considered in some designs. The twin problems of short-circuiting and electric shock have to be completely eliminated from any design incorporating electric circuits. Good electrical insulation is essential. The advantages of using a low voltage supply such as from a battery or transformer may have to be balanced against the advantages of using mains supply with its demand for more effective insulation.

Maintenance

All designs will need to be maintained in a good condition. This means they need to be regularly cleaned and serviced. At its simplest, maintenance may only refer to cleaning and dusting of furniture or to polishing of an item of silver ware. Maintenance can, however, also involve the replacement of parts of a machine as they become worn or damaged. Maintenance may also require making provision for easy access to places where dust, dirt or grease may be liable to accumulate. Problems involved in maintenance and how it can be carried out may need to be considered when solving a design brief.

Exercises—general

1. Design and make a piece of water sculpture which will be the main feature of interest in the new 'Waterfall Hotel'.

Your solution is to be no larger than a 1 metre cube. Any necessary electrical fittings and equipment may be purchased.   *Oxford*

2. You have been asked to study the use of stools in the home.

The following is the beginning of a design brief.

A stool is required for use with a dressing table; the height to the top of the seat should be approximately 420mm. The seat should be upholstered and drop into rebates in the top rails of the stool. Continue the design brief to include the timber to be used and a brief description of the dressing table it has to match (use your imagination to provide these details). Add any other items which will help you to design the stool and write the whole brief on your first piece of paper. Also on your first piece of drawing paper, carry out the following work.

(a) Freehand drawings of at least two alternative ideas for the stool.

(b) Draw to a small scale front and side elevations of the design which you prefer, in order to arrive at suitable sizes and good proportions. You may need to make several drawings. They should be accurate but need not be carefully finished.

(c) Work out *full size* on quick orthographic drawings the correct layout and sizes of the joints involved.

On your second piece of drawing paper, working to a suitable scale, which will probably be half full size, make accurate well-finished drawings of the front and side elevations of the stool. Include the joints either on the two views or as extra details, so that this sheet is a complete working drawing.

Add the main overall dimensions and, between lines 6mm apart, letter the title 'Dressing Table Stool', your name and index number.

Oxford and Cambridge

3. Small quantities of stationery sundries are required to be readily available on the study or office desk. Six such items are illustrated, approximately full size, in Fig. 1.

A unit has to be designed which will conveniently accommodate small quantities of these items as up to ten pencils or ball-point pens. The unit can be made in any suitable material or combination of materials.

Write a design analysis for the unit listing the problems to be solved and suggesting methods of overcoming them.

London

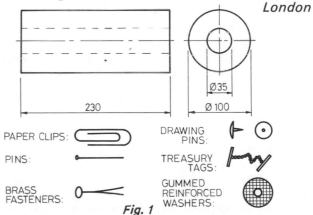

PAPER CLIPS:

PINS:

BRASS FASTENERS:

DRAWING PINS:

TREASURY TAGS:

GUMMED REINFORCED WASHERS:

Fig. 1

4. Design a storage unit for recorded cassettes. The unit should:
   (i) be free standing and completely self-contained;
   (ii) offer some method of quickly identifying and selecting any required cassette;
   (iii) give complete protection from harmful dust, grit, etc.;
   (iv) accommodate 10 cassettes.

Cassettes are normally 105 mm × 65 mm × 15 mm.   *Welsh*

Safety

When solving a design brief always make a note of any safety aspects which arise—Design With Safety in Mind. You have not completely solved a design problem if the solution is liable to cause danger to others or gives rise to situations which may be dangerous.

Some causes of danger

Sharp edges and corners
Sharp edges can cause painful cuts or bruises. Even if the design is one which will not be handled, all sharp edges and corners should be rounded off or covered. Not only will this remove a possibility of danger, but the resulting design will often have a cleaner, more smooth appearance. It will also 'look' safe to handle.

Inadequate strength
A completed design should be made of materials of adequate strength and sizes. It must be remembered that materials vary considerably in their strength values and a choice must be made accordingly. It is often wise to allow for extra strength. For example, a table may not only be used for working on, it may be stood upon by somebody wishing to reach a high shelf. The construction of a design should also be of adequate strength if the article is to be used with safety without collapsing or disintegrating. A model may often assist in solving strength problems.

Poor balance
Will the design be stable? Can it be put to use without either falling over or being easily knocked over? If the design is to carry another article, will the size or weight of the article cause the whole design to be unstable? A working model may be required to assist an assessment of stability.

Deterioration due to time
Corrosion and decay or the repeated use of parts of the design by movement or flexing may cause weaknesses to arise which make a design dangerous. The design may become too weak for its task or there may be a danger of collapse. Have good and correct materials been used? Are they protected against corrosion, decay or wear? If the design contains moving parts can they be replaced when they become worn?

Heat and fire
A necessary question may be 'Should non-combustible materials be used in this design?' if there is a danger of parts catching on fire. If an article which is to be heated, a saucepan for example, is being designed allowance must be made for heat proofing parts such as handles. Should such parts be made from heat proof materials, or should they be insulated with other materials or should they be designed so that rapid conduction of heat away from the handles allows them to be safely touched?

Electricity
Some people may become seriously ill or even be killed as a result of receiving a shock from mains supplied electricity. To ensure this doesn't happen from your designs consider the following when fitting any electrical circuitry:
1. Will a low voltage supply from a battery or from a transformer be suitable? Such low voltage supplies, 6 volt or 12 volt, are always reasonably safe.
2. Is the circuit you have designed the most suitable for the purpose it is to fulfil?
3. Is the circuit properly insulated at every part?
4. Check carefully for short circuits before switching on.
5. Use only good, approved electrical components and fittings.
6. Check that water cannot get into any part of the circuit.
7. If earthing is necessary check that it is firmly secured to a good earthing point.
8. When connecting a mains circuit always fit a fuse between the mains supply point and the circuit. The fuse should be rated no greater than is required by the circuit. Fuses are rated in amps. Check using the formula:

$$\text{amps} = \frac{\text{watts}}{\text{volts}}$$

Moving parts
If your design contains moving parts, will guards be needed to protect fingers or loose clothing from being caught up in the parts? Is the whole design sufficiently strong to withstand the strains caused by the parts moving? Will any vibration for example cause parts to work loose.

Dangerous materials
Some materials should be completely avoided in craft designs. Two examples are lead and asbestos. Lead should be avoided because of the dangers of lead poisoning. Asbestos should be avoided because of the bronchial diseases which may be caused by inhaling its dust.

Poor instructions
If any instructions are to be printed on your design, ensure that they state precisely and exactly what is intended. An example is ON and OFF printed against a switch in an electric circuit.

Appraisal

When a piece of craftwork has been made—after a design has been *realised*—an assessment of the degree of success of the results of the design should be attempted. This is best compiled in the form of a written *appraisal*. The appraisal may consist of a few brief notes or may take the form of a longer written report. Drawings and sketches may be thought to be necessary to amplify some of the notes. Tables in the form of those shown on this page may also be thought necessary to emphasise some aspects of the appraisal. The appraisal may contain information such as:

1. Does the design successfully meet the demands of the design *situation*?
2. Does the design successfully fulfil the requirements of the *design brief*?
3. Comments on the design as related to the *investigation*:
 – Does it function properly?
 – Is the design ergonomically sound?
 – Is its shape and form satisfactory? Could the shape and form be improved?
 – Are the materials which have been chosen the most suitable for the design?
 – Has the work been carried out economically?
 – Have the methods of shaping, forming and construction been suitable?
 – Are the fittings used the best which could be found?
 – Is the strength of the design sufficient?
 – Does the surface finish employed stand up to the conditions under which the design will be used?
 – Are there any special factors which seem to have been missed?
 – Is the design safe in all its aspects?
4. Suggest alterations where necessary.
5. Make notes on the results of any tests which were performed on, or with the design.
6. Suggest any improvements which could be made. This may involve quite detailed drawings.

Methods of assessment
Assessments may be required as to the degree of success of a design. There are several systems of indicating such assessments:
1. Very good; good; fair; poor; very poor.
2. A; B; C; D; E.
3. Mark out of 10, e.g. 6/10; 2/10.
4. Stars: *****; ****; ***; **; *; or 5*; 4*; 3*; 2*; 1*.
5. Percentages, e.g. 75%; 25%.

Diagrams
Diagrams may be included in an appraisal if it is thought they will clarify the report. Many forms of diagram may be suitable. Two examples are given. The table is one person's assessment of a screwdriver made in a craft room. The bar chart shows four people's assessment of a candle holder.

Screwdriver tests	
Inserting screws	
Extracting screws	
Handle grip	
Weight	
Strength	

Assessment table for a screwdriver

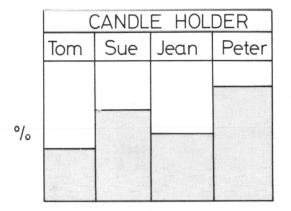

A bar graph comparing candle holders for appearance

Exercise

1. Collect, then test, three different pens: e.g. a ball-point pen, a common felt-tip pen and another pen of your own choice.

Make a list of what a good pen should be capable of doing, then see how good the pens are. Copy the chart below to help you get started, then add any extra tests you can think of at the bottom.

Pen test

	Pen 1	Pen 2	Pen 3
Writes on paper			
Writes on shiny plastic			
Writes upside-down (above eye level)			
Writes fast			
Writes without smudging			
Clips in a jacket pocket			
Cost			
Is point damaged easily?			
Always writes straight away			
Comfortable to use			
Looks attractive			

Exercises

1. Precious and semi-precious stones are frequently used in jewellery. Describe a piece of jewellery you have made which involved the setting of a stone. Illustrate your answers generously, with particular concern to show the aesthetic quality of your design.

Oxford and Cambridge

2. An amateur photographer wishes to use his camera tripod as a stand for the microphone of his tape recorder. Details of the camera tripod head and the microphone are given in Fig. 1.

Design an 'adapter' to enable the microphone to be mounted rigidly on the tripod head. Present your solution in the form of clear, bold, annotated diagrams. In note form give all details for its manufacture.

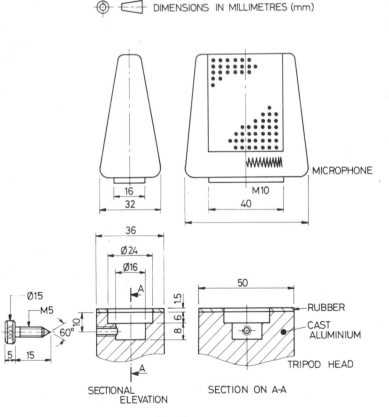

DIMENSIONS IN MILLIMETRES (mm)

Fig. 1

3. A clock movement is of the size and shape as shown in Fig. 2. The clock is to be used on the desk of a study furnished in the modern style. To be of use the clock movement must be supported in some way.

Write a design analysis for the 'support' listing the problems to be faced and suggesting ways of overcoming them. *London*

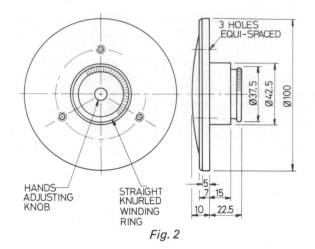

DIMENSIONS IN MILLIMETRES (mm)

Fig. 2

4. Fig. 3 shows the overall size of a roll of perforated kitchen paper. Prepare a design for a paper holder to the following specifications:
(a) It is to be made mainly of either solid wood or manufactured board.
(b) Paper rolls must be easily replaceable.
(c) The paper is to be protected by a cover.
(d) There must be a suitable arrangement to assist tearing of the paper.
(e) The holder is to be wall mounted.
  (i) With a long edge of a sheet of A2 size paper placed horizontally, rule a vertical line 200 mm from the left-hand edge. To the left of this line write out a full design analysis for the holder which covers all aspects of the problems. Set out each aspect clearly and letter each reference.
  (ii) On the right-hand side of the line make preliminary sketch solutions for each of the problems stated, lettering them to conform with your solutions in answer to (i).
  (iii) Prepare freehand sketches that clearly show the general overall outline of the final solution.
  (iv) Make a full size production drawing in orthographic projection giving all constructional details required to enable the holder to be made. Use sections, scrap views, full size orthographic details, freehand sketches, etc., if further clarification is required.
Clearly letter each part of your solutions (a), (b), (c), etc., to conform with your analysis.

London

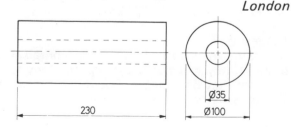

5. A magnifying glass, such as could be used in the examination of wood specimens or when engraving metal, is shown in Fig. 4. To enable both of the user's hands to be free for manipulating work or tools the magnifying glass must be supported from a base on the bench surface.

In use the glass must:

(a) always be held with the axis of the stem parallel to the bench surface.

(b) be capable of extension from the support so that large work may be accommodated.

(c) be capable of being raised or lowered to obtain the magnification desired.

(d) be capable of being rotated through 360 degrees about its horizontal axis.

Design a base and method of support which satisfies the brief set out above.

(i) With a long edge of a sheet of A2 size paper placed horizontally, rule a vertical line 200 mm from the left-hand edge.

(ii) To the left of this line list additional relevant design problems as they occur to you, lettering them (e), (f), (g), etc.

(iii) To the right of the vertical line, using clear diagrams with explanatory notes, set down your solutions to the design problems. Clearly letter each part of your solutions (a), (b), (c), etc., to conform with the brief given above.

(iv) Use the best solution to each individual problem to develop a complete solution which should be presented as a freehand pictorial sketch.

(v) Draw to a scale of full size a side elevation of the assembled magnifying glass support. Hidden detail is not to be shown. Compile a parts list for the completed support using the headings given in Fig. 5.

London

PROJECTION ⦶ ◁ DIMENSIONS IN MILLIMETRES (mm)

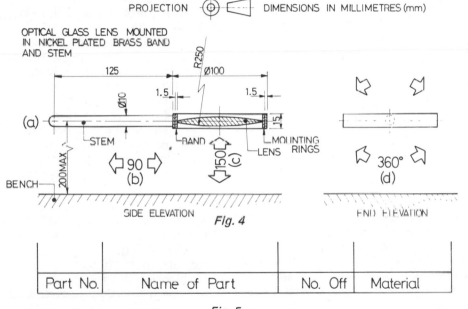

Fig. 4

Part No.	Name of Part	No. Off	Material

Fig. 5

6. A game of noughts and crosses is shown in Fig. 6. The pegs have a cross at one end and a nought at the other. The pegs are to be injection moulded in polyethylene. The mould is to be made in the school workshop.

Design a suitable mould in which the pegs may be formed.

London

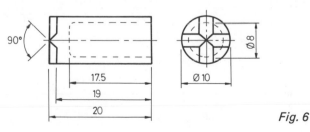

Fig. 6

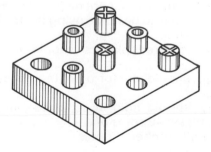

7. The grid in Fig. 7 represents part of an open plan house. The kitchen area is separated from a living–dining area by a room divider. Indicate clearly on the kitchen plan the position of the following items:

sources of light; power points; cooker; refrigerator; working surfaces; storage units and anything else you consider to be important. *Welsh*

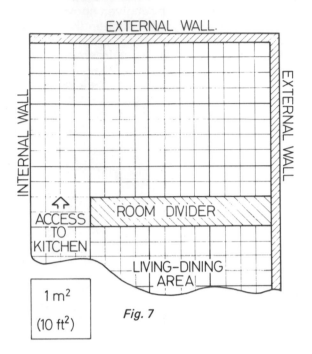

Fig. 7

8. You are to prepare a design for a 'tray' to be used as a receptacle for coins and notes at school fund raising activities. Each vendor will have a 'tray' into which he sorts the coins and notes he receives and from which change will be given. The sizes (in millimetres) of the coins and notes to which your design refers are as follows:

Notes: £5—145×76

Coins: £1—φ22·5×3 thick
50 pence—allow φ32×2·5 thick
10 pence— φ28×2·2 thick
5 pence— φ22×2·2 thick
2 pence— φ26×2 thick
1 pence— φ20×2 thick

When designing the tray, of which several are required, the following points should be noted:

It is to be made mainly, but not necessarily exclusively, in plastics; it is to be made using the facilities of a school workshop.

The use of coloured plastics should be considered.

Your design should conform to the following specifications:

(a) the 'tray' should hold in separate compartments at least 40 coins of each denomination and a small number of notes.

(b) there should be some form of cover to prevent coin spillage when the 'trays' are being collected.

You may use colour in your preparatory design work but *not* in your final working drawing.

(i) With the long edge of a sheet of A2 size paper placed horizontally rule a vertical line 200 mm from the left-hand edge. To the left of this line write out a brief design analysis for the container which covers all aspects of the problem. Set out each aspect clearly and letter each for reference. Additional design problems associated with formers, moulds, etc., should be included.

(ii) To the right of the line, using clear diagrams and/or sketches with explanatory notes set down several possible solutions to the design problems. Clearly letter each part of your solutions (a), (b), (c), etc., to conform to your analysis.

Answer parts (iii) and (iv) on a separate sheet of drawing paper.

(iii) Make a pictorial sketch or sketches that show clearly the general intention of the final solution you have evolved.

(iv) Make detail drawings in orthographic projection of the container and any formers needed for its production. These drawings should show all constructional details to enable the container to be made. The drawings may be done *either* with instruments to a scale of full size *or* freehand, approximately full size.

London

9. What specific materials would you select as being the most suitable for the following:
(a) die casting,
(b) vacuum forming,
(c) blacksmith's forging,
(d) steam bending (e.g. the rocker on a wooden chair),
(e) wooden pattern making for a short run.

In each case state three properties of the material you have selected that makes it eminently suitable for the particular job. Use the form of table shown in Fig. 8. *Oxford*

ITEM	MATERIAL	PROPERTIES
DIE CASTING		(i) (ii) (iii)

Fig. 8

10. The woodworker is often involved in structural work in the garden in which he meets other materials and techniques such as glazing, mixing concrete, etc. Make a freehand drawing of some piece of garden woodwork in which you have been involved, seen made, or would like to make, then write notes on the technical aspects under headings such as structure, materials, techniques.

Oxford and Cambridge

11. The work of the Craft Department is to be exhibited in the entrance hall of a modern school. Suggest ideas for an exhibition stand assuming that a floor space of approximately 3 m² (32 ft²) is available.

The exhibition stand should have:
(i) a number of horizontal surfaces at various levels for small three-dimensional work;
(ii) some vertical surfaces for graphic work.

Security is a factor which should also be taken into account.

Your ideas may be expressed by annotated sketches with constructional details enlarged. Name all materials used.

Welsh

12. You have been asked to consider the design of metal fittings which could be used in the home or garage/shed. You are to design a simple foot-operated door stop which could be used to secure in an open or closed position a wooden garage door or large shed door. It is stressed that the door stop must be entirely foot-operated. (A simple movable block is not considered adequate.)

On your first sheet of drawing paper, write down clearly, in *tabulated* form, the requirements that you feel are necessary if the door stop is to function successfully.

Now start to design the door stop which will satisfy the conditions you have stated. You should begin by making clear, annotated, freehand drawings on your first sheet of drawing paper. These drawings should cover *all* aspects of the design.

State clearly the materials you would use for the different parts and suggest suitable sizes. When you consider that adequate preparatory work has been done, take your second sheet of drawing paper and produce orthographic drawings which provide sufficient details to enable the door stop to be made. Include sectional drawings if you feel that they will explain details better.

Insert six of the main dimensions and, between lines 6 mm apart, letter the title 'FOOT-OPERATED DOOR STOP', your name and index number, in a suitable position on your paper.

Oxford and Cambridge

13. Design a dispenser for a roll of transparent adhesive or draughting tape. The dispenser may be used on a table or fixed to a wall. Provision should be made to allow the required length of tape to be easily torn off, leaving a sufficient amount to be gripped by the next user.

Welsh

14. Details of a salt cellar or pepper pot, required in large numbers, are given in Fig. 9 Use bold diagrams with explanatory notes to show your solution to *one* of the following problems relating to the quantity production of:
Either (a) the nylon body,
Or (b) the stainless steel cover, excluding the holes,
Or (c) the pepper sifting holes in the stainless steel cover.

London

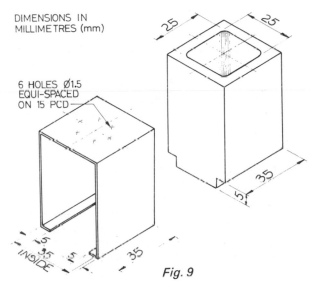

DIMENSIONS IN MILLIMETRES (mm)

6 HOLES Ø1.5 EQUI-SPACED ON 15 PCD

Fig. 9

15. Fig. 10 shows a drinking bottle commonly used for gerbils, hamsters, mice, etc. Make several sketch designs of a supporting bracket to attach the bottle to the side of a sheet metal cage.

The bracket can be cast, formed or fabricated from metal and/or plastics. Add brief notes to show how the chosen material has influenced your design.

London

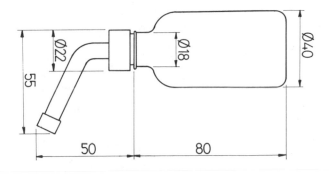

Fig. 10

16. Fig. 11 shows details of a plate for reinforcing the corners of boxes. Several hundreds of these are required. The plates are to be drilled prior to bending and to ensure uniformity a drilling jig is required.

Write a design analysis for the jig listing the problems to be faced and suggesting methods of overcoming them.

London

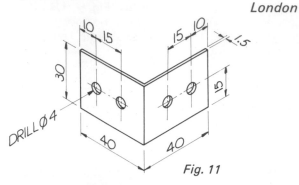

Fig. 11

17. Fig. 12 is a sketch of one end of a room into which a writing surface and storage compartment are to be fitted under a window. The outline of the fitment is shown by thick lines. The storage part of the fitment is to contain drawers and a cupboard suitable for holding stationery, writing materials, etc. The whole fitment is to be fitted permanently to the walls of the room.

On the A2 size drawing paper provided draw a vertical line 200 mm from the right-hand border.

Make *all* the following drawings:

In the space to the right of the line you have drawn:

(a) Draw *freehand* sketches showing a suitable design for the required fitment. Your sketches should include the methods of construction you intend using.

(b) Draw *freehand* sketches to show suitable methods of securing the fitment to the walls of the room.

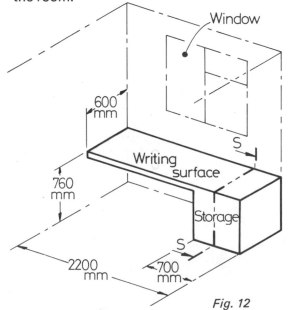

Fig. 12

In the space to the left of the line you have drawn:

(c) Using the freehand sketches as a guide draw accurately with instruments to a scale of 1:10:
   (i) A front view of the whole fitment;
   (ii) A sectional end view as seen in the direction of the arrows SS in Fig. 12;
   (iii) A plan.

The plan view (iii) must contain sufficient hidden detail lines to show clearly details of your design not fully shown in the front view and sectional end view.

Add the main dimensions to your drawing.

WMEB

18. You live in the semi-detached house shown in the plan Fig. 13. You wish to seek permission from the local council to erect a brick-built garage and garden store in the approximate position given.

The council requires from you detailed drawings showing front view, end view, and plan of the proposed building. The following details must be included in your drawing—overall dimensions; positions of doors and windows; type of roof; the internal arrangement of partitions, if any.

On the A2 size drawing paper provided draw a vertical line 200 mm from the right-hand border.

Make *all* the following drawings:

(a) In the space to the right of the line:
   Three *freehand* sketches showing different designs for your proposed building. Your sketches should include the details asked for by the council.

(b) In the space to the left of the line:
   Select the best of your designs and, using it as a guide, draw accurately, with the aid of instruments, to a scale of 1:50:
   (i) A front view,
   (ii) An end view,
   (iii) A plan.

Fully dimension your drawings.

WMEB

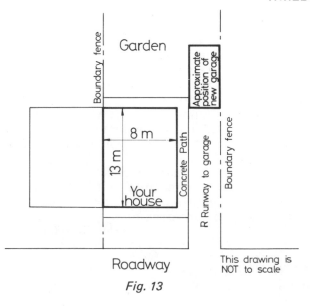

Fig. 13

Models

Why make a model?

1. Models are made to test the value of design ideas. Will the design function properly? This can often be tested in a model.
2. Wrong design ideas will show up in a model. You will not then have to scrap a completed piece of work, but only the model.
3. Proportions, stability and sometimes strength can be judged more clearly from a model than from drawings.
4. Models can be viewed from all directions—they are three dimensional, unlike your drawings which are only two dimensional.
5. Problems arising from designs can often be remedied in a model.
6. Models are cheap and easy to make. Having to scrap a final design can be expensive. So—solve problems at the model stage.

When should a model be made?

Start the making of a model when drawing possible solutions to your design brief. Even if you are reasonably satisfied with your drawings, test them in model form. This will give you a better opportunity of choosing a good, final solution with some degree of success. Certainly a model should be made before commencing a working drawing. You should be able to make your final design from a working drawing. The testing by model making must thus be completed before the working drawing is started.

Types of models

Before making a model you will need to decide which is the best type to suit your particular purposes. The main types are listed below.
1. *Full size models*   Of particular importance when testing ergonomics.
2. *Small scale models*   Possibly the most common type.
3. *Larger than full size*   Of value when designing small details such as jewellery parts.
4. *Cut-away models*   To show constructional details which cannot be seen from outside.
5. *Complex models*   To show only the more intricate parts of a complex design.
6. *Working models*   Not common in craft design. A train set is a good example.
7. *Layout models*   To show how a design fits into say, a room layout.

Materials for model making

Try to choose materials which have a similar appearance to the materials which will be incorporated in the final design. Some suggestions for materials are as follows.

To represent surfaces
Paper—Various stiffnesses and colours.
Cardboard—Various thicknesses, types, colours and surface finishes.
Plastic sheet—Celluloid, acetate, old film, vinyl.
Wood—Thin plywood, veneers, thin balsa.
Hardboard—Makes a good base for a model.
Metal—Thin sheet metal, tinplate containers.
Foil—Aluminium and plastic foils.

To represent linear parts
Wire—All types.
Wood strips—Off cuts from machine sawing.
Meccano—Easily assembled with Meccano nuts and bolts.
Plastic strip—Such as Meccano.
String—Also useful for holding parts together. Can be stiffened with glue.
Cotton

To represent solid parts
Wood—Blocks of softwood, particularly balsa.
Plastic foams—Rigid polyurethane foam is easily worked to shape; flexible polyurethane foam; polystyrene foam which can be obtained from packing materials.
Plasticine—One of the most valuable modelling materials.
Plaster of Paris—Sets hard in a few minutes. Can be cast to shape or can be filed and sanded when cast.
Clay—Shaped by fingers or with tools.
Modified clays—Set quite hard without firing.
Soap—A useful, easily procured model material.

Surface treatment of models

Models can be varnished or painted or shapes may be marked on their surfaces. Oil paints, poster paints or water colours are quite suitable. Pencils or felt pens will mark surfaces clearly.

Joining materials

Various types of adhesives, Sellotape, masking tape, pins, paper clips, solder wire, twining wire, knots, veneer pins, small screws can all be used for jointing parts of models. Plasticine makes quite firm joints when smoothed on to other materials. Bostik Blu-tack makes good temporary joints.

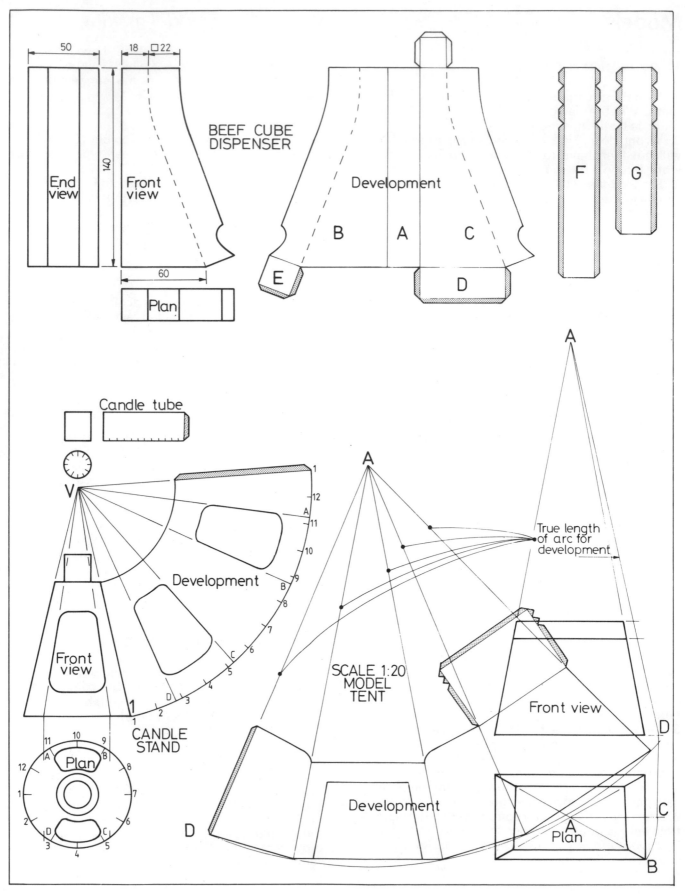

BEEF CUBE
DISPENSER

50

18   □ 22

140

60

End
view

Front
view

Development

B   A   C

E   D

F   G

Plan

Candle tube

V

Development

1
12
A 11
10
9 B
8
7
6 C
5
4
D 3
2
1

Front
view

1
CANDLE
STAND

11 10 9
A   B
12 Plan 8
1   7
2   D C 6
3   4   5

A

A

True length
of arc for
development

SCALE 1:20
MODEL
TENT

Development

Front view

D

D

C

Plan

A

B

Models made from sheet paper or cardboard

Many of the models required when you are designing can be made from sheet paper or cardboard in a variety of colours and thicknesses. These may be full-size or scaled models. When making models from such sheet materials, a 'development' of the surfaces of the design may have to be drawn. Three examples of surface developments are shown on page 108 opposite, and photographs of the models relating to the three developments are given on this page.

Development of model of meat-cube dispenser

This is a full-size model. The development is in three parts. The back (A), sides (B and C), bottom pieces (D and E) form one part. The rear of the meat-cube shute (F) and its front (G) form the other two parts. Note the tabs (shaded) for glueing the various parts of the development together.

Development of candle holder

This is another full-size model. A front view and a plan of the proposed conical design are first drawn. The plan circle is divided into twelve equal parts with a 30-degree set square. An arc of centre V and radius V1 is then drawn. Compasses are set to any one of the twelve spacings in the plan, and twelve of these spaces are marked around the arc of radius V1. Note the points A, B, C and D marked on the plan and transferred to the development to give points to which the sides of the holes in the cone can be drawn. Shaded tabs are for gluing the cone.

Development of model tent

This is a 1:20 scale model. The shape is derived from a rectangular pyramid. Front view and a plan of the pyramid are drawn, and the apex (A) of the pyramid is found. To obtain the *true length* of an edge of this pyramid: from A, in the plan, draw an arc of radius AB to meet a line drawn horizontally from A at C. Project C to the base line of the front view to give D. AD is the required true length. To draw the development, first draw an arc of radius VA. Step off along the arc the lengths of the four bottom edges of the pyramid. Then proceed as indicated in the drawing on page 108. The development of the top of the model tent is added to the top edge of the tent back. Shaded tabs are for gluing.

Gluing paper or cardboard models

Any paper glue or paper paste is suitable. Avoid instant glues—they can glue one's fingers together. One of the best glues for this purpose is white PVA wood glue. This glue is clean in use and provides a speedy 'tack', making the joining of the tabs to the surfaces of a development a fairly easy operation.

Note
In the photographs, two of the original developments of each model have been included, although in practice such developments would normally be drawn on the surfaces of the paper, or cardboard, from which the models are to be made.

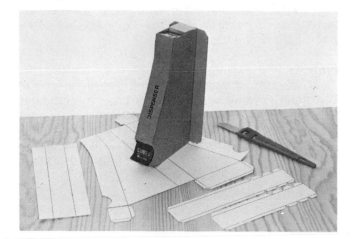

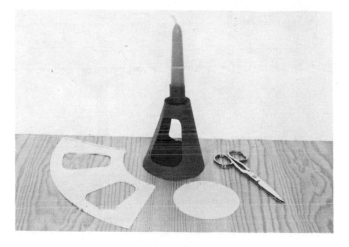

Tools required for model making
Only a limited range of tools is necessary. Because of this many models can be made at home. Tools such as sharp knives, scissors, paint brushes, felt-tip pens, sandpaper and small files are suitable. A tube of glue or a squeegee container of PVA wood glue will also be required. If you are working at a table, protect the surface of its top with paper or with sheet polythene. If using metal, a junior hacksaw and a pair of pliers will be useful.

Note
1. Models must be stored carefully—they tend to be fragile. Folding paper models may overcome this problem—they can then be stored flat.
2. Toys may be of help in solving some model problems. A good example of this is the use of movable plastic toy men to solve ergonomic problems.

Windvane. See page 30. Models to test whether windvane will function. Wood, cardboard, steel rod. Full-size model

Stools. Rigid polyurethane foam, Plasticine, wire, cardboard. Small-scale model

Radio case. A cardboard box with polystyrene foam handles. A black felt-tip pen was used for the markings. OFF and ON are dry-transfer letters.

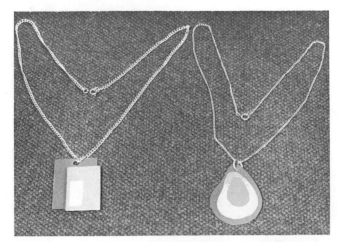

Pendants. Cardboard, coloured tapes, aluminium foil, neck chains. Full-size model

Door light. Polystyrene foam, cardboard, tracing paper, steel rod, wood, felt-tip pen. Small-scale model

The five photographs on page 110 and the five on this page demonstrate the variety of materials which can be employed when making models for craft designs.

Chess pieces and sculptures. Candles, Plasticine, steel rod, polystyrene foam. Small-scale models

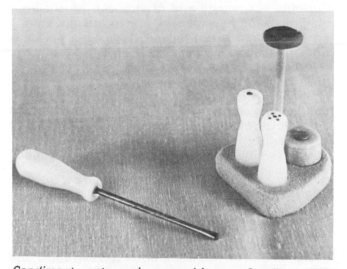

Condiment set and screwdrivers. Candles, rigid polyurethane foam, soap, Plasticine, wood dowel. Full-size models

Pen, pencil and rubber holder. Rigid polyurethane foam and cardboard. Full-size model

Cassette holder. Polystyrene foam and cardboard. Full-size model to test ergonomics of handling cassettes

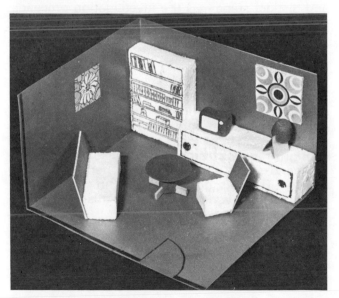

Room layout. Polystyrene foam, Plasticine, cardboard, wood strips, plastic sheet. A layout model

SECTION 3

Graphics and communication

Solutions

This is possibly the most important part of the design process. At this stage all the solutions to the design brief which come to mind can be explored. This is when you draw ideas on paper and, if your investigation is proceeding along the right lines, these drawings should lead to a good final design. You will have started taking notes during the early part of the investigation. You will by now know the important overall dimensions; have some ideas as to the ergonomic problems involved; you will have thought about proportions, shape and form as relating to your design brief. During the early part of the investigation there will be a need to begin making drawings. When several sketch solutions have been attempted you will have to go back to the investigation and think about shaping, jointing, fittings, strength and any special factors. These may influence your thinking and fresh solutions and ideas may arise. This stage—of producing solutions to the design brief—is interwoven with the investigation and is carried out at the same time. It is not a new and distinct stage—as the investigation proceeds, so will the drawing of solutions.

Drawing

The most common method of producing a variety of solutions to a design brief is by freehand drawing in pencil. Several different drawn ideas can then be compared and fresh ideas generated until there are enough drawings from which to make a final choice. Freehand pencil drawing is best because it is so speedy. There is nothing wrong in using instruments to assist your drawings, but this does tend to increase the time taken.

Types of drawing

Outline drawings—Outline only, no shading. Pencil of grade HB or B. Possibly the best form of design drawing.
Pen drawings—Some may prefer working in Indian ink, with Biro pens or with felt pens. This means inking over lightly drawn pencil drawings. Pen drawings make a greater impact in some work than do pencil drawings, particularly if colour is used.
Colour washed drawings—Colour washing of pencil or pen drawings can enhance certain features which need to be emphasised.
Shaded drawings—If you wish to shade your drawings, by all means do so. Shading may be by pencil, dry transfer shading, charcoal, chalk, etc.

Other methods

Cut outs—Drawings and photos can be cut from magazines or newspapers and mounted among your drawings. Do not copy these designs, but ideas from them may assist in arriving at a good solution.
Tracings—Tracings from books and other printed material can assist in finding good solutions.
Photos—If you can obtain original photographs and mount them among your solutions, these may also be a source of ideas. Photocopies from books and other printed matter can also be mounted.
Collages—Shapes built up from coloured papers, etc., glued to the drawing sheet.

Summary

1. Always attempt *at least* three solutions to the design brief. The more solutions you can show, the better chance you have of being able to choose a good final solution.
2. Draw any idea that comes to mind, no matter how silly it may seem at the time. The seemingly stupid idea may lead to some sensible solution.
3. Let your imagination run free. It is surprising how ideas develop from some detail seen in school or home, in books or magazines.
4. Add notes to your drawings. Details such as dimensions, materials or construction. You may later regret not making notes if you forget what was intended at the time a drawing was made.
5. Always check back to the function of the design. Are you satisfying the function?
6. Check the ergonomics of your solution. Many solutions require a drawing showing the ergonomic problem—how the design relates to the people who will be using it.

All the drawings on this page and on page 114 are unshaded, outline sketches. Methods for the shading, toning and colouring of sketches are given in pages 119 and 120 under Presentation.

Methods of drawing

There are four basic methods of freehand drawing. See also Working Drawings, pages 124 to 131.
1. Single view drawing,
2. Oblique drawing,
3. Isometric drawing.
4. Perspective drawing.

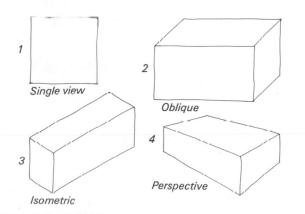

Boxing a drawing

To start off a freehand drawing outline a 'box' inside which the drawing can be constructed. With a sharp pencil (grade HB or B) draw the outline of the box in very faint lines. The overall proportions of the box should be similar to the overall proportions of the finished drawing. These faint lines are rubbed out when the drawing has been completed. The box acts as a guide keeping the finished drawing within its overall proportions. Fine lines drawn parallel to the box edges allow details of the drawing to be filled in to show the smaller proportions within the drawing. The box and guide lines provide much assistance in obtaining good, accurate drawings.

Drawing circular parts

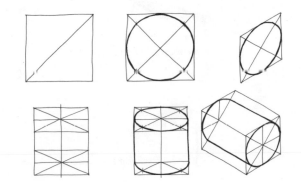

Producing the circular parts of a drawing may cause some difficulty. Faint, boxed guide lines assist in overcoming the difficulty. Circles should not only be 'boxed', but use made of the diagonals of the box for finding circle centres. Lines parallel to the box edges also assist.

Single-view drawings

Single view drawings are suitable for designs made from sheet materials, or where the details on one side of an article provide the most important features of the design. In the examples given the use of box outlines with guide lines within the boxes for smaller details are clearly shown. Notes with 'leader' lines drawn to the part to which the note refers are an essential feature of design drawings. Leader lines finishing on surfaces can end in dots. Those ending on the edge of a part can finish with an arrow touching the part. Some may prefer not to use dots or arrows, or even leader lines, but then the positioning of notes must show quite clearly the part to which the note refers.

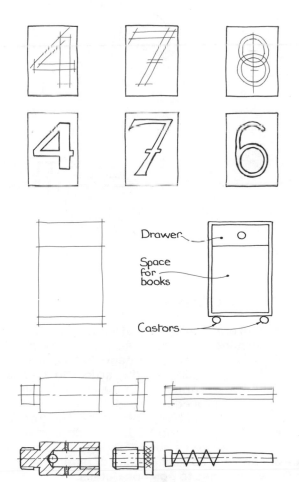

Idea for a safety valve
for a steam engine

113

Oblique drawing

The outline box of an oblique drawing starts with a single view box from the corners of which parallel lines are drawn at an angle of about 45 degrees. The 45 degree lines lead to the rear of the box, which is often the same shape as the face. The single view face of an oblique drawing should be the side of a design containing the most complicated shapes or those parts made up from circles, arcs or curves. The order of procedure for making an oblique drawing is as follows.

1. Select the face carrying the detail most difficult to sketch.
2. Draw the box containing that face—faint lines.
3. Draw lines at about 45 degrees from the corners of the single view face—faint lines. Complete the box.
4. Draw faint lines parallel to the box edges to locate the position of details within the drawing.
5. Add details of the drawing. Line in details with good black lines.

Oblique drawings of two tables and a plastic record rack are shown.

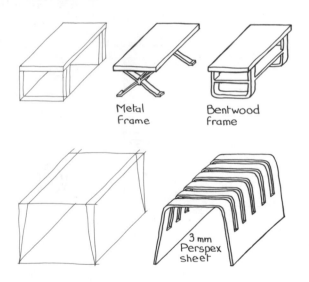

Metal
Frame

Bentwood
Frame

3 mm
Perspex
sheet

Isometric drawing

This type of drawing is of great value in design work. More difficult to draw than single view or oblique drawings, but with the advantage that the final work will look very much like the article to be made without the distortions which may occur in oblique drawings. The procedure is as follows.

1. Draw the outline box—faint lines. The front and one end of the drawing both slope from the front corner at an angle of about 30 degrees. The front, side and top will consist of pairs of parallel lines.
2. Draw faint lines to position details.
3. Complete and line-in all details.

Isometric drawings of a bathroom cabinet and a towel drying rail are shown.

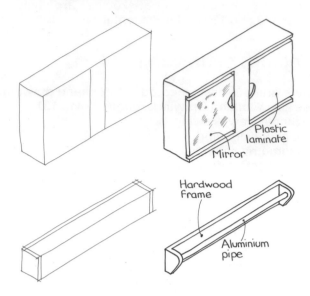

Plastic
laminate

Mirror

Hardwood
Frame

Aluminium
pipe

Perspective drawings

Perspective drawing takes account of the fact that when looking at any object, sets of parallel lines appear to meet in the far distance. This form of drawing produces sketches with the least distortion. In design work perspective drawing is of most value for producing room layouts or for articles taller than a person.

Two types of perspective freehand drawing are shown. In both the vanishing points (VP) are selected at about the height of the eyes of an average human. The distance of the VPs from the article are selected to give the best appearance to the sketch. In single point perspective start with a single view drawing and draw lines to the single VP. In two point perspective start with the nearest corner line and draw lines to the two VPs from its top and bottom.

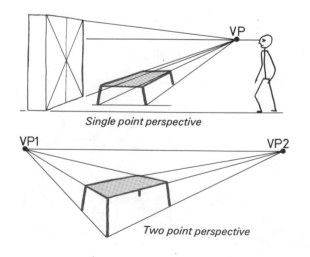

Single point perspective

Two point perspective

Other methods of drawing

Freehand drawing on centre lines

When making freehand drawings of articles containing circular parts, the circles and ellipses can be drawn around centre lines. Commence by drawing the sets of centre lines which pass through the centres of the circles and continue by drawing the various circles and ellipses based on the centre lines.

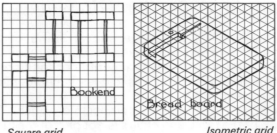

Square grid

Isometric grid

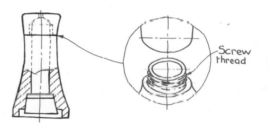

Perspective grid

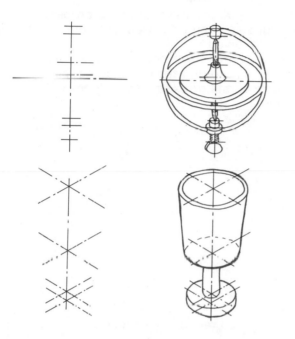

Small detail drawings

Small details in drawings can be emphasised by ringing within circles as shown.

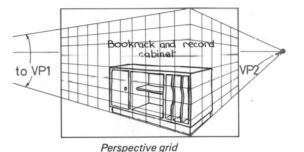

Grid papers

Square grid and isometric grid papers are made with 5 mm or 10 mm spacing between the lines. The grid lines are printed blue or green on white paper. Drawings can be made along the lines of the grids or drawn on tracing paper placed over the grid paper. The drawings on either the grid paper or the tracings can be glued, taped or pasted on the design sheets. Tracings can also be copied on to a design sheet by blacking over the rear of the tracing with soft pencil or by the use of carbon paper. The advantage of grid papers is that the process of producing freehand drawings can be speeded up. If a skill for drawing has not been developed, good design drawings can be made with the aid of grid papers.

Perspective grids can be purchased ready made or they can be drawn using architectural perspective geometry (an advanced technical drawing text book will explain this). Good, accurate perspective drawings can be speedily made on tracing paper over a perspective grid. Incidentally, grid papers are printed in blue because blue will not reproduce on the photographic negative material used when artists' drawings are being photographed for printing.

Perspective freehand drawing for interiors

One- and two-point perspective sketching can be employed when drawing interior room layouts. In the one-point perspective example shown the end wall is drawn as a single view drawing—it is a rectangle. A vanishing point (VP) is chosen at eye-level in a convenient position on the end wall. All lines other than verticals or parallels to the wall base are taken to the single VP. In the two-point example the vertical corner between two walls is drawn first, then two VPs are taken at eye-level in convenient positions. All lines other than verticals are drawn to the VPs.

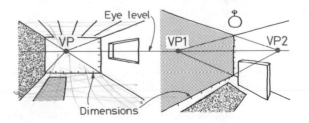

Examples of freehand drawing

The drawing on this page shows some of the methods of producing freehand work already described. The drawing gives a number of solutions to a design brief. The brief was to design a holder for a salt and pepper pot.

Drawing 1—A one-point perspective sketch. The design of the table and chairs is not part of the brief. They have, therefore, only been drawn in outline.

Drawing 2—The outline of the person has been traced from the 1:40 scale drawing on page 45. The table and chair have been drawn using single view sketches. Their proportions are based on the tracing of the human.

Drawing 3—The hand was traced from the drawing on page 45. Three sizes critical to the design brief are shown by A, B and C.

Drawing 4—A three-view freehand orthographic drawing which was traced over a square grid sheet. The drawing was transferred to the design sheet with the aid of carbon paper.

Drawing 5—An isometric freehand drawing. Could have been traced over isometric grid paper and transferred to this drawing. This example is suitable for isometric drawing because of the rectangular parts.

Drawing 6—An oblique drawing. Oblique type of sketching was chosen for this example because of the number of corner curves.

Drawing 7—A freehand drawing on centre lines. Very suitable method because of the number of ellipses involved.

Note—No notes have been added to this drawing sheet. This is so that the notes do not detract from the applications of examples of types of freehand drawing.

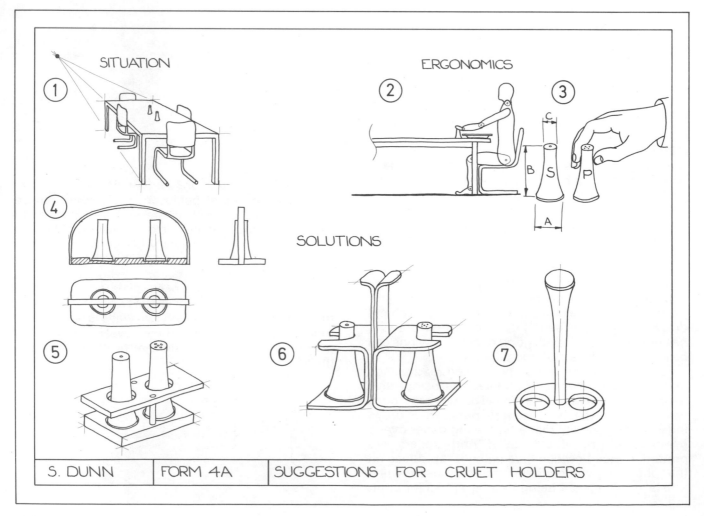

| S. DUNN | FORM 4A | SUGGESTIONS FOR CRUET HOLDERS |

Best solution

When a number of drawn solutions to a design brief have been made, the best of the solutions will be chosen for development. This may not be the actual design eventually made, because modifications may be necessary after a model of the chosen solution has been made. The best, chosen solution should be drawn as neatly and as accurately as possible. The method of drawing employed should be the one that will show the solution to its best advantage. The drawing should carry the following information:

1. *Shape and form*—This will usually be conveyed by the main sketch.
2. *Dimensions*—Overall dimensions and minor dimensions. Some of these may be drawn on scrap sketches associated with the main drawing.
3. *Construction*—Small additional sketches may be necessary to show constructions.
4. *Materials required*—Notes and leaders.
5. *Fittings required*—Sizes of these may be an important detail to be included.
6. *Finishes*—Add notes.

Other information may be required. This can be added in note form or in the form of small additional 'scrap' drawings.

The aim in making the best solution drawing should be to give sufficient information to allow both a model of the design to be made and the necessary working drawings to be produced. Try to think that somebody other than yourself will have to make the model and working drawings. If you give them all the necessary information they will not need to keep referring back to you.

Presentation

Because this best solution drawing, or series of drawings, is so important, its presentation on the design sheets should be such that the design can be clearly understood. Presentation is important—see the section on presentation on pages 146 to 151. Some of the ideas shown in those pages may be applicable to your chosen best solution drawing. A good plan is to present the best solution in such a way that it shows out clearly from the other solutions. Anybody looking at the design drawings should be able to see at a glance which is the chosen solution.

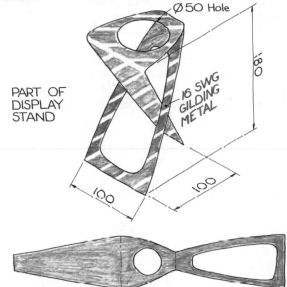

Shape of development

Exercises—General

1. You keep two rabbits as pets. Design a cage or pen in which the two pet rabbits can be kept. Your design must provide adequate shelter and area for sleeping, eating, exercise and play and must be capable of being easily cleaned and maintained. The cage/pen will be kept on a patio at the rear of your home in a position that is sheltered from the wind.

2. You are to make an occasional table which will have a top made from 15 mm thick chipboard, on to which 24 decorative ceramic tiles, each measuring 150 mm square, are to be fitted.

   Make sketches and notes which show various methods by which the tiles could be held permanently on the chipboard top. Make notes about the materials you would use to fix the tiles.

3. Recently a well-known oil company sponsored a design competition for schools. The subject of study was a small car which could be used as a means of transport in towns. Make a list of the factors which you would consider important in arriving at a design brief for such a vehicle.

Welsh

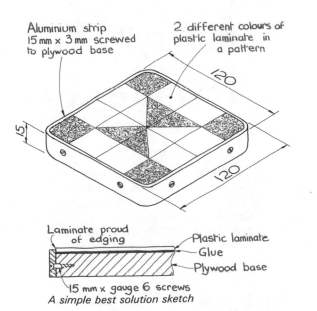

A simple best solution sketch

SECTION 4

Presentation

While working on a design brief the best methods of presenting the notes and drawings should be considered. Presentation of paper work should be regarded as an important part of designing. The paper work itself should be well designed.

1. All notes and drawings relating to a design brief should be contained in a folder, file or folio.
2. Notes should be clearly headed, neat, clear and precise.
3. Important drawings should show up clearly.
4. The appearance of layouts of notes and drawings should be interesting.

A design folder

Types of design folder
1. A single large sheet of paper or card folded centrally.
2. Large envelopes—usually lightweight card, often blue.
3. Artist's folders with flaps made from cardboard and linen, with closing tapes.

Inside the folder the sheets of paper relating to each design brief can be gathered together inside a single large sheet of paper or lightweight card, folded down its centre. Details of the design brief can be shown on the front of the folded sheet. Two examples are shown on this page. A further example is shown in a photograph on page 23. Drawing covers of this type should be well designed.

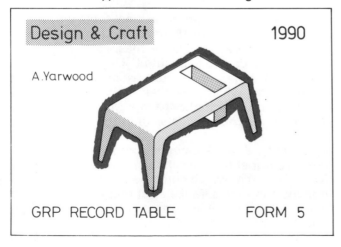

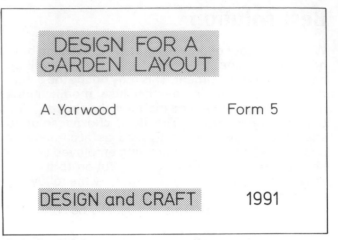

A design brief cover

Lettering

Good lettering on the design brief cover and on headings on the design sheets can be achieved by:
1. dry transfer lettering,
2. using letter stencils,
3. freehand lettering.

Dry transfer lettering
A good range of sheets of dry transfer lettering in a variety of type faces and sizes can be purchased. Each letter is transferred by rubbing with a Biro or pencil. See the photograph on page 123.

Stencil lettering
A photograph of a letter stencil in use is shown on page 123. The stencils contain letters, figures and punctuation marks. Designed for special pens and Indian ink. Common makes are Uno, Rotring and Standardgraph. Different heights and styles of letters are available.

THE DESIGN PROCESS
SITUATION   BRIEF
Investigation SOLUTIONS

Freehand lettering
Good quality freehand lettering comes with practice. Quicker than using dry transfers or stencils and requires no special equipment.

MATERIALS *models*

Presentation of the investigation

Methods of presenting the investigation notes are as follows.
1. By neat writing in longhand or in capital letters.
2. In pencil, Biro, pen or Indian ink.
3. Typed on typing paper which is then glued or pasted to the drawing sheet.
4. The whole of the investigation can be written, printed or typed on separate sheets of paper and presented separately from the design drawing sheets.

Headings for the various parts of the investigation can be presented by:
1. Freehand capitals underlined.
2. Freehand capitals within a shaped border.
3. Dry transfer lettering which can be bordered.
4. Stencilled lettering, which can be bordered.

function, ergonomics

Working drawings

shaping and forming

Some headings

Presentation of solutions

Outline sketches
This, the commonest method, is shown in the drawings on pages 112 to 117 under Solutions.

Colouring
Pencil crayons—Easy to apply. No special equipment required.
Wax crayons—Deeper colours than pencil crayons. Useful for outlining.
Felt-tip pens—Clear colours. Fade in time, particularly in sunlight.
Water colour washes—Either water colour or poster colour paints with water. For tinting the whole of a drawing surface with a coloured wash which does not cover up the lines of a drawing.
1. 'Paint' the surface to be washed with clear water.
2. Mix a pale colour wash in a palette.

3. Apply the wash to the surface which has been coated with clear water. Work from top to bottom.
4. Remove any surplus with a dry brush.

Dry tone transfers
Obtainable in sheets of clear colour or in a variety of greys. Applied to areas which are to be coloured or shaded by transferring from the tone sheets to the drawing sheet in the same way as dry transfer letters are applied. Many drawings in this book have been shaded with Letratone dry transfer tones.

Outline drawings
The drawings 1 to 17 show methods of presenting drawings such as a best solution sketch to which particular attention needs to be given.
1. *Straight line outlining*—Thick ruled lines in pencil or pen emphasise the outline of the set of wall shelves. Of most value when the drawing is composed of straight lines.
2. *Background emphasis*—Ink, pencil, felt-tip pens or wax crayons will produce this effect which strongly emphasises the shape of an article. A vase to be made from copper sheet.
3. *Background emphasis*—A 'squared' off background to a drawing of a fibre-glass magazine rack. Drawn with pencil, ink, wax crayon or dark water paint.
4. *Ruled line background*—Thick background outline emphasises the shape of this technical drawing instruments tray.

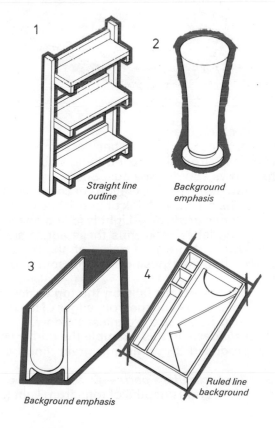

1
Straight line outline

2
Background emphasis

3
Background emphasis

4
Ruled line background

5. *Colour wash background*—The outline of the pottery vase is strengthened by a background formed by colour washing. The shape of the colour wash roughly follows the outline of the vase.

6. *Colour wash background*—In this example the box made from acrylic sheet is shown up against a background of colour wash 'squared' off at the corners.

7. *Dry transfer tone*—The dry transfer is placed over the drawing of a fibre-glass tray and cut to the outline of the drawing with a sharp knife. An irregularly shaped outline to the background emphasises the outline of the tray. A similar result could have been produced by colouring with crayons, felt-tip pen or paints.

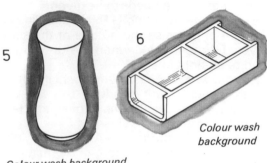

5

6

Colour wash background

Colour wash background

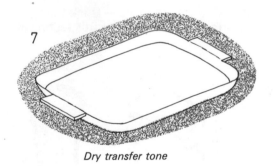

7

Dry transfer tone

Shade effects on drawings

In the examples 8 to 17 it has been assumed that the light source is from the top left-hand side as shown by the arrows above drawings. Shadings like these can be drawn with pencil, crayons or colour washes. Some can be drawn with ink or pencil lines.

8. *Three tones of shade*—Light is falling on the top edges of the letter rack, thus these edges are unshaded. Three degrees of depth of shade depend upon the supposed position of the source of the light.

9. *Two shades*—Light falls on the top of this box. The front of the box and the front edges of the raised pattern on its lid are in the darkest shadow.

10. *Two shades*—In this example the darker shading is produced by drawing grain lines close together.

11. *Shading circular parts*—Circular parts are shaded with various depths of tone from light (cen-

tral) to dark (right). The shades can merge if produced by pencil or colouring.

12. *Straight line shading*—Single thick lines along the length of a cylinder will emphasise its circularity.

13. *Straight line shading*—The spacing of the lines varies from wide to narrow both inside and outside this serviette ring.

14. *All round shading*—A drawing of a serviette ring showing two methods of circular shading.

15. *Thick line shading*—Compare with drawing 13.

16. *Line shading*—The conical shape of this coal hod is emphasised by straight line shading on its outside but with arcs on its interior surface.

17. *Surface shading*—Flat surfaces can be emphasised with black or striped shading.

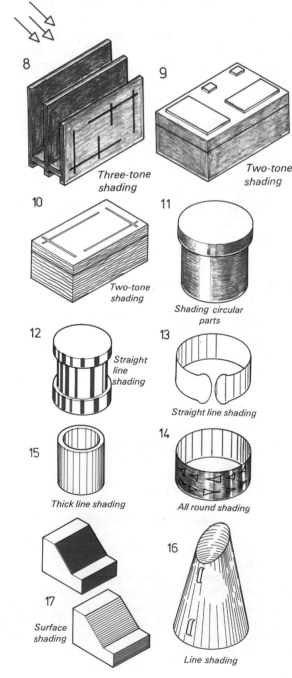

8

Three-tone shading

9

Two-tone shading

10

Two-tone shading

11

Shading circular parts

12

Straight line shading

13

Straight line shading

15

Thick line shading

14

All round shading

17

Surface shading

16

Line shading

120

Further examples of presentation

Simplifying complex design drawings

The radio circuit diagram shown can only be fully understood by those who have some knowledge of electronics. The simplified block diagram can be understood by the non-expert.

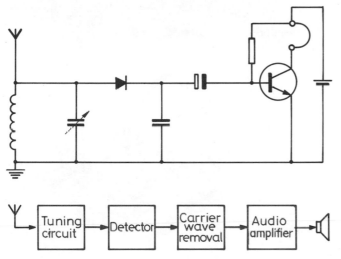

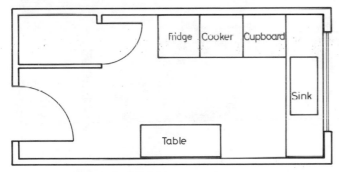

A radio circuit and its block diagram

Room and building layouts

Plans of rooms and building layouts drawn to scale may be necessary to show the position of a design in relation to other details in a room, house or garden.

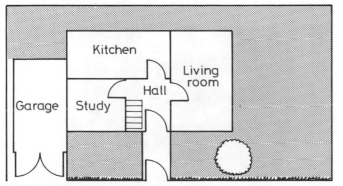

Room plan showing layout

House plan showing layout

Instructions without words

Could you start and use a gyroscope by following the sequence shown in the three simple line drawings? The method by which some designs operate may be presented by this method.

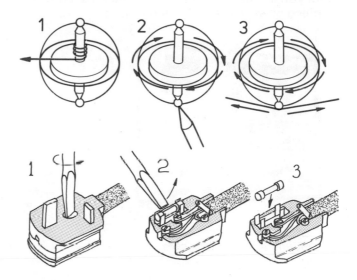

Exhibition layout in an art room

The photographs show how illustrations from newspapers, magazines and catalogues, or original photographs, can be presented on a design sheet. Illustrations like these may assist in solving a design problem by suggesting ideas. Remember, however, that you are not designing when you just copy from a piece of work seen in an illustration.

1

Shape cut out and mounted on coloured card

2

Cut out and outlined with coloured lines

3

Cut-out outline follows shape of doll's flat

4

Cut out and background crayonned in

5

Shape cut out and mounted on coloured card

6

Shape cut out and mounted direct on drawing

7

Outline in white colour wash and mounted on coloured card

8

Shape cut out to emphasise figures

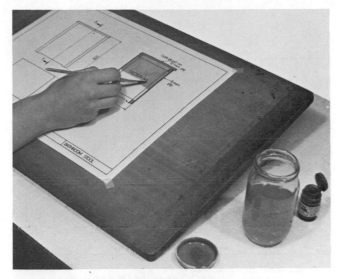

Colour washing with water paint

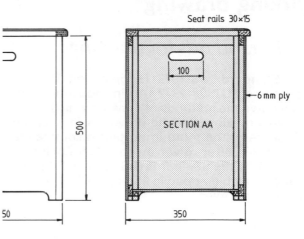

Seat rails 30×15

500

50

SECTION AA

100

6 mm ply

350

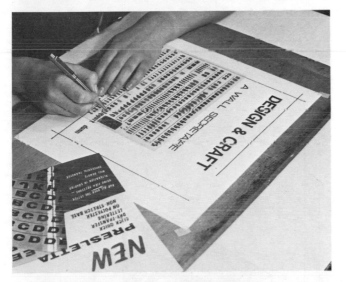

Applying letters from a dry transfer sheet

DESIGN & CRAFT

A WALL SECRETAIRE

stewart dunn

Letter stencilling with a Rotring ink pen

SITUATION

BRIEF

INVESTIGATION

Working drawings

British standards for drawings

British Standard 308:1972 (Engineering Drawing Practice) and PD7308:1977 (An Introduction to BS 308) lay down the methods of drawing which can be used when making working drawings for craft designs. Some of the more important recommendations from BS 308 are given on page 155. For further details refer to the Standards (BS 308 and PD 7308). They are available at public libraries. Most schools will also have copies.

Drawing sheets

When making your design drawings you will probably use A4 or A3 size sheets of drawing paper. For later work you may require A2 sheets. All drawing sheets in the A series are rectangles of the same proportions—side lengths in the ratio 1:√2. An A0 sheet is 1 square metre in area. An A1 sheet is half of an A0. An A2 sheet is half an A1 and so on.

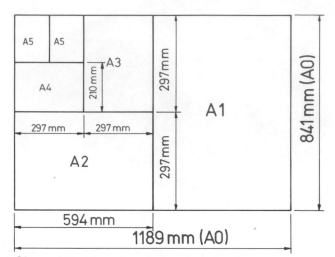

Sizes of the A series of drawing sheets

Types of working drawings

When you have decided which of your solutions to a design brief is the best, it will be necessary to make a working drawing. The working drawing should show *all* the information needed to allow the design to be made. Four working drawings are shown on this page and on page 125 opposite.

1. Simple one-piece article drawn in orthographic projection with instruments.

2. The same one-piece article drawn in isometric with instruments.

3. A design to be made from four parts. This drawing is divided into three. Details of each part are drawn. The assembly of the parts is drawn. A parts list is added.

4. A freehand drawing used as a working drawing. A clear freehand outline with added notes.

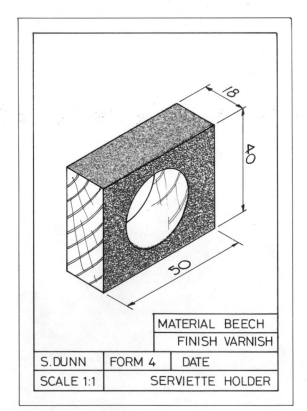

Single part drawing — pictorial

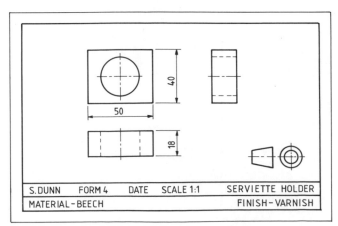

Single part drawing — orthographic

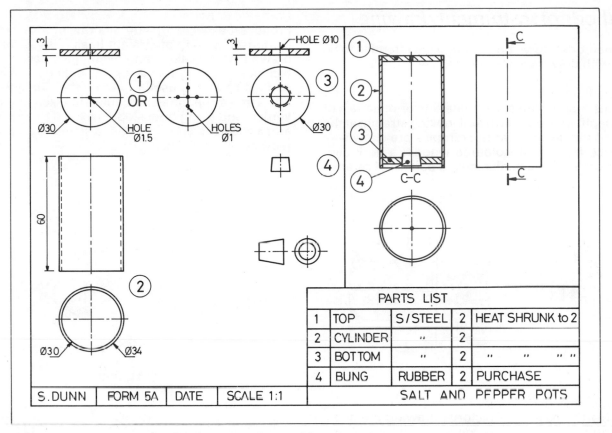

Combined drawing — details of parts and assembly

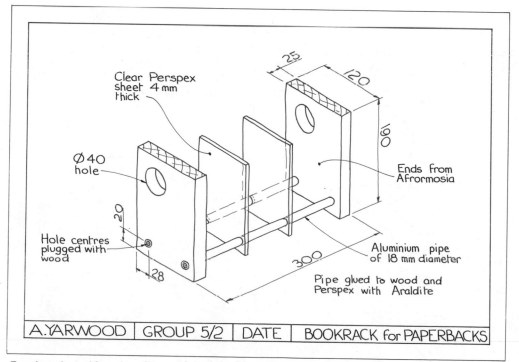

Freehand working drawing—pictorial with notes

Methods of instrument drawing

The methods shown on this page are intended to be used with drawing instruments.

Flat drawing

Designs made from sheet materials or materials of little depth may be drawn as if looking straight at the front of the design. Three examples are shown—a necklace from multi-coloured woods; a neck pendant from translucent Perspex; a pattern of ceramic tiles.

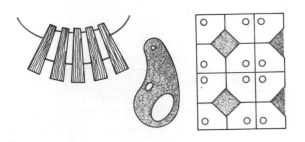

Oblique cabinet drawing

Possibly the easiest of pictorial drawing methods, most suitable for designs containing curves on one surface. The main surface is drawn as seen from the front—a front view. Half-length lines are then drawn from the front view with the aid of a 45 degree set square. Four examples are given—shaped supports in line; a pet's feeding trough; a box with lid; a spindle.

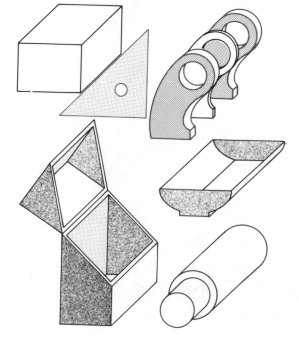

Isometric drawing

Produces excellent pictorial drawings of articles composed mainly of straight lines. Curves may be drawn isometrically using techniques described in technical drawing text books. The 30 degree angle of a set square is used to obtain the sloping lines. The same scale measurements are taken along the vertical and along both sloping axes. The examples are: a chessmen box in wood; a stainless steel toast rack; a match box stand.

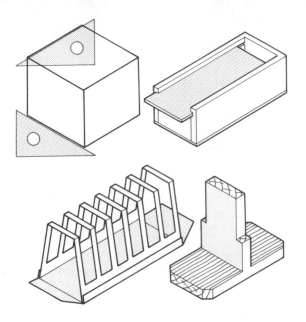

Single-point perspective drawing

This form of perspective drawing is sometimes suitable for larger designs. Another method is shown on page 105. A vanishing point (VP) at a scaled height of 1.7 metres (eye-level) is chosen and, after drawing a front view, or an end view of the object, all sloping lines are drawn to the VP. The examples given are: a house; a set of wall shelves; a table.

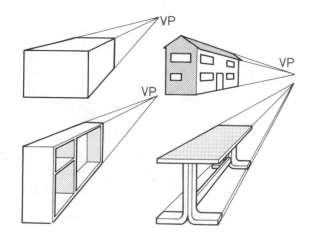

Producing working drawings

Using pictorial methods

Working drawings for simple, one-piece articles may be produced by making a sketch either freehand or using one of the methods shown on page 114. Dimensions and other details necessary for making the design must be included on the drawing.

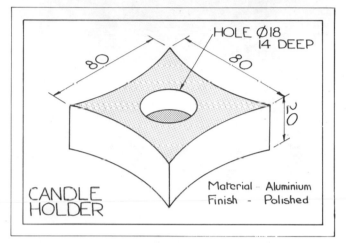

Simple working drawing using pictorial drawing

Using orthographic projection

The main method used for working drawings is orthographic projection. Two-view or three-view orthographic projections will usually describe a design completely, but four- or even five-view drawings are sometimes necessary. Dimensions and details, such as materials and finish, may be added.

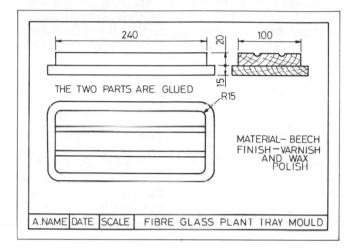

Drawings to include developments

Some sheet metal or sheet plastic designs will need a full size development constructed on the drawing sheet. Such developments worked on the drawing save the need for the development to be worked out while making the design.

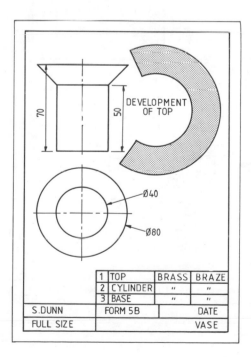

Drawings showing enlarged details

Either pictorial drawings or orthographic drawings may have enlarged detail added. The details may be drawn pictorially or in orthographic projection. The enlargement of details allows the main drawing to be made to a smaller scale, yet the details can be drawn to a sufficiently large scale to show their meaning quite clearly.

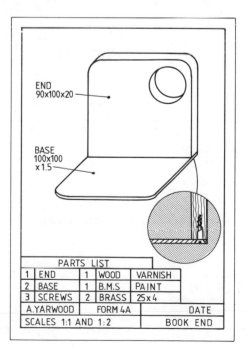

Working drawing—detail drawings

The working drawings of designs constructed from a number of separate parts which require to be glued or fitted together can be drawn in two stages. The first stage is to make drawings of each part of the design. From these detail drawings an assembly drawing can be made. The drawing on this page shows a typical example of details from such a design. Each component part is drawn in dimensioned orthographic drawings. These are clearly numbered for easy reference.

Exercise

Make an orthographic assembly drawing for the trolley shown on this page. Add a parts list to your drawing. The trolley body is made from coloured acrylic sheet, and the castors from aluminium sheet with acrylic rollers. Three castors are glued under the circular top being equally spaced around the circle.

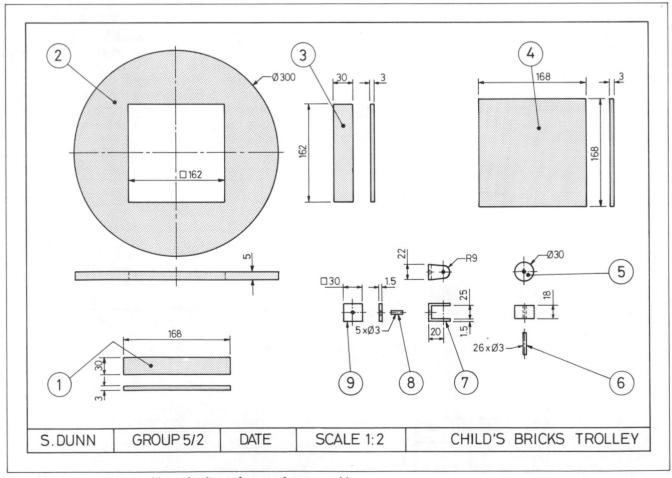

| S.DUNN | GROUP 5/2 | DATE | SCALE 1:2 | CHILD'S BRICKS TROLLEY |

Detail drawing — orthographic projections of parts of an assembly

Working drawings—assemblies

Assembly drawings are the most common form of working drawing. The drawing on this page is an assembly drawing of a tiled table. The drawing includes large-scale details of the methods by which the table is constructed. Note that the table can be constructed from reading the drawing. No further information is required.

Exercises

1. Make a cutting list of the wood required for making the tiled table. Add a list of parts which will have to be purchased from shops or ordered. Do not forget the tile cement.

2. Make a full size isometric drawing of the upper part of one of the legs to show the mortises which receive the rail tenons.

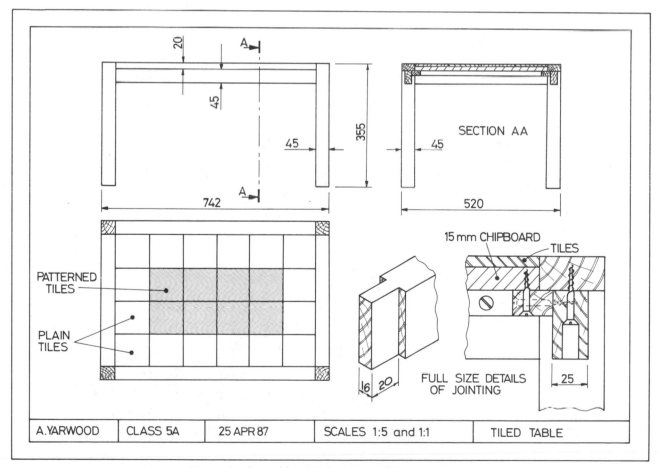

Assembly drawing—orthographic projection with added constructional details

Working drawings—combined

The drawing of a coats rack shows a typical working drawing involving a design made from assembling several parts. In this example the detailed drawings of each part have been drawn in orthographic projection and the assembly drawing is in isometric form. All details for the making of the coats rack are included. Note particularly the parts list added to the drawing. A full size parts list which you can trace for addition to your drawings is printed on page 132.

Exercise

Make a full size working drawing in orthographic projection of the assembled coat rack shown on this page. Your drawing should include a title block and a parts list and be fully dimensioned.

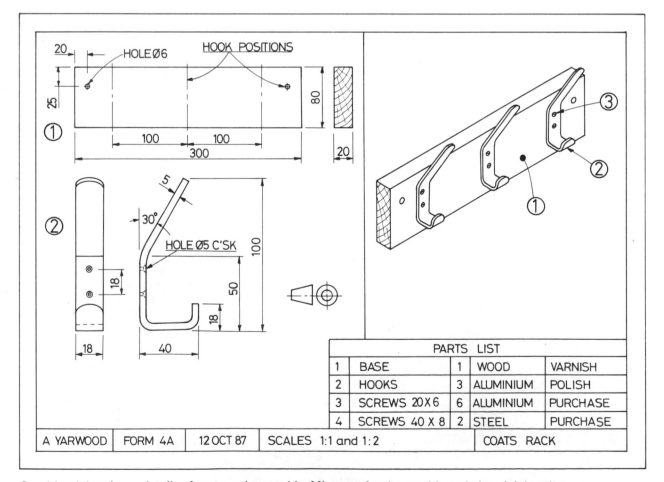

PARTS LIST				
1	BASE	1	WOOD	VARNISH
2	HOOKS	3	ALUMINIUM	POLISH
3	SCREWS 20 X 6	6	ALUMINIUM	PURCHASE
4	SCREWS 40 X 8	2	STEEL	PURCHASE

A YARWOOD	FORM 4A	12 OCT 87	SCALES 1:1 and 1:2	COATS RACK

Combined drawing—details of parts and assembly. Mixture of orthographic and pictorial drawing

Assembly drawings

Exploded views

Although quite difficult to draw, exploded drawings show clearly how the various parts of the assembly of a design are fitted in correct relationship to each other. A toy truck and a fishing net are shown in exploded drawings. These can be drawn using any of the pictorial methods shown on page 126, although isometric is the most usual method employed for exploded drawings. Freehand sketching methods can also be used for such drawings.

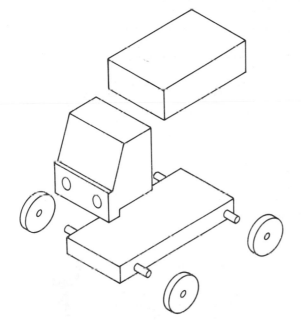

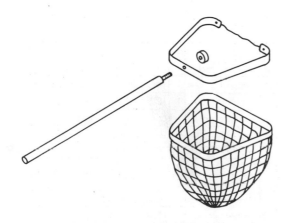

Part sectional views

This form of sectional drawing has the advantage of not only showing the external shape of a design but also shows how the parts of it fit together.

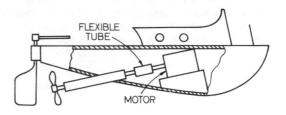

Drawing of internal structure

Sectional views or the use of hidden detail in orthographic drawings enable the shapes of parts which cannot be seen from the outside of an object to be clearly described in a drawing.

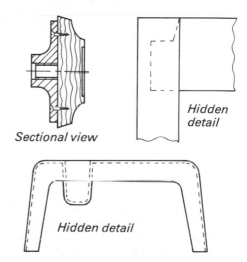

Sectional view   *Hidden detail*

Hidden detail

Part of a larger drawing

'Scrap' drawings showing a part broken from the main drawing can bring attention to bear on details which need further explanation in a working drawing. Such 'scrap' drawings are often drawn to a larger scale than the remainder of the drawings on the sheet.

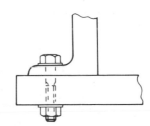

Parts lists

The drawing on this page can be traced for transferring to your working drawings. The thin lines are guide lines to allow you to print neatly and keep all your printing the same height. A parts list should include everything necessary to make your design. As each part is made, cut to size, ordered and obtained, it is advisable to tick it off on your parts list.

PARTS LIST				
Part No	DESCRIPTION	MATERIAL	No off	REMARKS

Parts list—this table can be copied on tracing paper

Cutting lists

If a design is made from a number of parts which will have to be cut out from material held in stock, such as in a school store, a cutting list may be required. Cutting lists can be written on a separate sheet of paper but should be written in a neat, table-like form as shown in the examples on this page. Three cutting lists are shown, the first a simple one for the coat rack in the drawing on page 130, the second, more complicated, for a small piece of furniture, the third for the windvane described on pages 30 and 31.

Sizes in mm   No allowance for waste

CUTTING LIST — WALL SHELVES						
Part No	DESCRIPTION		Length	Width	Thick	Remarks
1	ENDS	2	620	302	15	MAHOGANY
2	TOP	1	350	302	15	MAHOGANY
3	BOTTOM	1	342	298	15	MAHOGANY
4	BACK	1	616	342	3	HARDBOARD
5	SHELF	1	340	298	12	MAHOGANY
6	DOOR	1	590	320	12	BLOCKBOARD

Sizes in mm   No allowance for waste

CUTTING LIST — COATS RACK						
Part No	DESCRIPTION	No off	Length	Width	Thick	Remarks
1	BASE	1	300	80	20	RAMIN
2	HOOKS	3	165	18	5	ALUMINIUM

Dimensions in mm   No allowances for waste

CUTTING LIST - WINDVANE						
No.	Description	No.	L	W	T	Material
1	Vertical rod	1	495	$\varnothing$20		Mild steel
2	Support screw	1	140	$\varnothing$10		Tool steel
3	Rotating rod	1	105	$\varnothing$20		" "
4	Vane support	1	500	10	6	Mild steel
5	Letter rods	4	240	$\varnothing$10		Mild steel
6	Reinforcing rods	16	70	10	3	" "
7	Roof disc	1	$\varnothing$60		3	" "
8	Letters	2	100	70	3	" "
9	Pheasant vane	1	300	210	3	" "
10	Arrow vane	1	150	90	3	" "

Also required: $\varnothing$8 Ball bearings. Paints. Rivets 4mm C.S. Nuts.

Ordering parts

There may be parts needed for your design which cannot be obtained from your school's stores or from your own home. If you cannot purchase the parts in your locality, it may be necessary to order them from suppliers. You can order by phone or by letter. It is probably best to order by letter, keeping a copy for later reference. When you order, check on three items:

1. Is payment expected in advance?
2. Is Value Added Tax included in the price?
3. Is postage included in the price?

A typical letter ordering fittings

There are a variety of sources from which you can obtain the names and addresses of suppliers:
1. From your teachers.
2. From catalogues kept in your school.
3. From the Yellow Pages of a telephone directory.
4. From magazines and newspapers.
5. From the appendices in some books.
6. A librarian may be able to assist.

When writing a letter to a supplier check on all details:
1. Correct address.
2. Correct and full description of the items being ordered.
3. Quote a catalogue number if possible.
4. Correct size of the items.
5. Check that the money you send is correct.
6. Keep a note of a Postal Order number.
7. Check that prices are up-to-date.

Exercises

1. Using your own dimensions make a full-size orthographic assembled drawing of the toy lorry shown in the exploded drawing on page 131. Fully dimension your drawing, add a title block and a parts list.

2. The fishing net shown in an exploded drawing on page 131 is assembled as follows. The stiff support at the top of the net is held inside a metal hoop at the end of the handle. The hoop is held tightly to the net support by a sprung elastic strip which pulls the open ends of the hoop tightly over the net. The handle is held to the hoop by a nut which screws on to the end of the handle.

Using your own dimensions, make a half-size orthographic assembly drawing of the fishing net. Add all dimensions, a title and a parts list.

3. Make two drawings of the bookrack shown in the drawing on page 125. The first should be a fully dimensioned detail drawing of parts, the second a three-view orthographic drawing showing the bookrack assembled. Add a parts list to the assembly drawing.

SECTION 5

Materials

Introduction

Plastics

'Plastics' are a more recent addition to the range of materials used by man, although some 'plastics' have been with us for longer than is commonly thought. Celluloid, for example, was developed in the 1890s and Bakelite was made into large quantities of goods in the 1930s. A large number of different plastics have been developed, many of which are not available for craft work, having been manufactured for quite specific individual purposes. Plastics are materials made by chemical engineering, most often from crude oil. Plastics vary considerably in their strength values, from the comparatively fragile polystyrene foams used for packing to the very tough glass reinforced plastic mouldings made from polyester resin and glass fibre. Note the link between plastics and wood. The molecular structure of plastics is essentially of a large chain-linked polymer type. The basic material of wood, cellulose, is also of a chain-linked polymer molecule structure.

Metals

Metals are, on the whole, stronger than woods, size for size, but are heavier and more dense. Because of their greater strength, metals can be used in smaller sectional sizes and thicknesses than can woods. Metals, although obtained from minerals in the earth's surface, can be regarded as man-made. They are inorganic. Despite the wide range of different alloys made, pieces of metal of the same specification will all be similar. Variation in surface appearance and texture are the results of applications and/or polishing. Metals and woods harmonise well in design work if each is chosen with care. The stiffness, hardness of appearance and rigidity of metals is softened by the richness and softer appearance of woods. The smaller sectional sizes of metals can be set off by the necessary massiveness of wood. Some metals corrode when exposed to weathering; other metals have been deliberately made to resist this corrosion.

Woods

All woods have 'grain' and, as a result, possess grain direction. All woods are weaker along 'the grain' than across 'the grain' in that wood will split more readily along than it will across its grain direction. Except with a few species, wood is liable to decay unless protected against fungal attack. No two trees are the same, hence every piece of wood possesses individuality of colour, grain, density, strength and beauty. It is this individuality which makes wood such an important design and craft material. A large range of different species with different qualities means there will be a species suitable for most forms of design work. Good selection of that species is an essential part of good design.

Other materials

Clay

Potter's clay can be shaped or moulded and then fired in a kiln. Once fired it cannot be reshaped. Thinned with water it forms a 'slip' for pouring into plaster of Paris moulds.

Plastic cold clays will set hard without firing. They are polymers.

Concrete

Concrete is a mixture of cement and sand or cement and 'aggregate'. Common Portland cement is calcium carbonate from limestone and alumina and silica from clay. Limestone and clay are fired in a kiln, the resulting clinker is powdered and, with the addition of gypsum, forms the cement.

The mixture is mixed with water and allowed to set—a chemical, not a drying action. Concrete by itself tends to be brittle, but if reinforced with steel rods or wires, becomes very tough.

Fabrics

Wool tweeds, or tweeds containing polyester or acrylic fibres, and other furnishing fabrics may be used in upholstery work. PVC-coated fabrics suffer from the disadvantage that the PVC skin does not 'breathe' and so prevents ventilation through the upholstery which can cause discomfort. Printed, lightweight polyester (Terylene) or acrylic (Acrilan) cloth may be incorporated in fibre-glass mouldings.

Glass

Made from silica sand together with oxides of metals such as aluminium, boron, lead, potassium and sodium.

Soda lime glass is the common window and bottle glass. *Lead glass* is used in some optical work. *Borosilicate glass*, of which Pyrex is an example, is used for laboratory and oven ware. *Alumino silicate glass* can withstand temperatures of up to 850°C. *Fused silica glass* is possibly the most transparent glass.

Leather

Natural product, tough and decorative, but very expensive. Excellent upholstery material.

Plaster of Paris

Produced from gypsum which is quarried and heated in large steel vessels. Mixed with water, plaster of Paris sets within minutes. Used for making moulds.

Plasticine

A proprietary modelling material which can be used over and over again. One craft use is the making of models around which moulds can be cast—from plaster of Paris or from moulding rubbers such as Vinamould (a hot-melt vinyl rubber) or silicone rubbers (cold-setting polymer rubbers).

Choosing suitable materials

Three major considerations are involved when choosing the materials for a design.

1. The properties of the materials in relation to the functional requirements of the design.
2. Are the materials suitable for making the design? Is the necessary equipment available? Have I the necessary skills to work the chosen material?
3. Economic factors. The cost of the materials. Additional costs involved such as the making of moulds. The time to be spent in making the design. Choice of materials in relation to economy of line and space within the design.

Properties of materials

Tensile strength—The ability to withstand pulling without stretching or breaking.

Compression strength—The ability to withstand forces which may cause buckling or cumpling.

Stiffness—The ability to withstand bending and to resist deformation under loads.

Toughness—The ability to withstand impacts.

Hardness—The ability to resist wear. Cutting tools must be harder than the materials they are designed to cut.

Anti-corrosion—Air, water and pollution can cause materials to deteriorate.

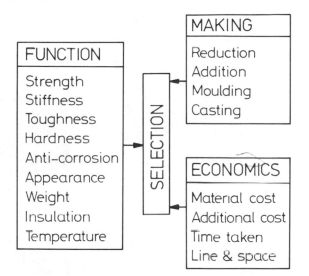

Appearance—Colour, surface finish, texture, surface patina, grain, direction of grain, 'figure', soft or hard appearance.

Weight—Relating to density. Metals are generally stronger, weight for weight, than woods or plastics. Some materials are strong in relation to density, some weak.

Insulation—The ability to withstand the flow of electricity or of heat or of noise. Light transmission may be considered under this heading—transparency or opacity, or somewhere between these two extremes.

Temperature—Increase or decrease in temperature can cause considerable changes in the properties of materials. Metals when heated usually become less strong, wood will burn and plastics degrade.

Making

The choice of materials often depends on the skills of the person making a design and on the availability of specialised equipment. It is no good, for example, considering vacuum moulded thermoplastic sheet if no vacuum forming equipment is available. There is little value in considering turned wooden parts in a design if the maker cannot use a woodwork lathe. Many designs will be limited as to whether or not they can, in fact, be made from materials at hand with the equipment installed.

Economics

In hand craft work of one-off designs, the cost of materials is rarely a limiting factor, although the use of expensive materials such as silver is usually not possible. However, design cost-effectiveness should always be considered. There is little value in making a design from costly materials when it could equally as effectively have been made from cheaper materials. In design work generally, consideration should always be given to the economic use of line, space and shape if effective designing is to be achieved.

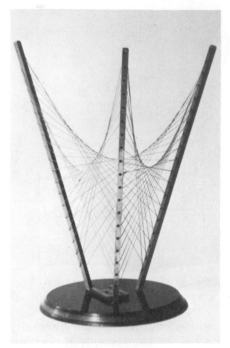

Sculpture from acrylic, aluminium square tubes and nylon twine

Chess board from mahogany and sycamore

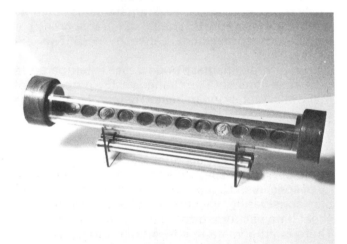

Coin display rack from Perspex tube, wood, Perspex sheet and stainless steel rods

Fishing stool from aluminium piping and seating canvas

Plastics

The materials we know as 'plastics' are products of the chemical industry. The raw materials from which the chemicals for plastics are obtained can be organic substances (carbohydrates) such as crude oil, coal, natural gas and plants or, in some cases, inorganic substances such as limestone, common salt, air and water. In present-day practice, oil is most frequently the basic raw material from which the chemicals are obtained. This is because oil can be transported more easily than can other bulky materials such as coal. Oil can be freely moved from place to place by pipes, sea, rail or road. Oil can be easily stored in tanks and drums from which it can be pumped to vehicles or to chemical plants.

The production of plastics from crude oil is broadly a two-stage process. First the chemicals (monomer molecules) are obtained from the raw material. Second the monomers are reacted to form the plastic materials. These plastic materials are made up from polymer molecules. The process from monomer to polymer is called polymerisation.

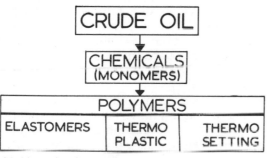

Making plastics

Polymers form in very long chains containing thousands of molecules strongly linked to each other. Monomers contain many fewer molecules, which are not chain linked.

Groups of plastics

Three general groups of plastics are produced:

1. Elastomers
Rubbers and rubber-like elastic substances. Elastomers have long polymer chains not cross-linked to each other.

2. Thermoplastics
When heated these become soft and can be moulded into shape. Further heating can lead to reshaping. Thermoplastics have long polymer chains which may have some cross-linking chemical bonds.

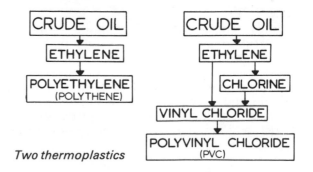

Two thermoplastics

3. Thermosetting plastics
Once formed into shape, thermosets cannot be re-formed. Thermosetting platics when heated in moulds become highly cross-linked forming hard, permanent substances with a three-dimensional bonding network.

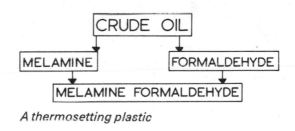

A thermosetting plastic

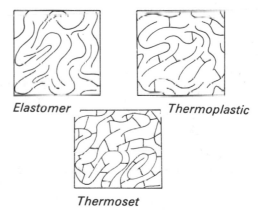

Elastomer —— *Thermoplastic*

Thermoset

Elastomers

Elastomers cannot really be regarded as a group of materials for design/craft but, because of their very wide range of applications, notes are given below about some of the more important of these polymers.

Natural rubber
Natural rubber is processed from latex obtained from rubber trees. It is a polymer of the monomer isoprene. A variety of materials are produced by the addition of fillers such as carbon black and silica to rubber. Natural rubber has excellent resilience and good resistance to abrasion. Its uses are well known —hot water bottles, rubber bands and carpet backings being but a few typical applications.

Isoprene

A synthetic natural rubber. Very similar properties to natural rubber but with higher extensibility.

Neoprene

Chemically similar to natural rubber. High resistance to oils and chemicals, natural light and ozone. Very resistant to permeability by gases. Applications such as footwear, V belts and motor mountings.

Styrene butadiene

Chemically similar to natural rubber. Very widely used particularly in tyres. Not resistant to oil or chemicals. Carbon black added to improve resistance to abrasion.

Butyl

Very high resistance to tearing, flexing and abrasion. Excellent resistance to permeability by gases. Not oil resistant but good resistance against chemicals. Applications—tyre inner tubes, hoses, diaphragms, cable insulation, seals for food and medicine containers.

Urethane

The strongest and hardest of the elastomers. Extremely good abrasion resistance. Good resistance to oils and fuels.

Silicones

A group of elastomers based on silicone and oxygen. Outstandingly good resistance to oils and chemicals at high or at low temperatures. Poor mechanical properties. Applications—seals and gaskets, insulation and encapsulation of cables and electronic components.

Thermoplastics in common use

A number of thermoplastic materials are in common use. Of these some have good design/craft applications. Thermoplastics can be moulded with ease when heated, but set firmly when cooled to room temperatures. After cooling, they can, if necessary, be reheated for further shaping.

Polythene

Properly called polyethylene, this is the most common of all plastics. Low density polythene (around 0.9 grams per cubic centimetre) is used as a packaging material and is available in sheet forms for this purpose. Low density polythene is also made into a variety of containers for liquids and foodstuffs. High density polythene (around 0.96 grams per cubic centimetre). is made into a wide range of products such as washing-up bowls. Waxy to the touch, excellent electrical and chemical resistance, and with very low water absorption (hence it is found in damp-proof courses in buildings). In craft work polythene has two main applications among others —as a powder for hot dip-coating of metals and as a release film for polyester resins.

Polypropylene

Light in weight and fairly rigid. Good resistance to many chemicals. One quite unique property is its ability to flex along the same line some millions of times without fracturing. This leads to it being used in hinging applications. In craft work polypropylene sheet can be vacuum formed or blow moulded to shape. Not easily joined but can be hot-air welded.

Polyvinyl chloride (PVC)

Very widely used. Basically rigid and stiff, but with the addition of suitable plasticisers can be made flexible. Applications of rigid PVC are in gutterings and pipes of many shapes and sizes, of flexible PVC in fabric coatings such as are found in upholstery work and in electrical cable coverings. Excellent chemical, electrical and weather resistivity. In craft work rigid sheet PVC can be vacuum formed or blow moulded and rigid PVC pipes are of value in some design work. PVC coated fabrics make good upholstery covers. Can be jointed with special PVC adhesives or by hot-air welding. Flexible between 90°C and 120°C but decomposes at 130°C.

Polystyrene foam

A lightweight rigid foam, white in colour, commonly found as a packaging material. A good material for model-making and large, temporary sculpture or display work. Can be easily and cleanly cut with hot wires between 200°C and 400°C. Dissolves if cellulose paint or polyester resin are applied to it, but a coat of emulsion paint will give protection against this problem. Many good craft applications.

Cellulosics

A group of polymers produced from cellulose obtained from wood pulp or cotton wastes. Tough materials which can be easily processed when suitable plasticisers are added. Photographic film is made from cellulose acetate. Cellulose acetate butyrate is moulded into chisel and screwdriver handles. Steering wheels may be made of cellulose propionate. Ethyl cellulose is suitable for helmets and gears. Not common craft materials.

Polyester film

Recording tapes are manufactured from polyester film. Do not confuse this thermoplastic with the thermosetting polyester resin which is the resin for fibre-glass work. Melinex is polyester film. Tough and flexible films of great mechanical strength. Excellent electrical and chemical resistivity. Some craft applications on a limited scale.

Acrylics

The plastics sold under the trade names Perspex, Oroglas, Plexiglas are acrylics. Excellent optical and weathering characteristics. Hard, stiff and strong but can be brittle. Applications are—illuminated signs, wind shields for motorcycles, substitute for glass, aeroplane windows. A valuable craft material, easily worked by most hand and machine tools. Rigid up to 85°C. Malleable and easily moulded from between 100°C and 175°C. Wide range of craft applications—jewellery, salad servers, signs, light shades, vacuum forming and blow moulding. Cemented with Tensol cements. Machined with zero or negative top rake on cutting tools.

PTFE (Polytetrafluoride ethylene)

Among the best of plastics as to chemical and electrical resistivity, even at high temperatures. Cannot be wetted by many liquids. Very low coefficient of friction. PTFE cannot truly exist in a molten state so cannot be moulded by conventional methods. Thus it is usually fabricated by compacting in powder form and then sintering. Non-stick coatings and plumber's sealing tape are two typical applications. A valuable engineering material because of its extremely low coefficient of friction. Not a craft material.

Nylon

A very important plastic with many practical applications—bearings and gears, door catches, hinges, locks, slides, etc.—as well as for stockings. Machines well but is not easily jointed except by mechanical methods such as rivetting, screwing, bolting and so on. A disadvantage of nylon is its comparatively high water-absorption rate. Of great value in craft work for small bearings and parts which need machining as well as in fittings such as hinges and catches.

Polyurethane foams

Flexible polyurethane foams are employed for padding seats of chairs and of stools and for general upholstery work. Available in a range of densities, the 'high' density foams being more suited to seats than the 'low' density foams which are better for backs and arms of upholstered work.

Rigid polyurethane foams can be easily cut to shape with knives, rasps, Surform tools and files and are thus suitable for model-making or as the basis of glass-fibre sculptures.

Thermosetting plastics

The number of different thermosetting plastics in common use is less than that of thermoplastics. This does not, however, limit their importance and in design/craft work polyester resins, which are thermosets, are probably used to a greater extent than any other plastic. This, together with thermosetting polymer glues, makes the thermosets as important in craft work as the thermoplastics.

Urea formaldehyde

When fully polymerised, urea formaldehyde is a light-coloured, hard substance. This plastic is manufactured into a large range of articles, the most common of which are probably light-coloured electrical fittings such as switch cases, plugs, sockets and lamp holders. Some excellent, strong and water resistant wood glues are urea formaldehydes, examples being Cascamite and the Aerolite range.

Phenol formaldehyde

Made into similar products as is urea formaldehyde, but dark brown in colour. Bakelite is a typical phenol formaldehyde. In addition to the manufacture of goods such as electrical fittings, kettle handles, hot iron handles and the like, phenol formaldehyde resins are available as glues for woods. Such glues are fully waterproof and are thus used in manufacturing plywoods such as the marine grades. One important application of phenol formaldehydes is in the making of plastic laminates such as 'Formica'. The backing-paper sheets of these laminates are impregnated with phenol formaldehyde.

Melamine formaldehyde

More expensive than the preceding two thermosets. Employed in the making of a large range of domestic items. Melaware crockery is made from this plastic. Melamine formaldehyde is impregnated in the patterned and surface papers of plastic sheets. Transparent, hard and good resistance to abrasion.

Epoxy resin

Valuable in craft work as adhesives or as 'fillers'. Epoxy resin glues are supplied in two-resin packs to be mixed together before application. Araldite is the best-known epoxy adhesive. Filled epoxy resins such as Plastic Padding are used for filling dents such as in damaged car bodies. The resins will adhere strongly to most known substances. They set hard at room temperatures and do not shrink as they polymerise. This makes epoxies valuable adhesives for metals, ceramics and glass.

Polyester resins

Polyester resins are used as the plastic medium in glass-reinforced plastics (GRP or fibre glass). Available in a range of types (see page 140). The resins set hard at room temperature after the addition of polymerising agents.

Materials for GRP work

Polyester resins

These are liquids which polymerise to thermoset solids at room temperatures when catalysts or hardeners are added. The thermoset solids are hard, brittle, not flexible and of low strength. When reinforced with other materials, however, polyester resins can be formed into tough, strong and flexible articles. Typical reinforcing materials are paper, cardboard, metal wires, rigid polyurethane foam, carbon fibres and glass fibres. By far the commonest reinforcing material is glass fibre. Hence the term fibre glass, or more properly, glass reinforced plastic (GRP).

Polyester resins can be cast without reinforcement. In craftwork this often means the encapsulation of objects of interest.

Polyester resins are usually sold in a pre-activated state. Small quantities of 'catalyst' or hardener, added to the resins just before use, will cause them to set hard within from about 20 minutes to an hour (or longer). The time taken to set depends partly on the amounts of catalyst added. Casting resins take much longer to polymerise—as much as twenty-four hours.

Types of polyester resins

Gel-coat resin—Slightly thicker than lay-up resin. The first coat to be applied to a mould when making a GRP moulding. Can have colour added.
Lay-up resin—This provides the bulk of resin within a GRP moulding.
Thixotropic resin—Thick resins for laying on vertical faces where they will not run off or for laying on to the frameworks of sculptures.
Clear resin—Thin, water clear for transparent work.
Casting resin—For encapsulations. Slow setting because casting resin contains only very small quantities of activator.

Catalysts

Although 'catalysts' cause polymerisation of the resin to occur, they are not really catalysts in the chemical sense because they are broken up during the polymerisation process. In craft work catalysts are usually peroxides which can be purchased as liquids or as pastes. Sometimes called 'hardeners'.

Glass fibre

Five common types.
Chopped strand mat—Random 50 mm lengths of spun-glass yarn bonded together in the form of a mat by an agent which dissolves in polyester resin. The most common form of glass fibre for GRP mouldings.

Woven cloth—For GRP mouldings where flexibility is essential. Spun-yarn glass is woven into a cloth.
Tape—Similar to woven cloth but in tapes of various widths. One common width is 50 mm. For reinforcing edges and corners of GRP mouldings.
Rovings—Strands of glass yarn filaments laid side by side. Commonly employed for making items such as lamp shades.
Surface tissue—Very thin, lightweight mat laid as a final surface on a GRP moulding. Provides a reasonably smooth finish to the moulding.

All glass-fibre materials may be cut to shape with scissors or with a sharp knife.

Storage of plastic materials

Some plastics may be regarded as fire risks. Once they catch fire they may smoulder for long periods. Thermoplastic sheet will distort out of shape if kept in a warm atmosphere. Some plastic materials, such as polyester resins and their associated liquids, will give off fumes which may be unpleasant and even dangerous to inhale.

Because of these factors plastics should preferably be kept in a cool, well-ventilated, dry brick-built store. Direct access of sunlight should be prevented. Polyester resins and their associated catalysts and cleaning fluids should be separated from each other within the store.

Some safety precautions

1. Good ventilation of working areas is essential when working with polyester resins.
2. Wear face masks and goggles when machining plastics such as acrylics.
3. Expanded polystyrene when cut by hot wire gives off styrene fumes, which can be dangerous if inhaled. Allow adequate ventilation.
4. If working with polyester resins, apply a barrier cream to the hands. If working with glass fibre it may be advisable to wear gloves. Polythene disposable gloves are suitable.
5. If catalyst gets into the eyes, wash well with water and *call a doctor*.
6. *Under no circumstances* should catalysts and activators be mixed. The mixture can be explosive.
7. When polyester resin has been catalysed heat is generated. Thus dowse any waste catalysed resin in water before throwing out.
8. Polyurethane foams can be made from chemicals. The mixing *must* be carried out in the open air. The fumes generated are toxic.

Polyester resin applications

The three photographs on this page give some indication of the very wide possibilities of how polyester resins can be employed in design/craft.

Bottom left photograph
Two biological specimens, a butterfly and a giant centipede, have been cast in clear polyester coating resin. They are being released from their moulding boxes after the resin has set. They are now ready for polishing.

Top right photograph
A small GRP (glass reinforced plastic) lay-up. A mould made of wood has been coated with polyurethane varnish and wax polished. A gel coat resin is then laid. This is followed with two layers of chopped strand mat and lay-up resin. A final glass-fibre layer of surface tissue, also in lay-up resin, will complete the moulding. After trimming the edges of the lay-up back to the mould edges, the moulding will be allowed to set and the bowl released from its mould.

Bottom right photograph
This photograph was taken in the showroom of Trylon Limited of Wollaston. Thixotropic resins have been coloured and worked on to a framework made from paper-wound wire. Some chopped strand mat would have been worked into the resin.

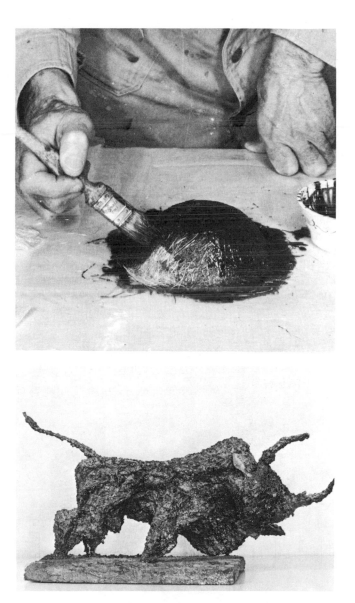

141

Shaping and forming plastics

Reduction

Thermoplastics such as acrylics, nylon, PVC may be cut into shape with the usual range of hand craft tools—by sawing, filing, screw cutting, turning and drilling. Polystyrene foam can be rapidly cut to shape with hot-wire cutters such as those illustrated.

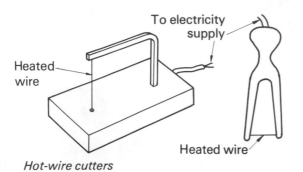

Hot-wire cutters

Addition

Mechanical jointing methods suitable for plastics are shown on pages 79 to 81. Thin sheet plastics, particularly polythene, can be heat welded with the aid of a heated roller tool. Polyester sheet film (Melinex) between the roller and the polythene will prevent any possibility of the heated roller sticking to the polythene.

Thicker thermoplastic sheet material may be hot-air welded. The hot air melts both the parent material and the filler rod along the line of the joint.

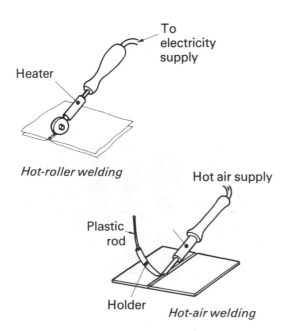

Hot-roller welding

Hot-air welding

Moulding

Thermoplastic sheet material-polystyrene, polypropylene, polythene, acrylic and PVC—may all be moulded into shape by a variety of methods—vacuum forming; blow moulding; by heating along a strip of the material and then bending along the heated strip; by placing heated sheet plastic between moulds and then keeping the moulds under pressure until the sheet cools.

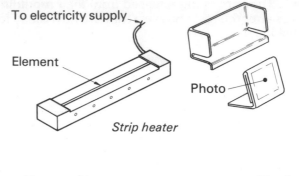

Strip heater

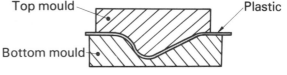

Moulding sheet plastic

The thermosetting plastic polyester resin is most often formed to shape by laying glass-fibre and polyester resin on to moulds to form glass reinforced plastic mouldings.

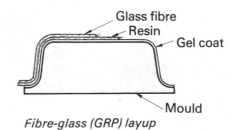

Fibre-glass (GRP) layup

Casting

The thermosetting plastics, polyester resins and epoxy resins can be poured while liquid into casting boxes and moulds. They will set solid at normal room temperatures.

Thermoplastic powder, notably acrylic and polythene, can be poured into heat resistant moulds, which can then be heated until the powders melt and flow in the moulds. This process is known as sintering.

Polyurethane foams may be formed into shape inside moulds by mixing two chemicals together. If this method is used, it must be remembered that the fumes emitted by the chemical reaction are toxic. Thus the process should be carried out in the open air.

Metals

Aluminium

In the earth's crust, aluminium is the most abundant of all metals. Its principal ore is bauxite in which aluminium oxide (alumina) is present in quantities of from 40% to 60%. Other compounds of the metal are common—they are found in the felspar of mica, in china clay, in corundum and in the mineral cryolite (as sodium aluminium fluoride).

One process by which the metal is obtained from its ore, bauxite, is shown diagrammatically on this page. The stages of the process are as follows.

1. The ore is crushed and heated under pressure in caustic soda (sodium hydroxide).
2. The resulting solution of sodium aluminate is filtered to produce a precipitate of aluminium hydroxide.
3. The precipitate is made into a solution and heated to produce alumina (aluminium oxide).
4. The alumina is electrolysed in solution in molten cryolite. As more alumina is added the cryolite is unchanged and can be used indefinitely. Aluminium collects at the cathode. The carbon anode is gradually oxidised away.

Properties of aluminium

After steel, aluminium is the most widely used of all metals at the present time. The pure metal has relatively low strength values, so it is either cold-rolled or alloyed in order to develop better strength properties.

A tough oxide film forms naturally on the surface of aluminium directly the fresh metal is exposed to the atmosphere. It is the presence of the oxide film which allows aluminium to resist corrosion to atmospheric conditions. Because of the very rapid formation of the oxide film, soldering, brazing and welding of aluminium can only be carried out using techniques and fluxes developed for the purpose. This oxide film is thickened and coloured in the process known as anodising. Hence anodised surfaces are very resistant to wear.

The low density of aluminium compared to iron (aluminium 2.7 grams per cubic centimetre, iron 8.0 grams per cubic centimetre) make it a light weight metal. Easy to work with both hand and machine tools.

Aluminium is a good conductor of both electricity and of heat.

The metal is very ductile and can be rolled into very thin foil sheets.

The melting point of aluminium is 660°C (compared with iron—1540°C.

Aluminium alloys

Many aluminium alloys have been developed for various and for specific purposes. Alloying elements are copper, manganese, magnesium, silicon, chromium, lead, tin and zinc.

One aluminium alloy of value in craft design work is commonly known as duralumin (a trade name). This is an alloy of aluminium and copper (2% to 6%). Duralumin possesses excellent strength properties (up to 5 times that of pure aluminium before hardening) combined with good ductility. Rather susceptible to corrosion, but more corrosion resistant than most common metals.

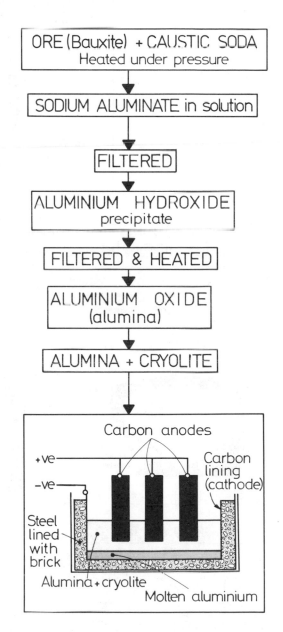

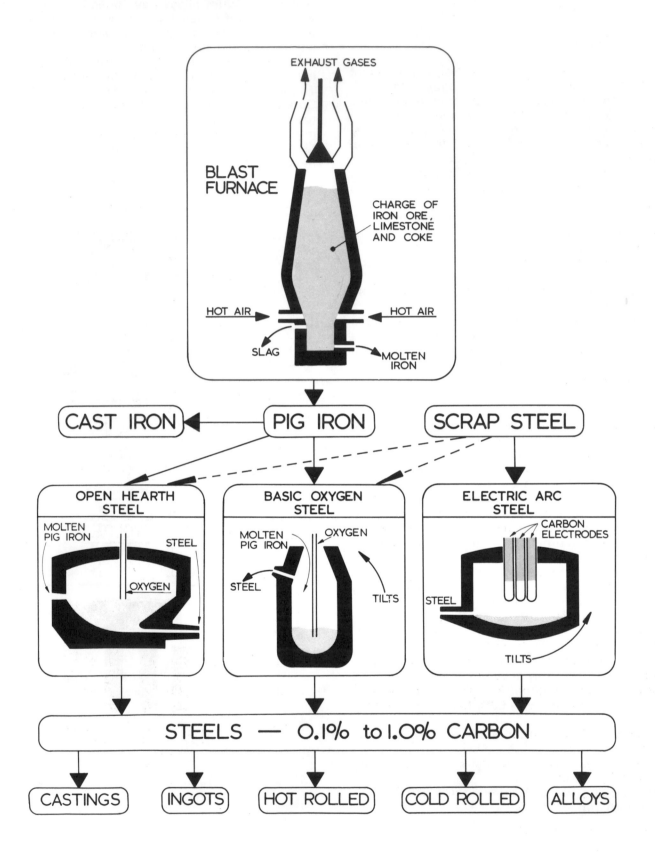

Ferrous alloys

Metals composed mainly of iron are known as ferrous metals or ferrous alloys. Metals containing no iron are known as non-ferrous metals. For craft and structural uses iron is alloyed with other substances to produce alloys, of which the most important is carbon tool steel. Other ferrous alloys are used in craft work. An example is stainless steel, which can be regarded as an iron/chromium alloy.

Production of carbon steels

The drawing on page 144 opposite shows, diagrammatically, stages in the production of carbon steels.
1. *Pig iron*—Crushed iron ore and coke, mixed with limestone, are heated in a blast furnace. Under the action of the heat provided by the burning coke, with the limestone acting as a flux, iron is melted from the ore to produce pig iron. The waste from the coke, limestone and ore forms a slag which floats on the surface of the molten iron in the blast furnace. The slag has many uses, one of which is as a road surfacing material. The molten metal is pig iron. Pig iron contains many impurities and needs further refining to obtain carbon steels. We are not concerned with cast iron here, it is not a craft material.
2. *Carbon steel*—Three methods of producing carbon steels from pig iron are shown. The more modern of these is the basic oxygen process. Molten pig iron is poured into crucibles, together with a proportion of scrap steel. Impurities are burned away with oxygen. Various methods of controlling this process will produce different carbon steels.
3. *Other ferrous alloys*—The common method of producing other iron alloys, of which carbon may be a constituent, is by the melting of scrap steel in an electric arc furnace together with alloying substances.
4. *Forms produced by steel works*—The products of the steel-forming processes are worked into various forms at the steel works. Some of these are shown—castings, ingots, hot or cold rolled plates, rods, strips and various alloys.

Note

Carbon steels are defined as those containing carbon up to about 1.0% carbon. Other alloying substances may, however, be included—up to about 1.5% manganese, a maximum of 0.5% silicon and as much as 0.5% copper. Residual elements may also be present, examples being sulphur (up to 0.05%) and phosphorus (up to 0.05%). Carbon, however, is the major constituent determining the characteristics of carbon steels.

Types of carbon steels

Dead mild steel

Up/to 0.1% carbon. Soft and ductile. Used for soft wires and tubing.

Mild steel

0.1 to 0.3% carbon. The most popular carbon steel. Tough, machines easily and will weld easily. Cannot be hardened. Used for bolts, general craft and constructional work, car bodies. Obtainable as black mild steel, or as bright mild steel in sheets, rods and bars in a wide range of thicknesses and sectional shapes.

Medium mild steel

0.3% to 0.6% carbon. A tougher steel of high tensile strength. Typical uses are for high tensile wires, bolts which undergo a strain, hammer heads.

High carbon steel

0.6% to 1.0% carbon. Tough and hard steels used in toolmaking. Often called carbon tool steel. Can be hardened and tempered to receive cutting edges. Uses—springs, tools for the working of many materials.

Stainless steels

Stainless steels are iron/chromium alloys. Their anti-rusting, anti-corrosion properties depend upon the formation of a surface chromium oxide film in the presence of oxygen in the air. This surface is non-porous, insoluble, self-forming and self-healing. About 12% chromium is necessary to achieve the surface, but as much as 30% chromium is present in some stainless steels. Other elements —aluminium, nickel, silicon and molybdenum, may also be present.

When working stainless steel, dirt, grease or machining swarf left on surfaces, may prevent the formation of the chromium oxide film. Surfaces must therefore be kept in a clean, bright condition.

High speed steels

Many different steels incorporating elements such as tungsten, vanadium, silicon, manganese, chromium and molybdenum have been developed for special tooling purposes such as machining tools —shears, dies, punches and lathe tools.

High speed steels developed for the making of machining tools are mainly alloys of iron and tungsten. As much as 20% tungsten may be present. High speed steels may also contain high carbon percentages. Other elements may also be present. High speed steels can overheat when machining at high speeds, without loss of cutting edges.

Tinplate

Tinplate is thin mild steel sheet with a coating of tin. The tin coating prevents the mild steel plate from rusting.

Copper

Copper is the world's third most important metal, measured in volume of consumption, after steel and aluminium. Although the almost pure metal is used on a very wide scale, it is also the principal element in a large range of alloys. Brasses, which are basically copper/zinc alloys; bronzes—copper/tin; cupronickels—copper/nickel; nickel silvers—copper/nickel/zinc. Copper was probably the first metal to be used to any extent by man and it will be recalled that the bronze age preceded the iron age in most parts of the world.

Production of copper

Copper ores as mined today are considered to be of a high grade if they contain above 2% to 3% of copper. Many ores with as little as 0.7% of the metal are mined on a considerable scale. Thus as much as 99% of the ore becomes waste. The ore is crushed and pulverised to a powder, which is then floated on liquid (often a pine oil) in tanks. The flotation separates the copper-bearing mineral parts of the oil from the waste. The powdered mineral is then mixed with a suitable fluxing agent and heated in a smelting furnace fired with a mixture of oil, coal powder and air. The product of the smelting is a copper of about 98% purity. This needs further refinement, most often by electrolysis before it is of commercial value—about 99.95% purity.

Properties of copper

Copper is a very ductile metal. It is moderately strong and can be moulded, bent or beaten to shape with ease. With a density of 9 grams per cubic centimetre it is 'heavier' than iron ($8\,g\,cm^3$).

Copper is an excellent conductor of electricity being second only to silver in this respect. It is also an excellent conductor of heat.

Copper is a red-coloured metal which naturally forms a surface film possessing good anti-corrosion resistance. The film changes the surface colour from red to dark green (the 'patina' of copper).

The pure metal's melting point is 1080°C.

The metal is very easy to work by hand.

Alloys containing copper

Brasses—Alloys of copper and zinc. Vary widely, e.g. gilding metal is 95% copper and 5% zinc; yellow brass is 65% copper and 35% zinc. Harder, and machines better, than copper. Electrical conductance less than copper. Corrosion resistant. Melting point lower than copper. Brazing brass approximately 50% copper, 50% zinc.

Bronzes—Usually alloys of copper and tin. Other elements added for special purposes, e.g. phosphor bronze—up to 10% tin and 2% phosphorus—used for springs and bearings.

Cupronickel—One example with 45% nickel used for precision electrical resistors.

Nickel silver—Contains no silver but is a copper/zinc/nickel alloy. Works like brass but very hard. Can be worked to a high polish thus is used for decorative applications.

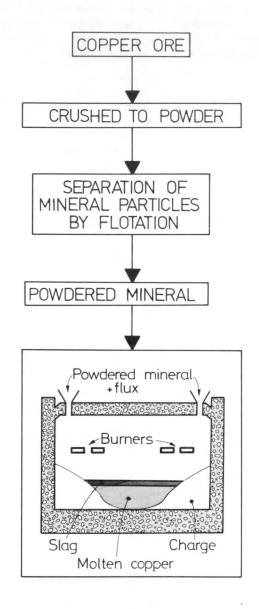

Zinc

Zinc cannot be regarded as a design/craft metal, although it can be purchased in rod, wire, bar and sheet form if required. In terms of the quantities used throughout the world, zinc lies in fourth place after steel, aluminium and copper. The importance of this metal lies in the following.

1. As a coating for steel sheet—galvanised steel —zinc enables the steel to resist rusting. This is due not only to the zinc itself being anti-corrosive, but

also because zinc is more electropositive than iron. Oxidation of the zinc thus occurs in preference to oxidation of the iron in the steel.

2. Zinc is a major constituent of brasses. See page 131.

3. The melting point of zinc is comparatively low —about 420°C. Thus zinc alloys containing traces of magnesium, up to 4% aluminium and sometimes about 1% copper, are extensively used for die castings. One common use of such castings is in motor car carburettor casings, but zinc die castings are found in numerous other situations.

4. In its commercially pure state, zinc is found in dry battery cell casings, weatherproof flashings in buildings and in electronics condensor cans, among other uses.

Tin

The importance of tin in design/craft work lies in its use as a coating for sheet steel—tinplate and also as a constituent of soft solders.

Tin is a white, silvery metal of about the same density as iron. It is very resistant to corrosion, which is why it is used as a coating to steel sheet. Tin is a very expensive metal. As a result tin-rich soft solders are now less extensively used than previously.

Tin foils are used in electrical condensors and tin lined copper pipes are used in the food and drink industries. Tin wire is used for electrical fuses.

Lead

The value of lead as a metal lies in the following:

1. Its heaviness. At 11.3 grams per cubic centimetre, lead is the heaviest common metal.

2. Its anti-corrosive properties. Lead is resistant to most natural environments as well as to many acids.

3. Its low melting point of 327°C. This, combined with its lower cost relative to tin, makes it suitable as a major constituent of soft solders. Soft solders may be melted with soldering 'irons' in situations where great joint strength is not essential.

4. Its softness and ductility. Lead can be easily worked to shape.

Lead is still extensively used, although not so comonly as previously. This is due not only to its increasing cost relative to other materials, but also to the problem of lead poisoning arising from its use in some domestic applications.

Lead is used in the manufacture of accumulator batteries. It is the principal shielding material used in X-ray apparatus. Sheet lead is used for weather 'flashings' in buildings. Sheet lead is employed for the deadening of noise in buildings. The metal is extremely malleable and can be rolled into foil as thin as 0.01 mm. Because it will reproduce very fine detail it is the major constituent of type alloys for printing purposes.

Precious metals

Although not used in school design/craft work to any extent, except in jewellery work, the precious metals—silver, gold and platinum—are of great importance. Of the three, silver being by far the most abundant in the earth's crust, is the cheapest. Platinum, on the other hand, being the least abundant, is the most expensive.

Silver
Pure silver as such is not used to any extent in school design/craft work, although being the best heat and electrical conductor of all metals, silver is used for many applications in scientific and electrical situations such as in fluorescent lamp and refrigerator switches and in relays as found in telephone circuits.

In craft work, sterling silver is used for high grade silver working. This is an alloy of 92.5% silver with 7.5% copper. Silver solder, which will form strong joints between most metals (not aluminium or zinc) contains between 10% and 80% silver.

Silver is very ductile and can thus be easily worked into quite intricate shapes. When cold worked, the soft metal hardens considerably. Although its surfaces will tarnish in ordinary atmospheric conditions, silver is very corrosion resistant and is not affected by most chemicals, although it will dissolve in nitric acid.

Gold
Yellow in colour, soft and very ductile, gold has extremely high resistance to corrosion. With a density of 19.3 grams per cubic centimetre it is one of the heaviest metals. For practical purposes, gold is alloyed with copper or with silver to increase its hardness. Electrical contacts in some circuits are gold-plated.

Platinum
White in colour and very ductile. Extremely resistant to corrosion, even at high temperatures. Does not oxidise even at high temperatures. High melting point (in the region of 1770°C). Often alloyed with other metals such as gold or iridium to increase its mechanical properties. Not a school craft/design material—far too expensive.

Other metals

Other non-ferrous metals may be of interest to the craft worker from time to time.

Bismuth

A metal of bright lustre, which is extremely brittle. Major use is in low melting point alloys—from 110°C to 300°C. Thus it is found in fire alarm and sprinkler systems, for safety plugs in gas tanks and for shut-off valves in heating systems.

Nickel

An important alloying metal. Silvery white, with a tendency to yellow, in colour. Slightly denser than steel (8.8 compared with 8). Nickel alloys are hard, stiff and strong and highly resistant to corrosion. Nickel and iron alloys are of special value for their magnetic properties.

Almost pure nickel is used for plating.

Cadmium

Dull silvery white. Found as an excellent anti-corrosive coating to steels as in bolts and nuts for motorcycles and cars.

Cobalt

Silvery white but faintly bluish in colour. The main interest in this metal will be in its use in alloys of special magnetic characteristics. When alloyed with chromium, used for bone replacement and in dentures because the alloys are not attacked by body fluids.

Tungsten

A metal of extremely high melting point (3400°C) and high density (similar to gold). Retains strength at high temperatures and this, together with its excellent electrical conductance, makes it suitable for use in light filaments. Also called wolfram.

Comparison table

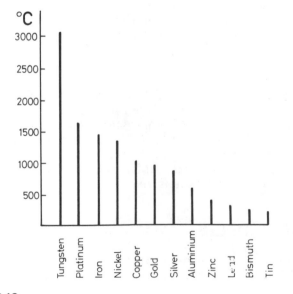

Heat joining of metals

Some of the most efficient methods of joining pieces of metal together are by melting other metals between the parts. The molten metal alloys with the parent metals to form strong, permanent joints between them.

Five basic methods are commonly employed:

1. Soft soldering

Solders made from lead/tin alloys containing up to 40% tin are melted between adjoining parts. Melting temperatures from 200°C to 250°C. The common 'tinman's' solder is a 70 lead 30 tin alloy. The heat needed to melt the solder causes the formation of oxides which prevent the solder fusing to the metals being joined. These oxides are dissolved in a paste or solution of zinc chloride applied to the joint area before heating. The zinc chloride is known as a 'flux'. Proprietary fluxes can be purchased. Another method is to apply a protective coating of tallow or resin to prevent the oxides forming on the metals.

2. Silver soldering

Very strong joins between metals such as copper, gilding metal and silver can be made with silver solder. Silver solders are alloys of silver and copper containing between 10% and 80% silver. Melting temperatures between 630° and 800°C. The melting point of these solders varies according to their composition. Thus some silver solders such as Easiflow melt at lower temperatures than others. The common flux for silver soldering is borax although proprietary fluxes are available.

3. Brazing

Brazing brasses are commonly alloys of copper and zinc in a 50/50 ratio. Used when joining metals such as copper and mild steel. The common flux is borax. Proprietary fluxes also sold.

4. Welding

Welding rods for melting between joints are usually of a similar composition to the metals to be jointed. Thus a mild steel joint from 0.3% carbon steel would entail a welding rod from about a 0.1% carbon steel. Welding a 0.6% carbon steel would entail say a 0.3% carbon steel welding rod. Flux incorporated in welding rods. Temperature range from 1200°C to 1500°C.

5. Aluminium brazing

Usually referred to as brazing but is really a form of welding. The main problem is to dissolve the rapidly forming oxides, for which special proprietary aluminium fluxes are employed. The welding rods are aluminium/silicon alloys with 10% to 12% silicon. Rods melting at about 25°C lower temperatures are alloys of aluminium silicon and copper. Temperatures in the region of 600°C are employed.

Woods

Woods are the most extensively used of all materials. They are being replaced naturally by replanting when trees are cut down to provide timbers. Woods were probably the first materials to be used by man. They are remarkably versatile materials, being strong, relatively light in weight, easy to work, obtainable in large sizes, comparatively cheap and available in any quantity. small or large. Woods are beautiful materials when worked with an appreciation of their colours, grains and 'figures'. Moreover, they can be successfully combined in design work with other materials.

Classification of woods

Woods fall into two main groups. These are classed as 'hardwoods' and 'softwoods'. A clearer classification would be to define the two broad botanical groups into which trees can be placed—'Angiosperms' and 'Gymnosperms'. However, the timber trade classification of hard and soft is in common use by craft workers.

Hardwoods

Hardwoods are derived from trees with broad leaves—'Angiosperms'. Woods from such trees are mainly cellular in structure. The woods are generally hard, examples being beech, oak, teak, ash, mahogany, although a few 'hardwoods' are quite soft—balsa being the most notable example of a soft 'hardwood'.

Softwoods

Softwoods are derived from coniferous trees—'Gymnosperms'. The leaves of coniferous trees are thin and needle-like in shape. Woods from coniferous trees are usually soft when compared with most 'hardwoods'. Examples are redwood (*Pinus sylvestris*), larch, spruce and hemlock. A few 'softwoods' are quite hard, for example pitch pine is a hard 'softwood'.

Production of wood from trees

Newly felled 'green' timber does not have much value for craft work. It is wet and therefore heavy, relatively weak, and very difficult to work. The production of timbers which can be used in our craft workshops follows the series of processes shown in the drawings on page 150 overleaf.

Trees felled—Trees are often felled with power driven, portable chain saws. Once the trees have been felled, branches are cut away either by sawing or by axing to leave the trunks in the form of logs. In some countries logs are squared off into baulks before transportation to saw mills for conversion into boards. The logs or baulks are transported by a variety of methods—floating by river, on lorries by road, by ships and barges or by any other method suitable for transporting the bulky logs. In some areas, the logs are sawn into boards in the forest near to the site of felling.

Saw into boards—Conversion of the logs into boards is usually carried out on large band saws, although frame saws and large circular saws are also in use in some sawmills. The method of sawing will depend on the uses for which the boards are intended. Hardwood logs may be slash sawn, quarter sawn or box sawn. Slash sawn timber, except for selected boards, have no distinct 'figure'. Some woods have a notable 'flash' figure from the medullary rays when quarter sawn or a distinct pattern of grain. Some boards show beautiful grain patterns when box sawn. With softwoods the aim when converting logs into timber is usually to obtain as much usable wood as is possible. The problem of figure is not often considered when converting softwoods into boards.

Season—The sawn boards are stacked into seasoning piles to allow the green wood to dry. This is an important stage in the wood producing process. Piling sticks are placed at regular intervals between boards in a seasoning stack to allow air to circulate between the boards and so hasten the process of drying.

Two major methods of seasoning are employed—open-air seasoning and kiln seasoning. Many hardwoods are now kiln seasoned. Kilns are purpose-built structures in which temperature and humidity of the air are under strict control. The seasoning stacks are built on trolleys which can be run by rail into the kilns. The close control of the drying conditions enables kiln seasoning to be not only more speedy than open-air seasoning, but the moisture content of the seasoned wood can be precisely monitored.

Saw to market forms—The seasoned timber is often machined into the shapes and forms required by the consuming public. Hardwoods are machined to a variety of board thicknesses and widths, into strips of specified dimensions, into mouldings and so on. Softwoods are machined into forms required mainly for constructional purposes such as flooring and roof joists, flooring boards, and battens.

Uses—Hardwoods are frequently manufactured into consumer items such as furniture. Softwoods are often used in the building of houses, house doors and window frames, and fencing. The two classes of wood overlap somewhat as to their uses. The design and craft worker will select the woods he wishes to use for other reasons such as—hardness, strength, colour, grain, figure, finish, cost and the general suitability of the wood for the particular item being designed.

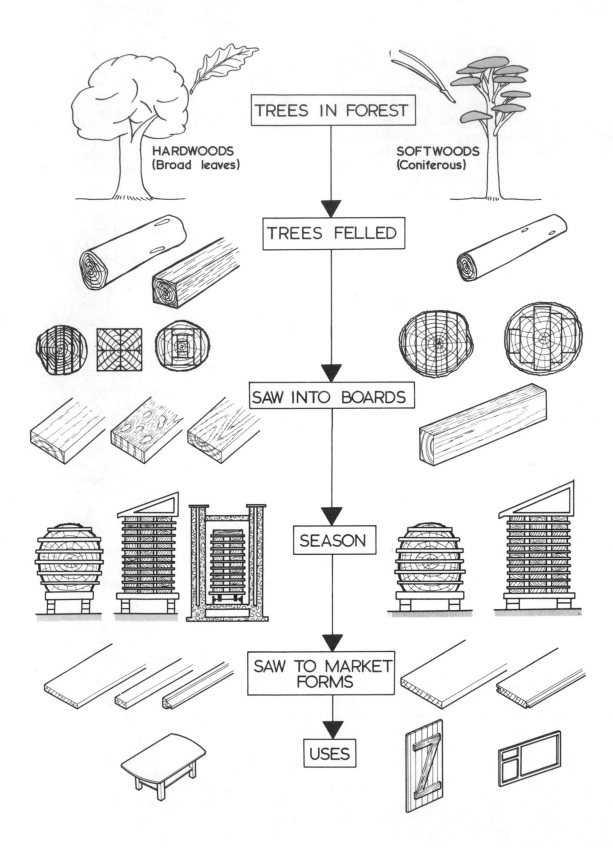

TREES IN FOREST

HARDWOODS
(Broad leaves)

SOFTWOODS
(Coniferous)

TREES FELLED

SAW INTO BOARDS

SEASON

SAW TO MARKET
FORMS

USES

150

Hardwoods and softwoods

Microscopic examination at a magnitude of 100 times of tiny pieces of wood macerated in chromic acid shows the essential structural differences between hardwoods and softwoods. Chromic acid dissolves the lignin in the wood. Lignin is the substance which holds together the constituent parts of wood.

Hardwoods
Five major constituents will be seen:
1. large spring vessels with thin walls;
2. smaller summer vessels with thick walls;
3. bundles of fibres, which give rigidity;
4. tracheids;
5. parenchyma cells—living cells found mainly in rays.

Softwoods
Two major constituents are present:
1. masses of tracheids—each up to 1mm long;
2. parenchyma cells mainly in the rays.
A third constituent appears in some softwoods:
3. resin canals.

The tracheids are hollow, roughly rectangular in section. In the tracheid walls are bordered pits (a). When sapwood changes to heartwood, the pits close (c) and fluids can no longer pass freely through the tracheids.

Constituents of a softwood:
(1) Tracheids
(2) Medullary parenchyma
(3) Resin canals (a) Bordered pit
(b) Pit open (c) Pit closed

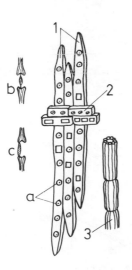

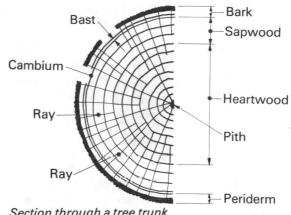

Constituents of a hardwood:
(1) Spring cells
(2) Summer cells
(3) Fibre
(4) Tracheids
(5) Medullary parenchyma

Cross-section through wood
Examination of a cross-section through any wood reveals the following features.
Bark—Protective layer.
Cambium—Growth layer. Usually green and sticky.

Growth rings—Usually one each year.
Rays—Radiating outwards.
Heartwood—Usually darker in colour than the
Sapwood—Contains living cells.

Section through a tree trunk

Shrinkage in wood
Wood is hygroscopic—it is sensitive to the fluctuations in atmospheric humidity. When moisture in the atmosphere increases, wood will absorb some of the moisture and, as a result, swell slightly in size. When moisture in the atmosphere decreases, wood releases some of its moisture to the atmosphere and, as a result, shrinks slightly in size.

The shrinkage varies in its effect according to the direction in which the shrinkage occurs. Thus shrinking along the grain of wood is so small that it can be ignored. Shrinkage along the annual rings —tangential shrinkage—is usually about twice that of the shrinkage which occurs across the annual rings—radial shrinkage.

These variations in the rate of shrinkage cause wood to distort out of shape when it dries. Some of the effects of this distortion are shown in drawings. Remember that shrinkage is greatest along the annual rings, which tend to shorten. This accounts for the shapes which occur as a result of the shrinkage caused by wood drying.

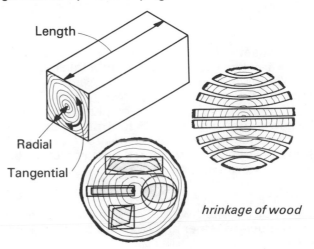

Shrinkage of wood

151

Wood forms on the market

Wood is sold in a large variety of forms, shapes, sizes, and species. It is purchased either as so-called 'solid' wood or as manufactured boards of various types. Some of the different market forms are shown in drawings.

Hardwood

Boards of hardwood are available in a range of thicknesses from about 5 mm upwards and in a range of board widths from about 150 mm to more than 300 mm according to the species of wood. Such boards are priced at so much per square metre, measured by the area of the surface of the board.

Strips of hardwood of various sectional sizes such as 50 mm by 25 mm, 75 mm by 15 mm, 30 mm square, are usually sold at so much per metre in length—referred to as so much per metre run.

Softwood

Softwoods are more often sold in standard sectional sizes than are hardwoods. Thus standard board widths and thicknesses such as 150 mm by 22 mm, 150 mm by 12 mm, as well as smaller standard sections such as 50 mm by 20 mm, 25 mm square, and so on are common. Most softwoods, as a result, are sold by the metre run, although some dealers may prefer selling by the square metre.

Hardboard

Hardboard in thicknesses from 2 mm upwards is cheap manufactured board made of chips from waste material from tree felling (branches, etc.) and of waste from factories (chips, etc.). The chips of wood are bound together in resins. Hardboard is most often a deep brown in colour with an upper face smooth and polished and a lower face textured. Hardboard is, however, made in a variety of types and finishes. Thus types with reeded or moulded surfaces, painted or veneered surfaces, low density board for pinboard, board with holes for pegboard, are all manufactured.

Plywood

If thin sheets of wood (veneers) are glued face to face with alternate pieces at right angles, a strong board known as plywood results. Made in a wide range of thicknesses and board sizes from a variety of different woods. The common plywood is 3 ply in thickness from about 1 mm to 4 mm. Thicker plywoods contain more plies—usually 5, 7, 9 and so on. Some plywoods are veneered with choice woods, plastics or even metals.

Blockboard

A type of plywood with a 'core' made of strips of wood glued together and faced on both sides with thick veneer.

Laminboard

A high quality blockboard with a core made from thin strips.

Chipboard

Made from wood chips set in polymer resins—most often urea formaldehyde. Unfaced chipboard is a low cost board. Chipboards can be purchased ready faced with wood veneers or with plastic veneers.

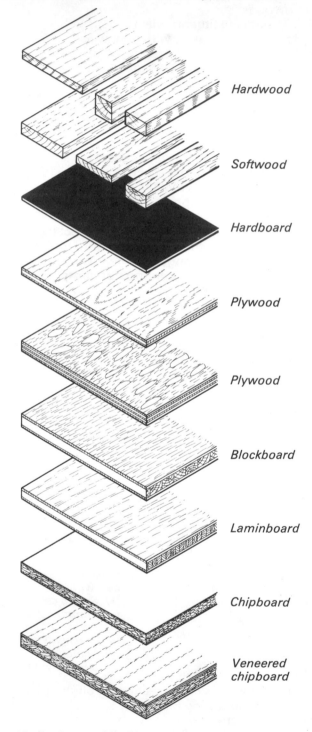

Market forms of timber

Manufacturing plywoods

The 'plies' of plywood are veneers which are most often cut from logs by a rotary process. The log is placed in a machine and made to rotate against a knife which is slowly moved towards the centre of the log as it rotates. The veneers are then cut into sheets. The sheets are glued together with the grains of alternate plies at right angles to each other. High quality veneers are usually obtained by slicing from 'flitches' of chosen woods. These choice veneers may be glued to the plywoods as facings.

Glues for making plywood vary according to the uses for which the plywood is being made. If it is to be exposed to weathering, waterproof glues such as phenolformaldehyde would be suitable. Other glues of many types are used according to cost and availability at the place where the plywoods are manufactured.

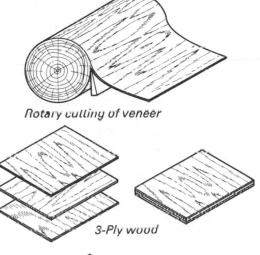

Rotary cutting of veneer

3-Ply wood

Veneered plywood

Knife cutting veneers

Advantages of manufactured boards

As explained on page 151 wood shrinks in response to atmospheric humidity. Along the grain, however, shrinkage is so small that it can be ignored for practical purposes. When manufactured boards are made, the fact that veneers are laid with alternate grains at right angles means that shrinkage across the grain of one ply is presented by the lack of shrinkage along the grain of the ply it is in contact with. Thus:
1. manufactured boards do not shrink in either direction;
2. manufactured boards remain flat;
3. manufactured boards do not twist, warp or split.
Also:
4. manufactured boards can be obtained in very wide boards.

Disadvantages

1. Manufactured boards are often unsuitable for framed constructions because when used in narrow strips their strengths across the piece are less than in strips of 'solid' wood.
2. Edges of manufactured boards are unsightly.
3. Special jointing techniques are often required unless 'solid' wood is used in conjunction with manufactured boards.

Quarter sawn v. slash sawn boards

Drawings on page 150 show that logs may be converted by sawing into boards in various ways. Boards resulting from this conversion fall into two types—they are either 'quarter sawn' or 'slash sawn'. To determine which group a board belongs to, look at its end grain. Quarter sawn boards possess advantages over slash sawn boards as follows:
1. Quarter sawn boards of some species have a distinct figure or grain quality which designers value. Examples are figured oak, quarter sawn sapele 'mahogany' and 'fiddle back' sycamore.
2. Because of the variation of shrinkage rate between the radial and the tangential directions, slash sawn boards will readily warp. Quarter sawn boards, on the other hand, remain flat if drying occurs, although they will be reduced in width and thickness.

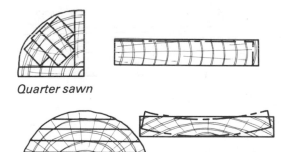

Quarter sawn

Slash sawn

Moisture contents

When boards are seasoned in the open air, their moisture content will be reduced to about 20% by weight from the original moisture content of the green wood. Green wood may well contain 50% (sometimes even more) of its weight in the form of water. Further seasoning to as little as 8% moisture

153

content can be achieved by kiln seasoning or by storing boards in a well ventilated position in a workshop for some time. It is not advisable to use freshly purchased open-air seasoned boards for your design work. The chart on this page shows typical uses for timber seasoned to certain levels of moisture content.

The moisture content of a piece of wood can be measured as follows.

Weigh a small portion of the wood—Wet weight
Dry the wood in an oven and re-weigh—Dry Weight
Then apply the formula:

$$\frac{\text{Wet weight minus dry weight} \times 100}{\text{Dry weight}} = \text{Moisture content}$$

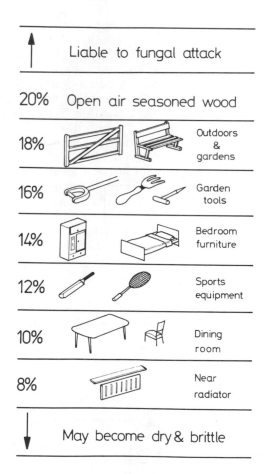

Moisture contents of wood

Some hardwoods

Afrormosia—A West African wood; heavy and hard; yellow brown in colour; straight grained. A good furniture timber.

Ash—A European wood; heavy, hard, tough and elastic; distinct grain; light brown in colour. Hammer handles, sports equipment.
Balsa—Mainly from South America; extremely light in weight; white to pale brown colour. An excellent modelling wood.
Beech—European. Heavy and hard; white to pale brown. Used for tool and bench making.
Box—European. Very hard and heavy; yellow with a fine texture. A good wood for turning.
Chestnut—England. Medium weight, works easily; light brown with distinct grain. A good furniture wood.
Elm—England. Reddish-brown; distinct and beautiful uneven grain. A good furniture wood.
Iroko—Central African timber. Heavy and hard; yellow-brown in colour. A good furniture timber.
Jelotung—Malaya. Soft; yellow in colour. Good for model-making.
Mahogany—Usually African. Not true mahogany, which comes from Central America. Medium weight; reddish-brown. Good furniture wood. Good decorative timber.
Oak—England. Heavy and tough; yellowish-brown; good flash when quarter sawn. An excellent all-purpose timber. Very resistant to weathering.
Sapele—West Africa. Medium weight; red-brown in colour; interlocking grain which shows as a fine stripe figure when quarter sawn. Furniture.
Sycamore—England. Medium weight; white colour. A good turning wood. Furniture.
Teak—From Burma. Heavy; golden-brown in colour; strongly resistant to decay. Good furniture timber.

Some softwoods

British Columbian Pine—Very distinct grain. A good constructional timber. Grain quality makes this a good decorative wood for some purposes.
Larch—Central Europe. Light in weight; reddish-brown in colour; straight grained. Pit props and telegraph poles.
Redwood—Northern Europe, Alps, Siberia. This is the most common of all constructional softwoods. Also called 'red deal' or 'yellow deal'. General joinery and carpentry work.
Spruce—Two types—white spruce (or white deal). Lightweight with a lustrous grain. Often pulped for paper. Sitka spruce which is a lustrous pink colour is very strong for its weight and is therefore used for gliders, boats and canoe paddles.
Western Red Cedar—Californian timber. Very light in weight; pink to dark brown in colour; straight grained. Very resistant to decay, this wood is mainly used for outdoor claddings, roof shingles and weather boarding.
Yew—Common in Europe. A heavy wood of very variable grain; orange to deep brown in colour. A very decorative wood suitable for turning.

Appendix

Letters and figures

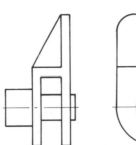

British Standards

On page 124 a reference was made to two British Standards. These two publications recommend methods for making working drawings:

BS 308: *Engineering drawing practice*
PD 7308: *Engineering drawing practice for schools and colleges*

If the methods shown in these publications are followed, your drawings can be understood throughout the world. This is because BS 308 is based on international (ISO) recommendations.

Another PD (Published Document) which could be of interest to those who wish to make design drawings is:

PD 7307: *Graphical symbols for use in schools and colleges*

Those details which are important for design working drawings are shown on this page and page 156 overleaf. These are followed on page 157 by those British Standard symbols which may be needed when drawing electrical and elctronics circuits. The British Standards containing these symbols, among many others are:

BS 3939: *Graphical symbols for electrical power, telecommunications and electronics diagrams*
PD 7303: *Electrical and electronic graphical symbols for schools and colleges*

Fuller details of the exact use of all the drawing conventions and symbols from these British Standards should be taken from the Standards concerned.

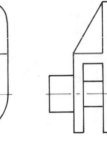

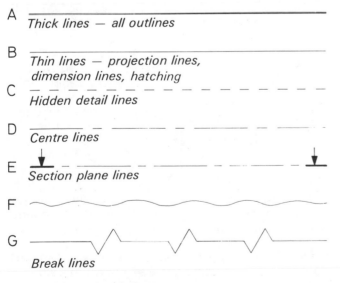

A ——————————————
  Thick lines — all outlines

B ——————————————
  *Thin lines — projection lines,
  dimension lines, hatching*

C – – – – – – – – – –
  Hidden detail lines

D —– – —– – —– – —
  Centre lines

E ↓—· — · — · — · —↓
  Section plane lines

F ∿∿∿∿∿∿∿∿∿

G ——\/——\/——\/——
  Break lines

Lines used in drawings

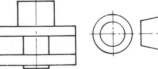

Note

All drawings in this book which have been made to orthographic drawing principles are in First Angle projection. Another orthographic projection is shown here for comparison with First Angle projection. This is Third Angle projection, which is in common use in the USA and is also used in the British Isles by some industrial undertakings.

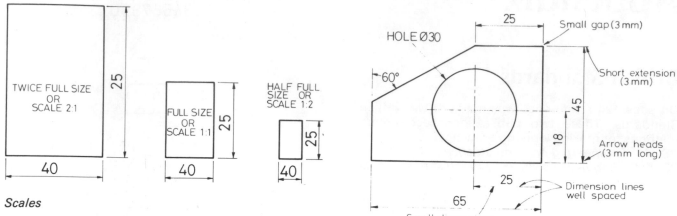

TWICE FULL SIZE
OR
SCALE 2:1

25

40

FULL SIZE
OR
SCALE 1:1

25

40

HALF FULL
SIZE OR
SCALE 1:2

25

40

Scales

HOLE Ø30

25

60°

Small gap (3 mm)

Short extension
(3 mm)

45

18

Arrow heads
(3 mm long)

25

65

Small dimensions
inside larger

Dimension lines
well spaced

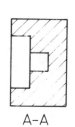

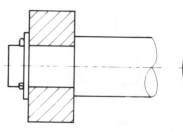

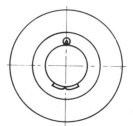

A

A-A

A

Sections

Ø20

Ø20

R7

R7

Dimensioning

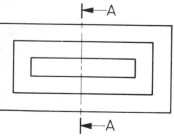

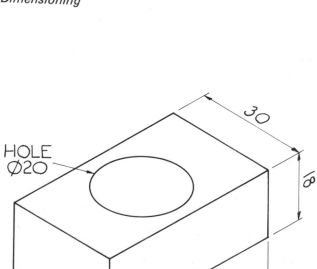

HOLE
Ø20

30

18

45

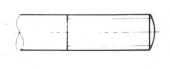

Screw threads

Dimensioning pictorial drawing

156

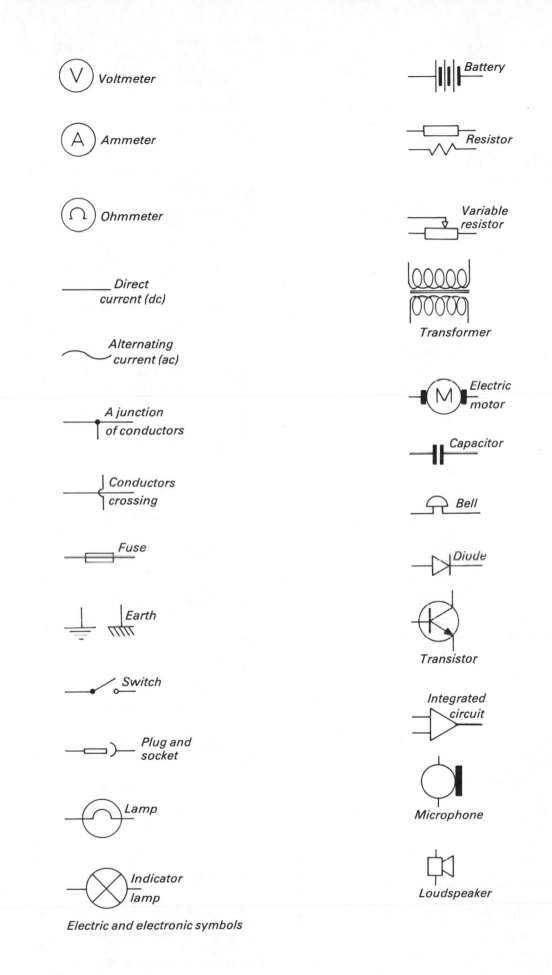

Voltmeter

Ammeter

Ohmmeter

Direct current (dc)

Alternating current (ac)

A junction of conductors

Conductors crossing

Fuse

Earth

Switch

Plug and socket

Lamp

Indicator lamp

Battery

Resistor

Variable resistor

Transformer

Electric motor

Capacitor

Bell

Diode

Transistor

Integrated circuit

Microphone

Loudspeaker

Electric and electronic symbols

Index

Acknowledgements

The authors wish to place on record their grateful appreciation of the help given by representatives of organisations who have permitted copyright photographs to be reproduced in this book. These organisations are:

The Central Electricity Generating Board—page 93 (cooling and suspension towers).

CIBA-GEIGY (UK) Limited—page 60 (boat assembly).

Dexion Comino International Limited—pages 86 and 121 (knock-down fittings).

The Ford Motor Company Limited—page 10 (six photographs).

Freeman, Fox and Partners—page 93 (Humber Bridge).

Galt Toys Limited—pages 46 and 52 (push horse and first construction kit).

Imperial Chemical Industries Limited—pages 46 and 50 (lampshades, garden secateurs and chairs).

The Pilkington Glass Museum—page 6 (glass vessel by Labino).

The Raleigh Cycle Company Limited—page 68 (bicycle).

Sir Robert McAlpine and Sons Limited—page 60 (entrance).

Selectus Limited—page 68 (Velcro).

The Tate Gallery—page 6 (sculpture by Denis Mitchell).

Trylon Limited—for allowing the photographs on page 154 to be taken in their showroom.

Danielle and Selwyn Holmes—for allowing the photographs on page 7 to be taken in their Craftwork Gallery at Abbotsbury, Dorset.

British Library Cataloguing in Publication Data

Yarwood, A.
  Design and craft.—2nd ed.
  1. Design
  I. Title   II. Dunn, S.
  754.4   NK1510

  ISBN 0 340 38625 8

Cover

The cover picture was produced by James F Blinn, Computer Graphics Lab, Jet Propulsion Laboratory, Caltech, Pasadena.

Examination questions

The following examination boards have allowed questions to be included from examination papers set in recent years.
Oxford and Cambridge Schools Examination Board.
Oxford Delegacy of Local Examinations.
University of London University Entrance and School Examinations Council.
Welsh Joint Education Committee.
West Midlands Examinations Board.